Public Workers in
Service of America

THE WORKING CLASS
IN AMERICAN HISTORY

Editorial Advisors
James R. Barrett, Thavolia Glymph,
Julie Greene, William P. Jones,
and Nelson Lichtenstein

*A list of books in the series appears
at the end of this book.*

Public Workers in Service of America

A Reader

Edited by
FREDERICK W. GOODING JR.
AND ERIC S. YELLIN

Foreword by
JOSEPH A. McCARTIN

Afterword by
EILEEN BORIS

© 2023 by the Board of Trustees
of the University of Illinois
All rights reserved
♾ This book is printed on acid-free paper.

Library of Congress Cataloging-in-Publication Data
Names: Gooding, Frederick W., Jr., editor. | Yellin, Eric
Steven, 1978– editor.
Title: Public workers in service of America : a reader / edited
by Frederick W. Gooding, Jr. and Eric S. Yellin ; foreword
by Joseph A. McCartin ; afterword by Eileen Boris.
Description: Urbana : University of Illinois Press, [2023] |
Series: The working class in American history | Includes
bibliographical references and index.
Identifiers: LCCN 2023000827 (print) | LCCN 2023000828
(ebook) | ISBN 9780252045172 (cloth : acid-free paper) |
ISBN 9780252087318 (paperback: acid-free paper) | ISBN
9780252054549 (ebook)
Subjects: LCSH: Civil service—United States—History—20th
century. | Discrimination—Government policy—United
States. | Government employee unions—United States. |
Collective bargaining—Government employees—United
States. | Neoliberalism—Political aspects—United States.
Classification: LCC JK691 .P987 2023 (print) | LCC JK691
(ebook) | DDC 352.6/309730904—dc23/eng/20230214
LC record available at https://lccn.loc.gov/2023000827
LC ebook record available at https://lccn.loc.gov/2023000828

This one's for Helena Sarah
—ESY

*To my beloved father-in-law, Ruthven Fernandes,
who hated getting up at four o'clock in the morning to
go labor, but who evidently loved his four kids more*
—FWG

Contents

Foreword *Joseph A. McCartin* .ix

Acknowledgments. xv

A Note on Language xvii

Introduction *Frederick W. Gooding Jr. and Eric S. Yellin* 1

PART I: THE POLITICS OF PUBLIC WORK AT
THE DAWN OF THE TWENTIETH CENTURY

1. Gender and Politics among Federal Indian Service
Employees, 1880–1930 *Cathleen D. Cahill*. 17

2. The Spoils as Reparations *Eric S. Yellin* 36

PART II: GOOD GOVERNMENT JOBS FOR WHOM?

3. Dead End Job? Black Public Workers Struggle to
See Light of Day *Frederick W. Gooding Jr.* 63

4. "We're the Backbone of this City": Women and
Gender in Public Work *Katherine Turk*. 85

PART III: ORGANIZING PUBLIC WORKERS

5. Police Unions and Public Sector
Labor Law and Policy *Joseph E. Slater*. 109

6. The Road to Memphis: Southern Sanitation Workers and the Transformation of Public Employee Unionism in the Postwar United States   *William P. Jones* 130

7. "They Won't Work for a Cop of Any Kind": The 1970 Sanitation Slowdown and the Struggle for Black Independent Politics in Philadelphia   *Francis Ryan* 149

PART IV: PUBLIC WORKERS IN THE NEOLIBERAL AGE

8. Sick-Ins, Feed-Ins, Heal-Ins, and Strikes: Labor Organizing at Chicago's Public Hospital in the 1960s and Its Legacy for the 1970s   *Amy Zanoni* 177

9. The Meaning of Teachers' Labor in American Education: Change, Challenge, and Resistance   *Jon Shelton* 209

Afterword   *Eileen Boris* 231

Contributors 237

Index 239

Foreword

JOSEPH A. McCARTIN

While public sector workers and their unions have been at the center of many of our biggest, bitterest fights over labor policy, law, and politics in recent years—becoming both the prime target of antiunionists and organized labor's most energetic incubators of innovation and militancy—these workers generally have yet to receive the attention they deserve from historians. This volume helps correct that problem and it could not be more timely. As the essays that follow make clear, the struggles of public workers have deeply impacted the status of all U.S. workers and unions, shaping the quality of our democracy, as well as its limitations for much of modern U.S. history. It is long past time that we give these workers their due.

For recent evidence of the central importance of public sector workers and labor struggles, consider what transpired between the Great Recession and the COVID-19 pandemic. As Wall Street's 2008 implosion triggered the largest downturn since the 1930s, a ferocious antiunion struggle erupted that targeted public workers. Republican governors used the recession to drive a wedge between laid-off private sector workers and workers who remained on government payrolls, opening up an all-out assault on public sector unions. Minnesota's governor, Tim Pawlenty, charged that government workers were "over-benefited and overpaid compared to their private-sector counterparts," while Indiana's Mitch Daniels called them "a new privileged class in America." For his part, Wisconsin's Scott Walker translated such divisive rhetoric into a policy breakthrough. In 2011 he pushed through Act 10, a law that effectively stripped most of Wisconsin's public workers of the right to bargain collectively. Inspired by Walker, a dozen states amended their laws within a year to weaken government workers' unions. The U.S. Supreme Court soon joined the fray.

In a string of decisions culminating with *Janus v. AFSCME* in 2018, the court invalidated laws that allowed unions to collect fees from the government workers they represented in contract negotiations and grievance appeals.[1]

That assault against government workers rippled far beyond the public sector. In state after state, attacks on government unions opened the door to a broader offensive against unions in general. Indeed, in Indiana and Michigan in 2012 and in Wisconsin two years later, attacks on the collective bargaining rights of government workers catalyzed enactment of "right to work" laws that weakened private sector workers' unions.[2] The decimation of these unions in key states like Michigan and Wisconsin in turn proved decisive for Donald Trump. In 2016 he narrowly won both of those states and with them the presidency. The targeting of public sector workers thus set the stage for the Trump era.

Yet, public sector workers and unions were not only targets of attack during these years, they were also agents of innovation and militancy, inspiring and sustaining the broader labor movement during challenging times. Teachers' unions played an especially important role in this regard. Beginning with the Chicago teachers' strike of 2012 and reaching a crescendo during the #RedforEd teachers' strikes and mobilizations of 2018 that spread from West Virginia to Arizona, teachers began pushing back against neoliberal education policies and fighting for the "schools our children deserve," as the Chicago teachers put it. Through these efforts, organized teachers almost single-handedly revived the strike after years of dwindling labor militancy. Thanks to the #RedforEd upsurge, more workers walked off the job in 2018 than in any year since 1986, and a staggering 89 percent of those strikers were employed in public education. During the pandemic, these same unions pushed hard for policies that would protect students and their families from COVID-19.[3]

Public sector fights not only revived militancy; they also helped revive social unionism through new initiatives such as Bargaining for the Common Good (BCG). BCG represented a transformative union strategy that was devised by public sector unions in the aftermath of the passage of Wisconsin's Act 10. It grew out of government workers' realization that they could not preserve their collective bargaining rights against the antiunion onslaught unless they began to ally their cause with that of beleaguered private sector workers and residents of working-class neighborhoods, expanding the scope of public sector bargaining in ways that addressed the issues of community members and private sector workers as well as government employees. Thus, teachers in St. Paul, Minnesota, demanded their school districts cease doing business with banks that would foreclose on students' families during the school year; Chicago teachers demanded a housing program that would deal with the growing homelessness and the impact of gentrification; Los Angeles municipal workers urged reforms in their city's relationship to financial entities, pointing out that LA spent more in fees paid to Wall Street firms than it did repairing and maintaining city streets; and LA teachers fought for an end to random student searches by public safety officers on school campuses. In these and many other BCG-style campaigns, public sector unions began using the collective bargaining process to fight for racial justice, immigrant rights, tax reform, and other demands important to their community allies.[4]

In many ways the growing racial and gender diversity of government workers' unions—whose ranks include more women and African Americans than the private sector workforce on average—was key to both their vulnerability to Act 10–style attacks and their BCG-style innovations. Their vulnerability became evident in the upsurge of right-wing populism during the Great Recession, as Daniel Martinez HoSang and Joseph Lowndes have shown, when right-wing populists used the prominent roles played by women and people of color in public sector unions to impose on them a set of racialized and gendered stereotypes that portrayed them as "the new welfare queens," as Jonathan Cohn memorably put it.[5] This trope was no more accurate than the original welfare queen myth, for in reality women and African American public employees suffered disproportionately from Great Recession austerity. Some 70 percent of the 765,000 state and local jobs cut between 2007 and 2011 were held by women; 30 percent by African Americans.[6] Yet it was also the vulnerability of public workers that incentivized them to lead creative new efforts like BCG. It is no coincidence that the majority of the advisory committee for the Bargaining for the Common Good network is made up of women and people of color.[7]

As this recent history suggests, the story of public workers and their struggles helps illuminate the clashing forces that are contending to shape America's future. To fully understand those forces requires that we step back to consider the changing dynamics of public employees and their organizations in multiple settings over a broad sweep of time, as the essays in this volume do.

Twenty years ago, U.S. historians had scarcely begun to tell the story of public workers and their organizations or to properly integrate them into the narrative arc of American labor history. "Where are the organized public workers?" historian Robert Shaffer asked in 2002, as he chronicled their near complete absence from U.S. history textbooks even as government workers were then on a trajectory to become one-half of the union movement's membership.[8] Fortunately, Shaffer was not alone in taking notice. A historiography of public workers and their unions was beginning to emerge, led by such works as Margaret C. Rung's *Servants of the State: Managing Diversity and Democracy in the Federal Workforce, 1933–1953* (2002) and Joseph Slater's *Public Workers: Government Employee Unions, the Law, and the State, 1900–1962* (2004).[9] Within a decade, the number of scholars "bringing the state's workers in" to U.S. labor history began to multiply.[10]

This volume builds on that foundational scholarship. Indeed, in many ways these essays represent a coming of age for the historiography of public sector workers and unions, illuminating the long-range historical processes that have shaped this current moment for public workers, the labor movement, and the nation.[11] The volume's able editors, Frederick W. Gooding Jr. and Eric S. Yellin, limn both the attractions and disappointments that federal government jobs have held for African Americans across the twentieth century. Katherine Turk and Cathleen D. Cahill demonstrate how gender has shaped public workers' experience in different settings and historical eras. William P. Jones, Francis Ryan, and Amy Zanoni show how the intersection of politics and race (and in Zanoni's case, gender as well) both animated and constrained public workers' organizing efforts in diverse settings. Joseph E. Slater and Jon Shelton, meanwhile, analyze the complex yet pivotal roles played by two strategically crucial groups of public workers—police officers and teachers—in shaping the historical trajectory of public sector unionism from the early twentieth century to the early twenty-first.

Taken together, these essays uncover the long roots of our contemporary conflicts, and by doing so they help shine a light on both the threats and the opportunities we now face as we struggle to deal with the twenty-first-century labor question. Most importantly, they remind us that if we hope to create a more just, sustainable, and democratic society in this century, we cannot afford to neglect the needs, aspirations, and energy of public workers.

Notes

1. Quotations from Joseph A. McCartin, "Convenient Scapegoats: Public Workers under Assault," *Dissent* 58, no. 2 (2011): 45–50; Joseph A. McCartin, "An Embattled New Deal Legacy: Public Sector Unionism and the Struggle for a Progressive Order," in *Beyond the New Deal Order: U.S. Politics from the Great Depression to the Great Recession*, ed. Nelson Lichtenstein, Gary Gerstle, and Alice O'Connor, 213–32 (Philadelphia: University of Pennsylvania Press, 2019); Martin Malin, "The Legislative Upheaval in Public-Sector Labor Law: A Search for Common Elements," *Labor Lawyer* 27, no. 2 (2012): 149–64.

2. For an overview, see McCartin, "Embattled New Deal Legacy," 213–32.

3. For detailed figures, see Bureau of Labor Statistics, *Work Stoppages Involving 1,000 or More Workers, 1993–2018*, https://www.bls.gov/web/wkstp/monthly-listing.htm/,

accessed October 26, 2019. Teachers' strikes were led by the following unions: West Virginia Education Association; Jersey City Education Association; Oklahoma Education Association; Kentucky Education Association; Colorado Education Association; Arizona Education Association; North Carolina Association of Educators; Tacoma Education Association; and Local 3299 of the American Federation of State, County, and Municipal Employees (AFSCME), which represents workers in the University of California system.

4. On Bargaining for the Common Good, see Joseph A. McCartin, "Bargaining for the Common Good," *Dissent* 63, no. 2 (2016): 128–35; on the St. Paul, LA, and Chicago examples, see McCartin and Marilyn Sneiderman, "Collective Action and the Common Good: Teachers' Struggles and the Revival of the Strike," in *Strike for the Common Good: Fighting for the Future of Public Education*, ed. Rebecca Kolins Givan and Amy Schrager Lang, 15–35 (Ann Arbor: University of Michigan Press, 2020); on the LA campaign against Wall Street, see Patrick Dixon, *Fixing L.A. and Remaking Public Sector Bargaining* (Washington, DC: Kalmanovitz Initiative for Labor and the Working Poor, 2016), https://lwp.georgetown.edu/wp-content/uploads/sites/319/uploads/Fixing-Los-Angeles-and-Remaking-Public-Sector-Collective-Bargaining.pdf/.

5. Daniel Martinez HoSang and Joseph Lowndes, "'Parasites of Government': Racial Antistatism and Representations of Public Employees amid the Great Recession," *American Quarterly* 68, no. 4 (2016): 931–54. HoSang and Lowndes borrow the concept of racial transposition from Natalia Molina, *How Race Is Made in America* (Berkeley: University of California Press, 2014); Jonathan Cohn, "Why Public Employees Are the New Welfare Queens," *New Republic*, August 8, 2010, https://newrepublic.com/article/76884/why-your-fireman-has-better-pension-you/.

6. Stephanie Luce and Ruth Milkman, "The State of the Unions 2015: A Profile of Organized Labor in New York City, New York State, and the United States," Joseph S. Murphy Institute for Worker Education and Labor Studies, 2015, https://www.gc.cuny.edu/CUNY_GC/media/CUNY-Graduate-Center/PDF/Communications/1509_Union_Density2015_RGB.pdf/; David Cooper, Mark Gable, and Algernon Austin, "The Public-Sector Jobs Crisis," in EPI Briefing Paper (Washington, DC: Economic Policy Institute, 2012), 1–22, https://www.epi.org/publication/bp339-public-sector-jobs-crisis/.

7. The BCG advisory committee includes Stacy Davis Gates of the Chicago Teachers Union, Cecily Myart-Cruz of the United Teachers of Los Angeles, and Merrie Najimy of the Massachusetts Teachers Association. See Bargaining for the Common Good, https://www.bargainingforthecommongood.org/advisory-committee/.

8. Robert Shaffer, "Where Are the Organized Public Employees? The Absence of Public Employee Unionism from U.S. History Textbooks and Why It Matters," *Labor History* 43, no. 3 (2002): 315, 331.

9. Margaret C. Rung, *Servants of the State: Managing Diversity and Democracy in the Federal Workforce, 1933–1953* (Athens: University of Georgia Press, 2002); Joseph E. Slater, *Public Workers: Government Employee Unions, the Law, and the State, 1900–1962* (Ithaca, NY: ILR Press, 2004).

10. Joseph A. McCartin, "Bringing the State's Workers In: Time to Rectify an Imbalanced U.S. Labor Historiography," *Labor History* 47, no. 1 (2006): 73–94.

11. The most relevant previous works of these authors are Cathleen D. Cahill, *Federal Fathers and Mothers: A Social History of the United States Indian Service, 1869–1932* (Chapel Hill: University of North Carolina Press, 2011); Frederick W. Gooding Jr., *American Dream Deferred: Black Federal Workers in Washington, D.C., 1941–1981* (Pittsburgh: University of Pittsburgh Press, 2018); William P. Jones, *The March on Washington: Jobs, Freedom, and the Forgotten History of Civil Rights* (New York: W. W. Norton, 2013); Francis Ryan, *AFSCME's Philadelphia Story: Municipal Workers and Urban Power in the Twentieth Century* (Philadelphia: Temple University Press, 2010); Jon Shelton, *Teacher Strike!: Public Education and the Making of a New American Political Order* (Urbana: University of Illinois Press, 217); Slater, *Public Workers*; Katherine Turk, *Equality on Trial: Gender and Rights in the Modern American Workplace* (Philadelphia: University of Pennsylvania Press, 2019); Eric S. Yellin, *Racism in the Nation's Service: Government Workers and the Color Line in Woodrow Wilson's America* (Chapel Hill: University of North Carolina Press, 2016); and Amy Zanoni, *Poor Health: Retrenchment and Resistance in Chicago's Public Hospital, 1950s–1990s* (PhD diss., Rutgers University, 2020).

Acknowledgments

Our first thank-you goes to Dr. Christopher Florio. Though Chris's scholarship does not appear in this book, his imprint is all over it. He made the book possible by using his own Society of Fellows funding at Columbia University to host a two-day symposium at Columbia's Heyman Center for the Humanities in March 2019. His generosity and sharp comments during the symposium made every chapter better.

Next, we wish to acknowledge the early faith placed in us by our former colleague at the University of Illinois Press (UIP), James Engelhardt. Before moving on, he made sure that there was a place for us and our ideas to be taken seriously. This burgeoning relationship and early ideation, shepherded as well by our fellow contributor William P. Jones, led to our successful partnership with Alison Syring at UIP. Alison was not only instrumental in providing cogent, concise, and encouraging feedback, but she was also able to work her wizardry in obtaining the thoughtful comments of series editor Julie Greene and two anonymous reviewers (who shall remain anonymous). It all fueled us with the motivation and good sense necessary to advance the project to this stage.

This volume is not just the product of congenial and collegial collaboration between us two coeditors; it is also the product of a larger coagulation of thought and practice among numerous scholars worth their salt (and then some). We remain indebted and grateful to the historians whose scholarship we are proud to showcase in this edited volume. The author contributions contained herein do more than validate our fundamental aim of correcting the undervaluing and overlooking of public sector labor's importance. Their presence and range validate the very principle that only with a multiplicity of trusted perspectives can we approach a holistic understanding of an important topic germane to numerous audiences: *public workers in service of America.*

Lastly, as both coeditors are members of immediate families of four, the ability to produce high-quality scholarship is often a delicate enterprise—most especially if one seeks to balance both the personal and professional spheres accordingly. We wish not to engender sympathy for what so many scholars have routinely done before us, but, rather, we wish to call attention to the loving individuals within our families who made "staying the course" even possible. The idea for this edited volume was prematurely teased at a first meeting in Washington, DC, in 2013, conceived in the Hartsfield-Jackson Atlanta International Airport in 2014, and formed in New York City in 2019. That travel and time away from home only hints at the ways our families made sacrifices so that this book could be written. We thank our families, for in so many ways, in addition to the stories within this volume we wish to resurrect, they too are the reasons why we labor.

A Note on Language

The spelling of "Black" with a capital "B" denotes that we are talking about more than just a color; we mean a set of lived experiences shared among those who identify as Black Americans in the United States. Although people identified as white can share experiences as well, we do not capitalize the "w," as that form has long been used by white supremacist groups. Moreover, "Black" is often used as an identifying adjective when most aspects of mainstream culture were not only white-dominated but also considered the default for "normal." The distinctiveness of Black experience is, in part, forged by the exclusion from normative white experience and culture.

Introduction

FREDERICK W. GOODING JR.
AND ERIC S. YELLIN

> We the People of the United States, in Order to form a
> more perfect Union, establish Justice, insure domestic
> Tranquility, provide for the common defense, promote
> the general Welfare, and secure the Blessings of Liberty
> to ourselves and our Posterity, do ordain and establish
> this Constitution for the United States of America.
> —Constitution of the United States of America, 1787

Who's Running the Country?

While editing this book about the history of public work in the United States, our thoughts turn to the most devastating failure of public infrastructure in living memory. During the COVID-19 pandemic, the United States was a world leader in infection and mortality rates. Certainly, the SARS-CoV-2 virus was the direct cause, but failures of national leadership and of governmental infrastructure helped to drive the nation's enormous caseload.[1] As journalist Michael Lewis and others have documented, the presidential administration of Donald Trump, at the helm for the first year of the pandemic, was not merely ideologically opposed to the basic tenets of government service; it was utterly absent. Crucial appointed positions remained empty long after the presidential transition period, while an unusually high attrition rate in the Senior Executive Service (SES) emptied federal offices of top leaders with little done to replace them. "The net loss of SES civil servants under Trump," explains statistician Daniel Lim, "marked the loss of many of the most educated and experienced members of the federal workforce."[2] Global pandemics can happen under any administration, but not every administration is functionally unable to meet the moment.

Even as Joseph R. Biden's administration made more efforts to control the virus and its impact on lives and jobs, the pandemic continued to expose both the importance of, and the underinvestment in, America's public workers. It was public workers at hospitals, in local health district offices, at the Centers for Disease Control and Prevention, in schools, and in so many other places who treated patients, traced contacts, distributed vaccines, vetted antiviral drugs, and addressed learning losses due to absences and "Zoom school." Like receiving a piece of mail delivered by the U.S. Post Office, encountering the virus almost certainly meant needing the labor of a public worker.

And yet, even as economic growth returned in 2021, employees in the public sector were left behind. The Bureau of Labor Statistics reported in August 2021 that four hundred thousand noneducation state and local jobs (park custodians, city hall clerks, police and corrections officers) were lost in the pandemic. As the economy improved and federal funding and tax receipts rose, state and local budgets were nonetheless kept at austerity levels. In addition, low wages, demoralization, and pandemic-related unpredictability made it more difficult for the government to recruit workers even when budgets allowed for hiring.[3] Finally, because the public sector has, historically, been an unusually fair practices employer, a reduction in public work meant losses in opportunities for marginalized workers, especially Black women.[4] Thus, another casualty of the pandemic was an exhausted, less representative public sector.

The history explored in this book makes one thing clear: the remedies for the crises of disease, economic collapse, climate change, inequality, disinformation, and racial injustice raging in twenty-first-century America are not likely to succeed *without* public workers. For what is novel about public sector workers is that they labor on a daily basis "to form a more perfect Union," even if its practical, daily existence is far from perfect. By maintaining and operating local, municipal, state, and federal governmental operations, the "general welfare" is promoted and the great experiment in self-governance that is American democracy continues for observation and improvement.

Despite its critical role, government, and the human beings who do its work at all levels of the American state, has long been a target of mistrust and, in many cases, derision due to conflicting agendas.[5] The public sector has always served as a scapegoat for larger societal failings. To wit, Aesop reportedly observed sardonically centuries ago, "We hang the petty thieves and appoint the great ones to public office."[6] Many years later, Alexis de Tocqueville noted that anyone with any brains in United States went into business, not governance: "A man does not undertake to direct the fortune of the State until he has discovered his incompetence to conduct his own affairs."[7] While the presumption of incompetence for all matters governmental is fairly well documented, far less well known are the individuals who publicly labor for the state on a daily basis to keep the general welfare out of jeopardy, despite failings of individuals from time to time. Tocqueville's friend Gustave de Beaumont hinted ironically that the secret ingredient of American public administration is its conspicuous absence: "Thus, all of the skill of the government, here, consists in not making itself felt, and the less the administration administers, the more content people are."[8] Through this edited volume, we endeavor to peel back the curtain a bit, to see who these people are, observe how they make their presence felt, and, in turn, make tangible the work of the American state.

Public workers run the gamut from white-collar executives to clerical workers in state agencies, from public school teachers to police officers, from mail carriers to laborers in government factories. In March 2020, nearly 20 million state and local government employees earned $89.3 billion in payroll.[9] With another 2 million permanent, civilian and nonpostal federal employees (the number rises closer to 10 million when military, postal, contract workers, and recipients of federal grants are included), public workers overall constitute about 15 percent of the American workforce.[10] Public employees, in short, represent both a significant and substantial portion of the U.S. economy.

The labor history of public workers reflects long-standing conflicts over the nature and goals of governing and the relationship between public good and private gain. Public workers are among the most organized and yet most threatened of workers in the contemporary United States. Tasked with meeting the needs of governance over and above their own needs as workers, they have been historically silenced and shoved to the background of the "real business" of America. These essays no longer permit taking for granted these crucial contributions; if anything, agency in these essays shifts to that of select groups of workers, moving dialogues away from the efficiency ratings of beleaguered governmental services that may lack in resources and toward analysis of the public work environments themselves.

This change in perspective provides historians with a better evaluation of what kind of employer is the state. Protecting civil servants from poor working environments precipitated conditions by which public employees built powerful protections and standards through law, unions, and administrative structures that inevitably spilled over into the private sector. These structures grew in complexity and scope, most especially after World War II and during a period of solid growth in tandem with the philosophical underpinning, underscored by the Great Depression, that the government indeed had a strong role to play in the growth and development of the economy.

America's New Deal largely survived the suspiciousness of the Eisenhower years and soon gave way to Lyndon B. Johnson's Great Society and Richard Nixon's grand ambitions—and the government continued to grow. In the 1980s, this growth trajectory altered considerably amid Ronald Reagan's efforts to "starve the beast" through federal tax cuts and "the new federalism" that pressured cash-strapped state and local budgets to meet citizen needs— for, as Reagan indicated in his presidential inaugural address, "Government is the problem." Such antigovernment politics decimated many of the key benefits of public work for a generation afterward.[11] All the while, public work was often pitted against private enterprise, as if the two were in direct competition.

We reject the binary competition model of public versus private sector enterprise to see both as vital to the daily maintenance of the United States. However, given the sheer volume of public sector employees nationwide, failure to account for the sum total experiences, practices, and lessons of public workers robs us of key knowledge about the U.S. workforce. In contrast to the word "private," the very nature of public sector work is that it is shared, open, and accountable. Accordingly, we aim to be open and transparent about the value these workers add to our lives. One thing is for certain: if these laborers execute their jobs correctly, then the positive results are there for all, or we the people, to see.

Defining Public Work

The essays in this book cover different periods in the twentieth century, places in the United States, and types of work and worksites. But the authors all understand "public workers" as people employed by the state—that is, those whose management and pay comes from within Max Weber's classic description of the state as the apparatus of power that governs, regulates, and institutionalizes violence, property, and society.[12] We have chosen the term "public workers" instead of "government workers" because the state has never been confined to spaces traditionally associated with "the government," such as bureaucrats in capital office buildings. Rather, the histories in this volume include people who worked at all levels of government and in all kinds of jobs, from laborers at government printing presses, to nurses at county hospitals, to drivers in municipal sanitation trucks. We move beyond the narrow boundaries of the formal civil service and the select ranks of appointed public officials. Public workers serve "the public" in numerous capacities, regardless of whether we always recognize them as "in government."

The history of public work examined here primarily occurred within the state. We have left largely untouched histories of the liminal space between the private and public sectors created by outsourcing and privatization, an equally broad and complex world of contract workers whose pay came from the state but whose employer was not a government agency. That other world of semi-public work expanded dramatically in the second half of the twentieth century, and its growth certainly affected our subjects.[13] So, while several of our essays are concerned with neoliberal privatization, we have focused on those workers whose labor was directly managed by public servants inside public institutions. Their paychecks came from the public, their work was publicly shared and inspected, their bosses were representatives of the government and its constituents.

Our definition of public workers is also rooted in a recognition that public work is inherently and uniquely political. Because sovereignty in the United States is held by "the people" and governed by republican and democratic structures, public workers work quite directly for "the people." As such, they have always been subject to the political system through which Americans organize, distribute, and execute public power, no matter how many civil service or other regulations attempt to insulate them from the political system. The American state bureaucracy is not autonomous; it is—and always has been—a creature of American politics.[14] Public employees' bosses are public officials and the people they serve are voters. Public workers, therefore, have always been bound to that political system, not just people hired to do a job. This obviously makes them distinct from those who work for private companies.

Visibility and political accountability have subjected public workers to surveillance, scrutiny, and political machinations unheard of in other employment sectors. No other sector's employees, not even companies with publicly traded shares or tax-exempt nonprofits, require the same levels of transparency as public workers. Public employees' salaries and wages are public information, regardless of seniority, position, or term of employment, including the president of the United States. "The people" have a right to know and publicly debate what their workers earn. This surveillance extends beyond pay, as well, to questions of productivity and efficiency and even to how public workers spend their time outside the office, school, hospital, or working vehicle.[15] The Hatch Act of 1939, for example, restricts the political activities of most federal employees, such as making campaign speeches or holding office in a political party. Regulations like Hatch stem from anti-corruption campaigns but also from widespread suspicions that public workers are inefficient and earn promotions in ways other than hard work. Therefore, they

Introduction   5

must strictly avoid even the appearance of impropriety, a standard from which numerous workers in the private sector remain shielded, if not liberated.[16]

While such transparency has led to monitoring and regulation, it has also led to advances in labor protections. It is no accident that laws ensuring decent labor conditions have been most extensive—and often first pioneered—for public employees, from the establishment of reasonable work hours to antidiscrimination regulations and procedures. Laissez-faire notions of private property, including ownership of one's labor, have long restrained efforts to intervene in the labor conditions of Americans in the private sector, but public work has never been the private property of its employers or its employees. Reformers, often acting in political arenas rather than union organizing, have had an easier road to making public work stable and secure than in the private sector.[17] This is not to say that public workers have never experienced precarity. Yet, constitutional requirements that the government pay its debts and the peculiar visibility and regulation of public sector work have provided opportunities for effective advocacy. Despite laws restricting public worker organizing and collective bargaining, public sector unions remain some of the most active and empowered unions today.

The distinctiveness of public work has not only been raised by liberals and labor organizers. Conservatives, too, have seen public workers as different and particularly subject to their own political aims. Arguments against public sector organizing have long been buttressed by concerns about the "common good" and the essential services public workers provide. Calvin Coolidge, of course, rose to national fame in 1919 for demanding that striking police officers in Boston go back to work for the public good, presaging a similar conflict between Ronald Reagan and the air traffic controllers in 1981.[18] More recently, Supreme Court Justice Samuel A. Alito Jr. expressed deep concern about the distinction between public and private employees in *Janus v. AFSCME*.[19] In his majority opinion striking down agency fees for public sector unions, Alito argued that such fair-share fees to public sector unions harm "the free speech rights of non-members by compelling them to subsidize private speech on matters of substantial public concern." The activities of public sector unions are distinctive, Alito contended, because as they advocate for their members' rights to decent compensation, their demands are linked to public concerns like the state budgets that pay their members' salaries. While the demands of private sector unions directly impact only the budgets of private companies, Alito insisted, the demands of public employees touch us all.[20]

Thus, the distinctiveness of the labor arrangements of public employees are clear enough to find grounds for agreement across the American political spectrum. Even as Alito argued for certain free speech protections of public employees, he took care not to imply that public employees are equally as free as private employees in all areas of activity, a theme Justice Elena Kagan picked up in her dissent to the majority opinion in *Janus*. Indeed, Kagan listed the occasions on which the Supreme Court has agreed that "'the Government has a much freer hand' in dealing with its employees than with 'citizens at large.'"[21] Ironically, public workers do not have the privacy nor the independence that are hallmarks of the Court's treatment of private sector employees, even though they diligently labor for private sector workers to retain such private privileges—from research scientists, to patent attorneys, to computer programmers.

As much as we agree that public work is different, we also share Kagan's assertion that public employment involves questions of both "the workplace" as well as "the broader public square." Indeed, one goal of this volume is to show the ways in which public work is both public (distinctive in labor history) and work (inextricably linked to labor history generally). As Kagan put it, "Arguing about the terms of employment is still arguing about the terms of employment."[22]

Labor historians have recognized the distinctiveness of public work, and the authors of this volume are the grateful inheritors of a now-established literature. From Sterling Spero's early investigations beginning in the 1930s; to Paul Van Riper's synthesis in 1958; to more recent work about public sector labor organizing by Michael Honey, Marjorie Murphy, and Joseph McCartin, historians have begun to get a handle on the lives and labors of federal clerks, municipal service workers, public school teachers, and air traffic controllers.[23] The grounding of a "field of study" is there.[24] And yet for all of this insightful work, our aim here is unique: no other volume has sought to make connections across the history of American public work. We have collected new scholarship covering different times, places, and kinds of work in order to invite readers to assess that field as it reaches maturity and to consider new directions it might now take.

Structure

This book is divided into three thematic sections that are also roughly chronological. Part I examines the way politics, identity, and labor operated together to offer opportunities to some federal workers in the twilight years of the nineteenth-century patronage system. Cathleen Cahill reveals how Indigenous and Anglo-American women used experience gained in the Federal Indian Service to launch professional and activist careers, even as the

Office of Indian Affairs' derisiveness toward Native Americans constrained the degree to which they could take advantage of their experiences and talents. Eric Yellin's chapter argues that African Americans, particularly Black men, found similar opportunities in the connections between their political affiliations and decent federal jobs in Washington, DC, opportunities that have largely gone unappreciated because of long-standing racist assumptions that Black government workers are either incompetent or corrupt. As the twentieth century began, women and men of color were beginning to find empowerment in public employment, even as they faced persistent and worsening discrimination in American life.

In part II, two essays delve into inequities that have undermined the opportunities in public work. Frederick W. Gooding Jr.'s chapter on Black federal employees after World War II forces us to contend with the reality that even as the public sector has been more inviting for Black workers than the private sector, this may say more about their exclusion from the United States' private sector than the fruitfulness of public work for African Americans. Katherine Turk carries this critical analysis to the history of women in public work, where women have found opportunities for both decent jobs and leadership but also frustration in their quest to have their work valued equally. Though federal and state governments have been among the leaders in fair employment practices, a close look at the experiences of marginalized workers, especially men and women of color, reveals ongoing struggles for fairness and equity.

Part III explores how public workers have organized themselves to demand better pay and working conditions. As Joseph Slater explains, public employee unions hold a distinct place in national labor law, a place defined by the actions and treatment of police unions since the 1919 Boston police strike. Generally not protected by the 1935 National Labor Relations Act, public worker unions have had to navigate legal barriers against certain job actions, such as strikes, and accusations that their organizing threatens the public good. In their chapters, William P. Jones and Francis Ryan drill down to the mid-twentieth-century experiences of municipal sanitation workers in Memphis and Philadelphia as they navigated racism in both city government and the American Federation of State, County, and Municipal Employees (AFSCME) to lay an unsteady foundation for blue-collar public worker organizing. This section makes clear that the history of public employee unions is one in which public workers have achieved stunning successes yet remained deeply embattled and vulnerable.

The book's final section, part IV, considers the history of public workers in hospitals and schools into the twenty-first century. Amy Zanoni's chapter tells the story of hospital workers in Chicago in the 1960s and 1970s who sought to ensure that their patients in an underfunded public hospital received the attention they needed, not just through medical care but also through their own organizing for better working conditions. In his chapter, Jon Shelton explores the conflicting images the public has held of public school teachers over time, from moral and civic guides to makers of human capital. Both essays reveal that public workers charged with caring for and educating the American public face difficult choices between executing their duties and maintaining their dignity, particularly as austerity budgets in the last quarter century have denied them the resources they need to do their jobs. That they have continually chosen the welfare of their patients and pupils over their own well-being is a fact that this history makes abundantly clear.

* * *

Taken collectively, the essays in this volume surface key themes in the history of public work in the United States, cutting across time and space: First, the public sector is, by virtue of its history as a site of opportunity for marginalized Americans, distinctly intersectional. Though the early history is often marked by a Black/white binary in terms of race and ethnicity, more recent clerical and government unions are making visible the work of Latinx, Asian American, and other people of color in public work, while categories of gender and class remain profoundly relevant to these workers' experiences. Second, public workers are distinctly visible, employed, as they are, by "the people," and subject to unique regimes of transparency and accountability. This visibility lends itself to symbol making, as public workers can be used for any number of agendas in the interaction of the American state and American society. Finally, these are workers who provide for the needs of "the people." Public workers exist because the public has defined a need and determined a way of meeting that need, from providing medical care, to cleaning our streets, to processing and managing the paperwork of modern corporate capitalism. This interaction between private citizens and government employees means that the history of public work consistently crosses the private/public binary, and attached to this theme of service are related concerns, such as sacrifice, compromise, servitude, and obligation. When are public workers merely ordinary employees with a job to do and a paycheck to collect, and when are they, more profoundly, "servants of the state," to borrow a phrase from public work historian Margaret Rung?[25]

These themes are present throughout the chapters in this book. Yet, our hope is that readers will identify more themes and avenues for research. Even as we try to distinguish "public work" from other types of labor, we refuse to resolve the complexity of American labor history. We show this in the variety of contexts described here and in our ready acknowledgment that we have left bases uncovered. Much more research is needed on the history of public sector labor, and we hope our volume is a touchstone for further work rather than a capstone of an endeavor completed.

We are cognizant that we address these overarching historical themes in a contemporary era of flux for public workers. The thirty-five-day shutdown of the federal government in the winter of 2018–2019 made many Americans more aware of the presence and importance of public workers as those people were forced to stay home—from FBI agents working to disrupt terrorist groups to food safety inspectors making sure our food does not sicken us—even as it also represented those workers' fundamental precarity in the face of political whims and grandstanding. As more and more teachers strike not just for decent pay and better working conditions but for a real commitment to education and the nation's youth, public work organizing has made clear the stakes for public institutions in our age of austerity politics. Finally, as we begin to appreciate the thousands of federal, state, and local public health officials and health care workers who labored around the clock to turn the tide of the COVID-19 pandemic in the United States and around the world, we can imagine no better time than the present for the public to sharpen their understanding of the history of public workers.

Notes

1. The Lancet Commission on Public Policy and Health in the Trump era estimated in February 2021 that 40 percent of deaths in the United States could have been prevented by a better response from the Trump administration. "Lancet Commissions: Public Policy and Health in the Trump Era," *The Lancet* 397 (February 20, 2021): 711, https://www.thelancet.com/journals/lancet/article/PIIS0140-6736(20)32545-9/fulltext/, accessed June 24, 2021.

2. Presciently, Michael Lewis notes that the Centers for Disease Control and Prevention had no nominee—let alone an appointed head—six months into Trump's presidency. Michael Lewis, *The Fifth Risk* (New York: W. W. Norton, 2018), 46; Daniel Lim, "Federal Workforce Attrition under the Trump Administration," *Government Executive* (December 28, 2020), https://www.govexec.com/management/2020/12/federal-workforce-attrition-under-trump-administration/171045/, accessed June 24, 2021.

3. Barb Rosewicz and Mike Maciag, "State and Local Government Job Growth Lags as Economy Recovers," *Pew Charitable Trusts* (September 14, 2021), https://www.pewtrusts.org/en/research-and-analysis/articles/2021/09/14/state-and-local-government-job-growth-lags-as-economy-recovers/, accessed March 22, 2022; "Unemployment

Rates during the COVID-19 Pandemic," *Congressional Research Service*, CRS Report R46554 (August 20, 2021), https://crsreports.congress.gov/, accessed March 22, 2022.

4. Jung Ho Parl and Yongjin Ahn, "Government Employees' Experience and Expectation of COVID-19 Hardships: The Moderating Role of Gender and Race in the United States," *American Review of Public Administration* 52, no. 1 (2022): 15–35.

5. A 2019 Pew Research Center poll reported, "Just 17% say they trust the government in Washington to do the right thing always or most of the time." "Little Public Support for Reductions in Federal Spending," *Pew Research Center*, April 2019, https://www.pewresearch.org/politics/2019/04/11/little-public-support-for-reductions-in-federal-spending/, accessed June 25, 2021. On the long history of ambivalent governance in the United States, see Brian Balogh, *A Government Out of Sight: The Mystery of National Authority in Nineteenth-Century America* (Cambridge: Cambridge University Press, 2009); Gary Gerstle, *Liberty and Coercion: The Paradox of American Government from the Founding to the Present* (Princeton, NJ: Princeton University Press, 2017).

6. Lewis D. Eigen, *The Obama Political Appointee Primer* (Potomac, MD: BEA Enterprises, 2009), 172.

7. Quoted in Louis Smith, "Alexis de Tocqueville and Public Administration," *Public Administration Review* 2, no. 3 (1942): 230.

8. Ibid.

9. U.S. Census Bureau, "Annual Survey of Public Employment and Payroll Summary Report: 2020," *U.S. Department of Commerce* (May 13, 2021), https://www.census.gov/content/dam/Census/library/publications/2021/econ/2020_summary_brief.pdf/, accessed June 25, 2021.

10. Public data on federal employment can be found at the U.S. Office of Personnel Management's data portal FedScope at fedscope.opm.gov; "Fed Figures 2019: Federal Workforce," Partnership for Public Service, https://ourpublicservice.org/wp-content/uploads/2019/08/FedFigures_FY18-Workforce.pdf/, accessed June 25, 2021; Fiona Hill, "Public Service and the Federal Government," *Brookings Institution* (May 27, 2020), https://www.brookings.edu/policy2020/votervital/public-service-and-the-federal-government/, accessed June 25, 2021.

11. On the distinctiveness of the austerity and antigovernment politics of Reagan's "new federalism," see Monica Prasad, *Starving the Beast: Ronald Reagan and the Tax Cut Revolution* (New York: Russell Sage Foundation, 2018); Timothy J. Conlan, *From New Federalism to Devolution: Twenty-Five Years of Intergovernmental Reform* (New York: Brookings Institution Press, 2010); and Paul C. Light, *A Government Ill Executed: The Decline of the Federal Service and How to Reverse It* (Cambridge, MA: Harvard University Press, 2008), 36–38.

12. Margaret Levi, "The State of the Study of the State," in *Political Science: The State of the Discipline*, ed. Ira Katznelson and Helen V. Milner (New York: W. W. Norton, 2002), 40; Brian Balogh "The State of the State among Historians," *Social Science History* 27, no. 3 (2003): 455–63.

13. Scholars have begun to connect privatization with the United States' global role

after World War II. Andrew Friedman, *Covert Capital: Landscapes of Denial and the Making of the U.S. Empire in the Suburbs of Northern Virginia* (Berkeley: University of California Press, 2013); Amy C. Offner, *Sorting Out the Mixed Economy: The Rise and Fall of Welfare and Developmental States in the Americas* (Princeton, NJ: Princeton University Press, 2019).

14. The question of the civil service's autonomy from sociopolitical development is an important topic in the history of public administration, but it is clear that American public workers have never been as cut off from politics as those in Britain, Japan, and other developed nations. Nor have they been insulated from broader social movements. Hugh Heclo, *Government of Strangers: Executive Politics in Washington* (Washington, DC: Brookings Institution, 1977), 49; Bernard S. Silberman, *Cages of Reason: The Rise of the Rational State in France, Japan, the United States, and Great Britain* (Chicago: University of Chicago Press, 1993), 231–32; Eric S. Yellin, *Racism in the Nation's Service: Government Workers and the Color Line in Woodrow Wilson's Washington* (Chapel Hill: University of North Carolina Press, 2013), ch. 2. On the development of the U.S. civil service, see Stephen Skowronek, *Building a New American State: The Expansion of National Administrative Capacities, 1877—1920* (Cambridge: Cambridge University Press, 1982); Sar A. Levitan and Alexandra B. Noden, *Working for the Sovereign: Employee Relations in the Federal Government* (Baltimore: Johns Hopkins University Press, 1983); Martin Shefter, *Political Parties and the State: The American Historical Experience* (Princeton, NJ: Princeton University Press, 1994); Daniel P. Carpenter, *The Forging of Bureaucratic Autonomy: Reputations, Networks, and Policy Innovation in Executive Agencies, 1862—1928* (Princeton, NJ: Princeton University Press, 2001); Paul Johnston, *Success While Others Fail: Social Movement Unionism and the Public Workplace* (Ithaca, NY: ILR Press, 1994).

15. While public work in general is highly regulated, legal scholars have noted that the specifics of those regulations, especially regarding organizing and collective bargaining rights, vary dramatically from state to state and across levels of government. See Ann C. Hodges, "Lessons from the Laboratory: The Polar Opposites on the Public Sector Labor Law Spectrum," *Cornell Journal of Law and Public Policy* 18 (2009): 735–74; Joseph E. Slater, *Public Workers: Government Employee Unions, the Law, and the State, 1900—1962* (Ithaca, NY: ILR Press, 2004).

16. William A. Herbert, "Public Workers," in *City of Workers, City of Struggle: How Labor Movements Changed New York*, ed. Joshua B. Freeman (New York: Columbia University Press, 2019), 142.

17. Ibid., 143.

18. Steve Fraser and Joshua B. Freeman, "In the Rearview Mirror: A Brief History of the Opposition to Public Sector Unionism," *New Labor Forum* 20, no. 3 (2011): 93–96; William A. Herbert, "The Chill of a Wintry Light: *Borough of Duryea v. Guarnieri* and the Right to Petition in Public Employment," *43 U. Tol. L. Rev. 583* (2012): 585; Joseph A. McCartin, *Collision Course: Ronald Reagan, the Air Traffic Controllers, and the Strike That Changed America* (New York: Oxford University Press, 2013).

19. *Janus v. American Federation of State, County, and Municipal Employees, Council 31, et al.*, 585 U.S. ___ (2018), https://www.supremecourt.gov/opinions/17pdf/16-1466 _2b3j.pdf/.

20. As labor scholar William A. Herbert has noted, Janus fits into a long history of American activism to curtail closed union shops. William A. Herbert, "*Janus v. AFSCME, Council 31*: Judges Will Haunt You in the Second Gilded Age," *Relations Industrielles / Industrial Relations* 74, no. 1 (2019): 162–73.

21. *Janus v. AFSCME, Council 31.*

22. Kagan noted that *Janus* represents a legal earthquake: "There is no sugarcoating today's opinion. The majority overthrows a decision entrenched in this Nation's law [*Abood v. Detroit Board of Education* (1977)]—and in its economic life—for over 40 years. As a result, it prevents the American people, acting through their state and local officials, from making important choices about workplace governance. And it does so by weaponizing the First Amendment, in a way that unleashes judges, now and in the future, to intervene in economic and regulatory policy." *Janus v. AFSCME, Council 31.*

23. Sterling Spero, *Government as Employer* (New York: Remsen Press, 1948); Paul P. Van Riper, *History of the United States Civil Service* (Evanston, IL: Row Peterson, 1958); Michael J. Honey, *Going Down Jericho Road: The Memphis Strike, Martin Luther King's Last Campaign* (New York: W. W. Norton, 2008); Marjorie Murphy, *Blackboard Union: The AFT and the NEA, 1900—1980* (Ithaca, NY: Cornell University Press, 1990); McCartin, *Collision Course.* On the value of Spero's pioneering work, in particular, see William A. Herbert, "Public Sector Labor Law and History: The Politics of Ancient History?," *Hofstra Labor and Employment Law Journal* 28, no 2 (2011): 345–58.

24. For an important call for this work, see Joseph A. McCartin, "Bringing the State's Workers Back In: Time to Rectify an Imbalanced U.S. Labor Historiography," *Labor History* 47, no. 1 (2006): 73–94.

25. Margaret Rung, *Servants of the State: Managing Diversity and Democracy in the Federal Workforce, 1933–1953* (Athens: University of Georgia Press, 2002).

PART I

The Politics of Public Work at the Dawn of the Twentieth Century

Historians typically date "the modern civil service" to the late nineteenth-century federal reforms designed to wring patronage, favoritism, and politics from the offices doing the nation's business. From the 1883 Pendleton Civil Service Reform Act forward, politics and personal advancement were imagined to be suppressed aspects of public work; primary was professional, selfless service to the nation, state, municipality, or local community. But did public workers really shed their personal and political ambitions so quickly? The essays in this section take an intersectional approach to the politics of public work at the turn of the twentieth century to reveal how questions of race, class, and gender shaped public workers, their workplaces, and their place in the American democracy.

While scholars have shown that women came to Washington, DC, to take advantage of the increasing "feminization" of federal clerical work in the late nineteenth century, Cathleen D. Cahill argues that the results of this process varied markedly for different women, depending on their identities and their intentions. While many white women found new routes to empowerment and middle-class status through political connections and public work, the hopes of Native American women for full citizenship, political relevance, and welfare were often run aground by racial ideologies and gendered expectations.

For African Americans, Eric S. Yellin provocatively suggests, work in the federal service has long constituted an attempt to recover some of what has been repeatedly taken from them: financial investment in their lives and communities. Learning to work within the parameters of the patronage system after emancipation, Black men in particular sought what nearly every federal worker hoped to draw from political and public work: a decent salary and the pursuit of happiness. That these ordinary ambitions came to be understood as corrupt and illegitimate, Yellin argues, is a function of how white supremacist ideas came to define Black labor and politics in the Progressive Era—a legacy that became readily apparent after Black voters and Black public workers earned new relevance after the civil rights movement.

CHAPTER 1

Gender and Politics among Federal Indian Service Employees, 1880–1930

CATHLEEN D. CAHILL

The 1922 edition of *The History of Woman Suffrage* proclaimed, "More women hold office in Washington than in any city in the world because of their very extensive employment by the National Government." The editors then offered examples of highly placed female civil servants, including Florence Etheridge, who had been appointed Office of Indian Affairs (OIA) probate attorney in Oklahoma.[1] Indeed, white suffragists had looked to the OIA as a site of women's empowerment through employment for several decades.

There were large numbers of female employees in the Indian Service (the workforce of the OIA). They were the result of the OIA's post–Civil War colonial agenda, which focused on assimilating Indigenous people into the nation as individual citizens. It created a variety of employment opportunities—including positions of high-ranking authority for white women—that were unique at the time. The office's goals and strategies also resulted in the employment of many Native women whose experiences were very different from their Anglo counterparts. For both groups of women, however, Indian Service employment influenced the development of their activist philosophies and national conversations about feminism. For white feminists, the Indian Service offered examples of competent women in positions of authority, countering stereotypes about women's unfitness for the public sphere. But federal Indian policy was premised on Native women's incompetence, and therefore Native women in public service had different experiences. Their firsthand knowledge of the difficulties Indigenous communities encountered at the hands of Indian Service employees and their own frustration with the bureaucracy shaped their Indigenous feminism, which often focused on calls for a new relationship between the federal government and Native nations that recognized tribal sovereignty.

Several decades ago, historian Cindy Aron revealed large numbers of women working in the federal civil service in Washington, DC. Despite these findings, only a few scholars, such as Amy Butler, have followed Aron to ask how such employment may have influenced women's political activities.[2] This is especially striking considering the fact that Washington, DC, became the site of suffrage political theater with the National Woman Suffrage Parade in 1913. It was also an important center for many other groups. For our purposes, it is relevant that Washington became a hub of intertribal Indigenous activism with the founding of the Society of American Indians (SAI) in 1911 headquartered in the capital city. The National Federation of Federal Employees, founded in 1916, also had its headquarters there.[3] Indeed, female Indian Service employees played an important role in all three of those movements: suffrage, intertribal activism, and union work.

* * *

The Indian Service was unusual among many federal bureaus in that it was an early employer of women, especially women in white-collar and high-ranking positions. This was the result of its particular mission and labor needs. Charged with assimilating Native people into the citizenry through education, imposing new legal regimes, and property (re)distribution, the OIA was unlike most other offices in the government in both purpose and personnel. Female employees were especially visible in its educational arm, the Indian School Service. By 1898 women made up 42 percent of the total Indian Service employees and fully 62 percent of the 2,649 employees in the Indian School Service. Moreover, the rhetoric used by administrators encouraged the employment of women. They often described Indian Service employees as missionary-like or serving in a parental relationship with Native people who were federal wards, especially the Native children in boarding schools. Because of nineteenth-century ideas about white women as naturally maternal and moral, this language solidified the sense that white women were particularly well-suited for these positions.[4]

The Indian Office also had a history of appointing white women to high positions. In the 1880s, the commissioner of Indian Affairs named several women, including Helen Hunt Jackson, Merial Dorchester, and Alice Fletcher to special agent positions. In 1898 Estelle Reel became the second-highest-ranking official in the Indian Office (and possibly the highest-ranking woman in the government) when she was appointed superintendent of the Indian schools.[5]

As the section from *The History of Woman Suffrage* that opened this essay suggested, suffragists were well aware of these women's appointments and looked to the Indian Service as a potential site of women's empowerment. For example, in February 1891, Anna Howard Shaw, later president of the National American Woman Suffrage Association (NAWSA), addressed the second annual conference of that organization. She had been campaigning for a woman suffrage referendum in South Dakota with Susan B. Anthony the previous fall, and just weeks after the 1890 election, the U.S. Army perpetrated the massacre at Wounded Knee. Native people and federal governance were both on her mind when she wrote her speech. She advocated for more women in governance: "I know of nothing which would settle the Indian question in this country like putting women at the head of Indian Affairs. Let Miss Alice Fletcher [applause] who is now a special Indian Agent . . . have full management in settling this question," she argued.[6] She was not the only suffragist to tout female Indian Service employees. Lucy Stone Blackwell, editor of *The Women's Journal and Suffrage News*, often printed articles about Indian policy and Indian Service employees, including Dorchester, Fletcher, and Reel. Readers also received updates on Native women, several of whom would become national voices of Indigenous feminism.[7]

But this empowerment primarily accrued to white women. Their employment was premised on racialized notions that white women were ideal mothers, while Native women were not. As a result of these ideas, Native women's children were removed from them and sent to boarding schools where white female employees served as surrogate mothers for them. Those white employees were also meant to be object lessons to Native girls and women who would learn true womanhood and appropriate behavior from them. In theory, they would then raise the next generation of Native children in a civilized manner, who could then blend seamlessly into the U.S. citizenry as individuals. This would solve "the Indian Problem" of the existence of sovereign nations with original claims to U.S. territory. The importance of social reproduction to federal Indian policy, and white women's particular fitness for it, opened up multiple employment and promotion opportunities for them.[8]

Ideas about Native women's unfitness for motherhood also gave policymakers incentive to hire them, as they argued that employment would be instructional. But Native women also provided a cheap source of labor necessary to run the perpetually underfunded federal Indian schools. As a result, they often held lower-paying menial or assistant positions and were paid at a lower "Indian rate," especially in comparison to white women. Many Indigenous women took these jobs despite their disadvantages because there were few other wage-earning positions available to Native people, and the posts offered them some opportunity to resist federal efforts of breaking up Indigenous families and nations by remaining close to their children and communities.[9]

For both groups of women, work in the Indian Service could lead to political activism, though often with different goals. For the growing number of white women, the politics of suffrage and labor activism addressed issues they had encountered upon entering the workforce, such as a glass ceiling. Because the Indian Office hired so many educated women, some emerged as leaders in these struggles, especially those employed in the Washington office. A handful of Native women who held positions in the Indian Service were also national activists, but their activism was often informed by their criticism of federal policy and in service to their agendas of tribal sovereignty and justice for Native peoples. What is clear is that the activism of some members of the OIA influenced the entire suffrage movement, the labor movement, as well as what has been termed the "red power" or "Native nationalism" movement.[10]

The Law, Feminism, and Civil Service

Law was essential in Indian affairs as well as feminism, and these two often came together in Washington, DC. Native nations had treaty relations—a specific diplomatic relationship—with the United States government. As the capital of the United States, the District of Columbia held an important symbolic and diplomatic place in the relations between Native nations and the federal government. Indigenous leaders and tribal diplomats had been traveling to the city to discuss that relationship as long as the city had existed.[11] Moreover, the diplomatic nature of the relationship and the fact that treaties were often contested or broken created a rich environment for lawyers.

Also, as the federal bureaucracy developed after the Civil War, so too did the role of attorneys. Women in Washington recognized that being a lawyer opened up a range of options. They also understood that the legal profession was changing. Rather than reading law with an established practitioner, as many of the first female attorneys had done, one increasingly needed a law degree to enter the profession, but law schools refused to enroll women. To address this, Ellen Spencer Mussey and Emma Gillett established the Washington College of Law (WCL) in 1896 to train women. Perhaps not surprisingly the WCL was a center of feminism and trained a generation of female lawyers in its first two decades. Between 1896 and 1916, 148 women received their LLB degree and 47 earned an LLM.[12] It is important to note that Howard University did enroll men and women (both Black and white) in its law courses, which the founders knew, as Gillett had graduated from Howard.[13] But they touted their school as the first "white" law school to be coeducational, and the school excluded African Americans until the 1950s.[14] They did not seem to exclude Native Americans, Jewish people, or applicants from Latin America.[15]

Indeed, the WCL had a specific connection between federal Indian policy and law. Belva Lockwood served as one of the school's board members. Lockwood, famously the first woman admitted before the bar of the U.S. Supreme Court and one of the first women to run for president of the United States, made her living by defending Indian claims cases.[16] That she chose this niche indicates the frequency of Native people in the courts of law in Washington. In 1875 Lockwood had taken a case for Jim Taylor, a Cherokee lobbyist for the Eastern Band of Cherokee Indians from North Carolina, and successfully argued his nation's case in the Court of Claims. Taylor and Lockwood made a deal in which he would bring her Native clients, and she would give him a cut of the fees. Soon afterward, she represented the Eastern and Emigrant Cherokees in their lawsuit against the United States, a case that required her to do years of research into treaty rights. It was for that case, *United States v. Cherokee Nation*, in 1906 that she argued before the Supreme Court for the second time.[17]

Three years later, Lockwood took Jean B. Bottineau's case, using her familiarity with treaty rights and claims to her advantage. Bottineau, an Anishinaabe or Chippewa man, had been serving as the attorney for the Turtle Mountain Chippewa Nation. He had been in Washington for over a decade contesting that nation's 1882 treaty with the United States. His daughter, Marie Bottineau Baldwin, joined him as his legal clerk, though in 1904 she had become an employee in the Indian Office. Bottineau had hired Lockwood to sue two former congressmen he had hired to help him but who had settled the case in favor of the federal government and taken payment. Maria Bottineau Baldwin testified during that trial and certainly met Lockwood. It is possible that watching Lockwood in the courtroom encouraged her to enroll at the law school a few years later.[18] Or perhaps she was motivated by the general desire of a civil servant to enroll in a professional school for promotional opportunities.

Indeed, like their male counterparts, female civil servants turned to the district's many professional schools to help give them promotional opportunities. For women seeking a law degree, the WCL was the obvious choice (unless they were African American). Given the close connections between Indian policy and law and the Indian Service's gendered hiring policies, it

Figure 1.1. Marie Louis Bottineau Baldwin, a woman of French and Ojibwe descent, first moved to Washington, DC, as legal clerk for her father, Jean Baptist Bottineau, tribal member and attorney for the Turtle Mountain Chippewa Nation. She lived in the city for much of the rest of her life, working as a clerk in the federal Indian Office. Like many women in the capital, she was politically active, but her engagement was shaped by the intersection of her gendered and Indigenous identities. (Photo from Louise Seymour Houghton, *Our Debt to the Red Man: The French-Indians in the Development of the United States* [Boston: Stratford Company, 1918], 173.)

is not surprising that the school also attracted a number of other Indian Service employees. Baldwin became one of the first Native women to train as a lawyer in the nation when she earned her LLB in 1914. She then went further, enrolling in an LLM program and graduating in 1915. She also acted as a mentor and served as a reference for some of her colleagues who applied to the college. This included an Eastern Shawnee woman from Oklahoma, Ida Prophet-Riley, who applied but withdrew her application due to financial constraints.[19]

With a few exceptions like Baldwin and Prophet-Riley, most of the WCL applicants from the Indian Office were white women.[20] Baldwin's OIA colleague Flora Warren (later Seymour) also graduated with her LLB in 1915, while a second colleague, Florence Etheridge, had graduated in 1912 and earned her LLM in 1913. The additional degree seems to have benefited all three of the women professionally. Etheridge and Baldwin received promotions. Baldwin was eventually supervisor of three white clerks. Upon receiving her LLB degree, Etheridge transferred from the Pension Office to the higher position of legal clerk in the Indian Office and, as we will discuss below, was later promoted to probate attorney. Upon her graduation, Flora Warren, who had been working for the Indian Office since 1909, resigned and married John Seymour. They moved to Chicago and both practiced law in the city. She would move back into the Indian Service orbit a few years later.[21]

Despite these women's seemingly similar career paths, their political activism and engagement differed dramatically. This was a direct result of their identities as white or Indigenous as well as their relationship to the Indian Office and its policies. For Native women, their work in the colonial bureaucracy of the Indian Service gave them firsthand experience from which to formulate a critique of federal policy. White women, on the other hand, found that while they still encountered glass ceilings in the civil service, federal Indian policies elevated them to prestigious positions in the bureaucracy. Suffrage and women's rights activism as well as labor activism became spheres in which women from these two groups attempted to communicate with each other across their different concerns.

Female Federal Employees and Political Activism

The women's time at the Washington College of Law also coincided with the revived suffrage movement in the capital. Not surprisingly, the school was a hotbed of DC feminism. A number of the teachers and students were involved in the planning of the famous 1913 suffrage parade the weekend of Woodrow Wilson's inauguration. Though later attributed to Alice Paul, the parade was Florence Etheridge's idea, proposed while she was the president of the Washington, DC, State Suffrage Association in 1912.[22] It may also have been Etheridge who generated the idea of having a float representing Native women. *The Woman's Journal* (and many other newspapers across the country) reported, "An Indian float is being prepared by the clerks in the

Indian Department. On it will be real Indian women." Other papers explicitly stated that Marie Bottineau Baldwin was planning the float. It "will portray the high position which Indian women [are] held in certain parts of the country under the old tribal regime—a position relatively higher politically than the position occupied by white women in this country today."[23]

Such coverage was consistent with white feminists' divided thinking about Native people, a dichotomy embedded deep in American culture. On the one hand, they often celebrated Native women as matriarchs with political power in their original societies that were, sadly, disappearing into the past. This was akin to the "Princess" or "Noble Savage" stereotypes. On the other hand, white suffragists often vilified Native men as "savages" who could potentially receive the vote before white women or with whom white women were unfairly classed as nonvoters. At the same time, anti-suffragists often used the imagery of the downtrodden "squaw" to deride suffragists for stepping out of their sphere and thus losing the respect due to women who maintained proper gender roles. This was similar to the imagery the Indian Office used to justify the removal of Native children from their mothers.[24]

Baldwin ultimately chose not to create the float. She did not disagree with the argument that Native women held power in their societies. In fact, she herself had made the case that "in a large number of tribes she [Native woman] was on absolute equality with her sons and brothers," and her speeches and newspaper interviews likely helped spread these ideas to white feminists.[25] But it is more likely that her work with a new organization, the Society of American Indians, founded in 1911, influenced her decision. She likely wanted to reject the idea that Indians were trapped in the past and disappearing. Instead, she proudly marched as a modern woman with her fellow lawyers. Baldwin's white colleagues at both the WCL and the Indian Service became nationally known because their work for the Indian Office advanced them to high positions. This fit their expectations for their employment, but they still sometimes encountered frustration due to their gender.

Etheridge was celebrated for her promotion to probate attorney for the OIA in 1917. It occurred just as Washington feminists were pushing for appointments in the city's judicial courts.[26] Etheridge, however, was also an example of the frustration white women encountered in federal employment. She disliked the rigid systematization of the civil service. She wrote that because the service was seen as "avocational . . . it has been easy for the government worker to fall into the error of believing himself to be something other than a workman" and thus accept lower pay and other poor labor conditions. The Indian Office's rhetoric of employees as missionaries certainly reinforced that. Her frustration, and that of others, came to a head in 1916 when a bill introduced by Rep. William P. Borland added an hour to government employees' workdays but also classified them such that they could not receive overtime pay. Moreover, because employees in Washington, DC, could not vote unless they could afford to return to their home districts, their concerns did not trouble most congressmen. The employees, therefore, turned to the American Federation of Labor (AFL) and organized a union, the National Federation of Federal Employees (NFFE). Etheridge had vowed that "she would do as much as might be done to abolish forever the circumstances that made possible, in what was supposed to be the honorable service of one's country, conditions which would not be tolerated in a modern factory." So she not only joined the union but also became an active leader.[27] She was appointed the first treasurer, one of two female officers (the other was recording secretary). The following year when she was elected fourth vice president, she was the only woman serving on the executive board and was the only female delegate (out of fifty-one) to the union's first annual convention.[28]

She was also a constant contributor of union news as well as poetry and fiction to its new magazine, *The Federal Employee*.[29] Etheridge's writing often addressed the issues female employees faced. For example, her article "On Women in the Government Service—And Elsewhere" emphasized the importance of "equal pay for equal work." At the 1917 convention, she successfully urged the union to endorse the "principle of woman suffrage" in face of opposition, including charges that women were taking men's jobs because they were willing to accept lower pay. (Etheridge responded that women accepted lower-paying jobs because they were not unionized.)[30]

Another WCL graduate, Flora Warren Seymour, also leveraged her Indian Service work into prominence. In 1922 President Warren Harding appointed her to the Board of Indian Commissioners (BIC). She was the first woman to serve in the board's fifty-five-year existence. Though not the Indian Service per se, the BIC served in an advisory relation to the commissioner of Indian Affairs. Members were "prominent people." Her previous work in the service as well as her law degrees were certainly both essential to her appointment, which was supported by both of Illinois's senators and the Chicago Bar Association.[31]

Seymour drew on all of those experiences to set herself up as an authority on Indians, becoming a popular author of a number of books about Native Americans. A 1925 article described her as an "Authority on Indian Culture and History" who "Serves as Federal Commissioner." It went on to say she was "one of the few people who really know Indian life." The article asserted that she was a great collector of Native objects and books on Native people. She was also an author herself, having already published "a number of descriptive and historical books on Indians" as well as "four small handbooks on Indian tribes": *History of the New York Indians, Five Civilized American Indian Tribes, Story of the Sioux Indians,* and *Indians of the Pueblos,* all published in 1924.[32] She later published *The Indians Today* (1926), *Story of the Red Man* (1929), *Women of Trail and Wigwam* (1930), *We Called Them Indians* (1941), and *Indian Agents of the Old Frontier* (1941) as well as the biography *Sacagawea: Bird Girl,* for young readers, in 1945.[33]

Indeed, as I have argued elsewhere, the Indian Service privileged white women as ideas about their female moral authority opened jobs for them and gave them power over Native people. For some women, like Etheridge and Seymour, this was further magnified by the high-ranking positions they received. Many of those white employees held racist ideas about Indian people, though some were certainly worse than others. Etheridge, for example, who vigorously protested against the "squaw drudge" stereotype used to characterize and dehumanize Native women, still wrote casually about "dirty" Indians or used caricatures to amuse her readers.[34] Seymour recognized that the Indian Service warranted criticism but argued that the problems arose merely from white employees' unfamiliarity with Native people. Speaking at a Society of American Indians conference in 1916, she argued that most employees were well-meaning but ignorant. Perhaps this is why she turned to writing, as a way to educate a broader white audience.[35]

* * *

Native employees also found ignorance about Indigenous people to be part of a larger criticism they had of federal Indian policy. In order to combat stereotypes and the federal policies that were built on them, Marie Baldwin, along with a group of fifty Native people who were well educated by the terms of Anglo America, founded the Society of American Indians in 1911. They imagined it as a "race organization" for "the purpose of the protection and advancement of [the] race." It sought to promote a positive image of Indianness to white Americans and to address a variety of concerns shared by Native people, especially federal policy.[36] Many of those founders were either current or past employees in the Indian Service.[37] Lawyers were also well represented among them. For Native people, the law was an important weapon in their fight for tribal sovereignty. Marie Baldwin knew this firsthand, as she had moved to Washington to clerk for her father as he fought for treaty rights. She pointed out in an interview that while all women should study law, it was especially important for Native women, as "to a race whose lands and property of other kinds are so valuable, it is all-important."[38]

26   THE POLITICS OF PUBLIC WORK

Despite the large number of SAI members who had been federal employees, the question of working in the Indian Service became a point of contention in the organization. Indeed, many had grave concerns about federal Indian policy but differed on the solution. For example, at the 1916 conference, some people, like vocal critic Carlos Montezuma (Yavapai-Apache), previously a doctor for the Indian Service, called for the immediate abolition of the OIA and castigated those members who worked for it as race traitors. Both Marie Baldwin and Gertrude Simmons Bonnin, also known as Zitkala-Ša (Yankton Dakota), insisted that Native employees were not the problem. They did, however, call for a gradual abolition of the OIA. (This was the same conference at which Seymour argued for a better-educated labor force).[39] Their experience as Native employees definitely shaped their thinking about federal policy. Their work experiences made them incisive critics of those policies, while their shared relationship with the federal government often contributed to their sense of a shared political identity across Indigenous nations.

This was the case for SAI founder Laura Cornelius Kellogg of the Wisconsin Oneida Nation. The Oneida are part of the Haudenosaunee (or Iroquois) Confederacy and had been removed from upstate New York to the area just south of Green Bay in the early nineteenth century. Kellogg came from a long line of powerful Haudenosaunee women, and her maternal grandfather was Daniel Bread, an important civil leader who had helped the nation during their relocation.[40]

Like many other SAI members, Kellogg had been an Indian Service employee. Her graduation with honors from the girls school Grafton Hall in Fond Du Lac, Wisconsin, in 1898, had received national newspaper coverage. She had hopes of a literary career, but like many other educated Native women, she found that jobs were scarce, so she joined the Indian Service. She was appointed as a teacher at the Sherman Institute, a federal boarding school in Riverside, California, where she served from 1902 to 1904. During that time, she witnessed the eviction of the Cupeños, Indigenous Californians, from their land at Warner's Ranch in northern San Diego County. Though they had never ceded their land rights, the U.S. Supreme Court ruled that the Cupeños had waited too long to assert them and therefore lost title to the land and that the non-Native owner could have the Cupeños removed. Kellogg again made national headlines as "the Indian Joan of Arc" when she made a speech to the Cupeños sympathizing with them and emphasizing Indigenous resilience. In an interview that year, she announced that she wanted to work "for the uplifting of her race" and to advocate "for the Indian point of view."

She soon quit her position at Riverside to study law at Stanford University. Though she remained at Stanford only briefly, she never stopped being an advocate for Native rights.[41]

Gertrude Bonnin also moved on from the Indian Service to advocacy work. In 1917 she was elected secretary of the SAI. She and her husband, Raymond, resigned their positions in the Indian Service at the Uintah and Ouray reservation in Utah and moved to the organization's headquarters in Washington, DC. The couple had worked in the service for two decades. Gertrude Bonnin had been born on the Yankton Dakota (Sioux) reservation in South Dakota and was taken to a missionary school in Indiana when she was only eight years old, an action that forever altered her relationship with her mother. She later enrolled at Earlham College in Indiana. After graduation, Bonnin took a position at Carlisle Indian School in Pennsylvania, the government's flagship boarding school. She was conflicted by the work and left the position to study music and write. She published a series of short stories under her Dakota name, Zitkala-Ša, in the prestigious *Atlantic* and *Harper's Monthly* magazines. They were semiautobiographical snapshots of federal Indian policy from an Indigenous point of view. They emphasized the sorrow of families torn apart by federal policy and the frustration Native employees experienced as they became disillusioned with the federal bureaucracy. She returned to the Indian Service after her marriage to Raymond Bonnin in 1902. They moved to Utah, where Raymond held the position of clerk in the Indian Service. Gertrude also held various positions during their time in Utah, including clerk and temporary teacher. She requested a permanent teaching position, but despite her stellar credentials, she was denied. Committed to helping the community, she was frustrated by the lack of support she received for her social work among Ute women but was especially aggrieved by the racism she and Raymond faced from other employees, especially a supervisor. As she wrote after Raymond's forced resignation in 1913 (he was later reinstated), "Somehow these officials hate to ever admit a mistake which is plainly theirs! They shield one another! There is no hope for an Indian to look to them for justice."[42]

For both Bonnin and Kellogg, their frustrating experiences in the service and with white federal officials contributed to their criticism of federal policy in their publications and speeches. Both women advocated for woman suffrage, not as the ultimate marker of "civilization," as assimilation policy would have it, but as a way to defend tribal sovereignty. However, most Native women were left behind by the ratification of the Nineteenth Amendment in 1920. Even after all Indians were granted U.S. citizenship in 1924, state laws kept many from voting, and the federal government maintained oversight of property. After 1920 they appealed to newly enfranchised white women to work for justice for Native people.

In Washington, for example, Bonnin often advocated for an end to federal wardship and oversight of Native nations and for Native citizenship. This was especially powerful against the backdrop of World War I. But she did not see U.S. citizenship as incompatible with tribal self-government. In her speeches, she was developing a series of arguments she would publish in her 1921 book, *American Indian Stories*. In one speech, "Bureaucracy versus Democracy," Bonnin contrasted Native wards controlled by federal agents with the exercise of self-governance. She illustrated this contention with two circles containing the elements of each system, one described as "What We Have" and the other, "What We Want." Clearly drawing on her own experiences, she elaborated on the problems of bureaucracy: "American Congress Gives Discretionary Power to Superintendents [and] Indians [are] Absolutely under the control and jurisdiction of superintendents." Instead of a democracy, "Indians [lived] on reservations without citizens' association[.] Without voice in their own affairs and expenditures of their moneys." She called on white Americans to grant Native nations tribal sovereignty and self-government as well as U.S. citizenship and the right of suffrage to facilitate that self-governance.[43]

Laura Cornelius Kellogg also spent those years writing and would publish her book of political theory, *Our Democracy and the American Indian*, in 1920. Like Bonnin, she argued that Indigenous people under federal wardship were not free. Indian agents who supervised reservations were "absolute despots." Why couldn't Native nations coexist with the United States while maintaining their sovereignty and land base? she asked. She advocated a plan called Lolomi, calling for tribally held property in terms familiar to Americans: the corporation, with tribal members as investors. According to Kellogg, Lolomi involved "federal incorporation of a self-governing body." Individuals would pool their allotments into shared property that would support all tribal members, and each would have a single vote. A very modern model, it would do away with "the status of semi-citizenship (the status of wardship), which is at once unconstitutional and chaotic." Incorporation also clarified the relationship of the Oneida Nation to the United States because it "presuppose[d] a state of self-government" free from Indian Office oversight and more akin to the position of the states within the union.[44]

Kellogg's and Bonnin's castigation of the Indian Office as despotic was not hyperbole but grew out of their specific experiences as federal employees. Their solutions also reflected their experiences. In place of bureaucracy and oversight by federal employees, each articulated a vision of tribal sovereignty based on communally held tribal lands and self-governance with a nation-to-nation relationship to the United States.[45] Both women ultimately quit the Indian Service to work for Native people, finding government employment a dead end in that regard.

* * *

The Native and white women examined here shared a number of things in common: they worked for the federal Indian Service, they believed in women's rights, they were politically active, many of them were authors, and several pursued law degrees. But despite those similarities, their identities significantly shaped their work experiences in civil service and their activism. While white women could advance in their careers by claiming authority over Native people, Indigenous women faced a bureaucracy that was constructed specifically upon the idea that they were unfit and needed to be "civilized." Even those who were extremely well educated by Western standards faced difficulties due to the prejudices and assumptions of non-Native employees and supervisors.

Further Reading

Aron, Cindy S. *Ladies and Gentlemen of the Civil Service: Middle-Class Workers in Victorian America.* New York: Oxford University Press, 1987.

Butler, Amy E. *Two Paths to Equality: Alice Paul and Ethel M. Smith in the ERA Debate, 1921–1929.* Albany: SUNY Press, 2012.

Cahill, Cathleen D. *Federal Fathers and Mothers: A Social History of the United States Indian Service, 1869–1933.* Chapel Hill: University of North Carolina Press, 2011.

Jacobs, Margaret. *White Mother to a Dark Race: Settler Colonialism, Maternalism, and the Removal of Indigenous Children in the American West and Australia, 1880–1940.* Lincoln: University of Nebraska Press, 2011.

Lewandowski, Tadeusz. *Red Bird, Red Power: The Life and Legacy of Zitkala-Ša.* Norman: University of Oklahoma Press, 2016.

Ramirez, Renya K. *Standing Up to Colonial Power: The Lives of Henry Roe and Elizabeth Bender Cloud.* Lincoln: University of Nebraska Press, 2019.

Wilkins David E., and K. Tsianina Lomawaima. *On Uneven Ground: American Indian Sovereignty and Federal Law.* Norman: University of Oklahoma, 2001.

Notes

1. Suffragists celebrated a number of other high-ranking women in federal positions beginning with Julia Lathrop's appointment as head of the Children's Bureau in 1912. Ida Husted Harper, ed., *The History of Woman Suffrage*, vol. 6 (New York: J. J. Little & Ives, 1922), 110–12.

2. Cindy S. Aron, *Ladies and Gentlemen of the Civil Service: Middle Class Workers*

in Victorian America (New York: Oxford University Press, 1987); and Jessica Ziparo, *This Grand Experiment: When Women Entered the Federal Workforce in Civil War–Era Washington, DC* (Chapel Hill: University of North Carolina Press, 2017). For women's political participation in "a parallel political culture" in the period before they were a large part of the federal workforce, see Catherine Allgor, *Parlor Politics: In Which the Ladies of Washington Help Build a City and a Government* (Charlottesville: University Press of Virginia, 2000). See also the essays in *Women and the Unstable State in Nineteenth-Century America*, ed. Alison M. Parker and Stephanie Cole (Arlington: University of Texas Press, 2000), especially Allgor's essay, "'A Lady Will Have More Influence': Women and Patronage in Early Washington City" (37–60) and Elizabeth R. Varon's essay, "Patriotism, Partisanship, and Prejudice: Elizabeth Van Lew of Richmond and Debates over Female Civic Duty in Post–Civil War America" (113–138); Amy E. Butler, *Two Paths to Equality: Alice Paul and Ethel M. Smith in the ERA Debate, 1921–1929* (Albany: SUNY Press, 2002), 7–8, 13–23.

3. On intertribal politics of Native people in cities more broadly, see Renya K. Ramirez, *Native Hubs: Culture, Community, and Belonging in Silicon Valley and Beyond* (Durham, NC: Duke University Press, 2007); Kent Blansett, Cathleen D. Cahill, and Andrew Needham, eds., *Indian Cities: Histories of Indigenous Urbanism* (Norman: University of Oklahoma Press, 2022). Washington was also an important site for African Americans; see, for example, Kate Masur, *An Example for All the Land: Emancipation and the Struggle for Equality in Washington, DC* (Chapel Hill: University of North Carolina Press, 2012); Chris Myers Asch and George Derek Musgrove, *Chocolate City: A History of Race and Democracy in the Nation's Capital* (Chapel Hill: University of North Carolina Press, 2017).

4. See Cathleen D. Cahill, "'You Think It Strange That I Can Love an Indian': Native Men, White Women, and Marriage in the Indian Service," *Frontiers: A Journal of Women Studies* 29, nos. 2/3 (2008): 106–145; and Cahill, "Seeking the Incalculable Benefit of a Faithful, Patient Man and Wife': Families in the Federal Indian Service, 1880–1925," in *On the Borders of Love and Power: Families and Kinship in the Intercultural American Southwest*, ed. David Wallace Adams and Crista DeLuzio, 71–92 (Berkeley: University of California Press, 2012).

5. See "Appendix of Employees," in *Annual Report of the Commissioner of Indian Affairs* (Washington, DC: Government Printing Office, 1898), 631–74. In 1898, of the 1,636 women in the School Service, 718, or 43.8 percent, were Native. Alice Fletcher was appointed as special allotment agent in 1882. In 1883 Helen Hunt Jackson, author of *A Century of Dishonor* and *Ramona*, was named special inspector to investigate the Mission Indians in California. In 1889 Commissioner Morgan appointed Merial A. Dorchester as special agent in the Indian School Service. During the 1890s and into the twentieth century, many well-educated women came to occupy other high-ranking positions. For instance, Molly Gaither and Clara True served as superintendents of individual boarding schools. Cathleen Cahill, *Federal Fathers and Mothers: A Social History of the United States Indian Service, 1869–1933* (Chapel Hill: University of North Carolina Press, 2011), 64–65.

6. Ida Husted Harper, ed., *The History of Woman Suffrage* (National American Woman Suffrage Association, 1922), 110–11; Anna Howard Shaw, "Indians versus Women," *The Woman's Tribune* (May 9, 1891), 147.

7. Articles from *Women's Journal and Suffrage News* include Alice Fletcher, "Concerning Women" (vol. 12, no. 50), December 10, 1881, 393; "The International Council" (vol. 19, no. 14), April 7, 1888, 114; and "Among the Omahas," (vol. 13, no. 6), February 11, 1882, 46–47; Merial Dorchester, "News and Notes" (vol. 21, no. 29), July 19, 1890, 229, and "Concerning Women" (vol. 21, no. 52), December 27, 1890, 409; Estelle Reel, "The Education of Indian Children" (vol. 32, no. 32), August 10, 1901, 255; "Miss Reel's Report on Indian Schools" (vol. 32, no. 50), December 14, 1901, 394; Zitkala-Ša (Gertrude Bonnin), "With Our Exchanges" (vol. 31, no. 3), January 20, 1900, 24; and "The December Magazines" (vol. 33, no. 51), December 20, 1902, 406–407; Marie Baldwin, "Parade Will Be Mass of Color" (vol. 45, no. 5), February 1, 1913, 38; Laura Cornelius Kellogg, "Women Lawyers," (vol. 36, no. 8), February 25, 1905, 30; and "Indian Squaw for Self-Government" (vol. 47, no. 15), April, 8, 1916, 113.

8. Margaret E. Jacobs, *White Mother to a Dark Race: Settler Colonialism, Maternalism, and the Removal of Indigenous Children in the American West and Australia, 1880–1940* (Lincoln: University of Nebraska Press, 2011).

9. Cahill, *Federal Fathers and Mothers*; and William Bauer, *We Were All Like Migrant Workers Here: Work, Community, and Memory on California's Round Valley Reservation, 1850–1941* (Chapel Hill: University of North Carolina Press, 2009). For the example of Ojibwe activist Elizabeth Bender Cloud, see Renya K. Ramirez, *Standing Up to Colonial Power: The Lives of Henry Roe and Elizabeth Bender Cloud* (Lincoln: University of Nebraska Press, 2018).

10. Fred Hoxie, ed., *Talking Back to Civilization: Indian Voices from the Progressive Era* (Boston: Bedford/St. Martin's, 2001); Lucy Maddox, *Citizen Indians: Native American Intellectuals, Race, and Reform* (Ithaca, NY: Cornell University Press, 2006); Tom Holm, *The Great Confusion in Indian Affairs: Native Americans and Whites in the Progressive Era* (Austin: University of Texas Press, 2005); Kent Blansett, *A Journey to Freedom: Richard Oakes, Alcatraz, and the Red Power Movement* (New Haven, CT: Yale University Press, 2018).

11. Herman J. Viola, *Diplomats in Buckskin: A History of Indian Delegations in Washington City* (Washington, DC: Smithsonian Institution Press, 1981); C. Joseph Genetin-Pilawa, "The Indians' Capital City: Diplomatic Visits, Place, and Two-Worlds Discourse in Nineteenth-Century Washington, DC," in *Beyond Two Worlds: Critical Conversations on Language and Power in Native North America*, ed. James Joseph Buss and C. Joseph Genetin-Pilawa, 117–36 (Albany: SUNY Press, 2014).

12. Virginia G. Drachman, *Sisters in Law: Women Lawyers in Modern American History* (Cambridge, MA: Harvard University Press, 1998), 154.

13. Grace Hathaway, *Fate Rides a Tortoise: A Biography of Ellen Spencer Mussey* (Philadelphia: John C. Winston, 1937), 105–106. The school's origin story in the book was that Delia Sheldon Jackson, daughter of Sheldon Jackson, Presbyterian missionary and educator working in Indian education in Alaska, convinced Mussey to train

her. Delia Jackson was later DC chair for the National Woman's Party; see "Official Program," *The Suffragist* 9, no. 1 (1921): 342.

14. Ellen Spencer Mussey, "The Law and the Lady," *The Suffragist* 8, no. 5 (1920): 93–94.

15. See Applications files, box 118, Washington College of Law Library Archives, Washington, DC.

16. Lockwood first argued before the Supreme Court in 1880. Jill Norgren, *Belva Lockwood: The Woman Who Would Be President* (New York: NYU Press, 2007), 81–83, 86–88, 106.

17. *United States v. Cherokee Nation*, 202 U.S. 101 (1906); Diana Klebanow and Franklin L. Jones, *People's Lawyers: Crusaders for Justice in American History* (New York: Routledge, 2002), 32–35. See also Norgren, *Belva Lockwood.*

18. Norgren, *Belva Lockwood*, 81–83, 86–88, 106; and *Maddux v. Bottineau* in *Reports of Cases Adjudged in the Court of Appeals of the District of Columbia from November 2, 1909, to April 5, 1910*, ed. Charles Cowles Tucker, vol. 34 (34 App. D.C.) (Rochester, NY: Lawyers Co-operative Publishing Company, 1910), 119–30.

19. Washington College of Law Library Archives, box 118, folder "Applications for Admission 1915–1916, Mrs. Winifred E. Ayers-Allen recommended by Florence Ether-idge and Mrs. M.L.B. Baldwin," and folder "Applications for Admission 1915–1916, Miss Ida Prophet-Riley recommended by M.L.B. Baldwin and Florence Etheridge," both in Pence Law Library, American University Washington College of Law, Washington, DC. On Riley, see Ida Prophet-Riley, Census no. 136; 1923, Quapaw Agency Census; 1923; Roll: *M595_413*; Line: 33; Agency: *Quapaw* Ancestry.com. *U.S., Indian Census Rolls, 1885–1940* [database online]. Provo, UT, USA: Ancestry.com Operations Inc., 2007.

20. Washington College of Law Library Archives, box 118, folder "Applications for Admission 1909–1910, Mrs. Lilly McCoy"; folder "Applications for Admission 1911–1912, Florence Etheridge"; folder "Applications for Admission 1912–1913, Hellen Saville Rapley of California with a reference from Hon. Charles F. Hauke 2nd Assistant Commissioner of Indian Affairs and Hon. Edgar A. Merritt, Law Clerk Office of Indian Affairs"; folder "Applications for Admission 1913–1914, Eunice K. Warner and Adele Smith"; and folder "Applications for Admission 1914–1915, Miss Nellie Nance," all in Pence Law Library, American University Washington College of Law, Washington, DC.

21. "Law College Graduates Twenty-Six Students," *Evening Star* (Washington, DC), May 28, 1915, 10; personnel files, Florence Etheridge and Marie Bottineau Baldwin, National Personnel Records Center, St. Louis, MO.

22. *Official Program of the Woman's Suffrage Procession, Washington, DC, March 3, 1913, Library of Congress*, https://www.loc.gov/resource/rbpe.20801600/; Harper, *History of Woman Suffrage 1900–1920*, vol. 6, 105.

23. "Parade Will Be Mass of Color," *Woman's Journal* 45, no. 5 (1913), 38; and "Equal Suffrage among Indians," *Los Angeles Times*, January 31, 1913.

24. See Sally Roesch Wagner, *Sisters in Spirit: Haudenosaunee (Iroquois) Influence*

on Early American Feminists (Summertown, TN: Native Voices, 2001); Margaret E. Jacobs, *Engendered Encounters: Feminism and Pueblo Cultures, 1879–1934* (Lincoln: University of Nebraska Press, 1999); Philip Deloria, *Playing Indian* (New Haven, CT: Yale University Press, 1999); and Rayna Green, "The Pocahontas Perplex: The Image of Indian Women in American Culture," *Massachusetts Review* 16, no. 4 (1975): 698–714.

25. *Report of the Executive Council on the Proceedings of the First Annual Conference of the Society of American Indians* (Washington, DC, 1912), 58. See also "Indian Women the First Suffragists and Used Recall, Chippewa Avers," *Washington Times*, August 3, 1914.

26. See "Women Lawyers in D.C. to Organize," *Evening Star*, March 14, 1917, in Ellen Spencer Mussey Scrapbook, 1904–1918, Washington College of Law Historical Collection, American University Digital Archives, https://auislandora.wrlc.org/islandora/object/wcl%3A14268/, accessed January 5, 2019. There are a number of similar articles in the scrapbooks.

27. Florence Etheridge, "The Point of View," *Federal Employee* 3, no. 5 (1918): 428–29.

28. Officers of the NFFE, *Federal Employee* 2, no. 10 (1917): n.p.; see foldout photos between pp. 372 and 373 and pp. 600–601. An Osage man, Wallace Springer, was included in the photograph as representative from Pawhuska, OK. See also Etheridge's report of the convention, "National Federation of Federal Employees," *Federal Employee* 2, no. 10 (1917): 573–600.

29. "Board of Representatives" and "Why the Federal Employees Union," in *Federal Employee* 2, no. 10 (1916): 12, 15.

30. Florence Etheridge, "On Women in the Government Service—And Elsewhere," *Federal Employee* 1, no. 5 (1916): 178–80; and Florence Etheridge, "National Federation of Federal Employees," *Federal Employee* 1, no. 5 (19176): 585.

31. "Woman on Indian Board," *McPherson (KS) Daily Republican*, November 20, 1922.

32. Henry Harrison, "Indians Not Held on Reservations but White Man May Not Enter," *Brooklyn Daily Eagle*, December 20, 1925.

33. "Flora Warren Seymour," http://encyclopedia.jrank.org/articles/pages/4778/Seymour-Flora-Warren-1888-1948.html/, accessed January 28, 2019. See, for example, her author biography in G.E.E. Lindquist, *The Indian in American Life* (New York: Friendship Press, 1944). "Flora Warren Seymour, LL.M., is a lawyer, traveler, and author whose lifelong study of Indians and the history of the West has resulted in an extended list of books. . . . She spent six years in the United States Indian Service and was the first woman appointed by the President to serve on the Board of Indian Commissioners." John Holst, another collaborator with Lindquist, also pointed to his own Indian Service credentials.

34. Florence Etheridge, "The Odyssey of a Federal Employee," *Federal Employee* 8, no. 7 (1918): 676; and Florence Etheridge, "The Odyssey of a Federal Employee," *Federal Employee* 3, no. 8 (1918): 823.

35. Flora Warren Seymour, "The Indian Service—An Opportunity," *American Indian Magazine* 5, no. 4 (1916): 315–17.

36. On the SAI, see Hazel Hertzberg, *The Search for American Indian Identity: Modern Pan-Indian Movements* (Syracuse, NY: Syracuse University Press, 1981); Maddox, *Citizen Indians*; and "The Society of American Indians and Its Legacies: A Special Issue of SAIL and AIQ" *American Indian Quarterly* 37, no. 3 (2013).

37. Cahill, *Federal Fathers and Mothers*, 229.

38. "Indians of Today Realize the Value of Education as Principal Asset of the Race," *Washington Times*, March 20, 1916. See also "Newspaper Comment," *American Indian Magazine* 4, no. 3 (1916): 268–69.

39. Hertzberg, *Search for American Indian Identity*. See also the 1916 SAI conference coverage in *American Indian Magazine* 4, no. 4 (1916).

40. Laura Cornelius Kellogg, *Our Democracy and the American Indian*, ed. Kristina Ackley and Cristina Stanciu (Syracuse, NY: Syracuse University Press, 2015); and Philip J. Deloria, "Four Thousand Invitations," *American Indian Quarterly* 37, no. 3 (Spring 2013): 25–43.

41. Kellogg, *Our Democracy and the American Indian*; and Doug Kiel, "Competing Visions of Empowerment: Oneida Progressive-Era Politics and Writing Tribal Histories," *Ethnohistory* 61, no. 3 (2014): 436.

42. Quoted in Tadeusz Lewandowski, *The Red Bird: The Life and Legacy of Zitkala-Ša* (Norman: University of Oklahoma Press, 2016), 76–77. See also Susan Rose Dominguez, "The Gertrude Bonnin Story: From Yankton Destiny into American History, 1804–1938" (PhD diss., Michigan State University, 2005).

43. Zitkala-Ša (Gertrude Bonnin), "Indian Study," box 8, folder 201, May Walden Papers, 1870–1972. Newberry Library, Chicago, IL.

44. Kellogg, *Our Democracy*, 260n73, 9, and 89–98.

45. Potentially Seymour was listening, though she heard only part of the message. It is intriguing that that one of the characters in her play, "What Do We Mean by Indian?" from the 1940s, was a Wisconsin Oneida with the first name Cornelius (admittedly a familiar name among that nation). The play offered a strong critique of federal wardship, similar to those articulated by Kellogg, but ultimately Seymour offered individual citizenship rather than Kellogg's defense of tribal sovereignty as the solution. Flora Warren Seymour, *What Do We Mean by Indian?* (New York: Home Mission Council of North America, n.d.), 1.

CHAPTER 2

The Spoils as Reparations

ERIC S. YELLIN

In his second State of the Union Address, in January 2019, President Donald Trump took special aim at the federal bureaucracy, demanding that Congress unravel rules that prevented him and his executive appointees from unilaterally firing civil servants who "undermine the public trust or fail the American people."[1] Surely, Trump hoped to erode the government's regulatory power by rooting out the so-called deep state that was resisting his authoritarian impulses.[2] Yet, even putting aside Trump's campaign to deny President Barack Obama's citizenship and presidential legitimacy, his rhetoric should be understood as trading in a long-standing racist trope that the disproportionately Black federal workforce is corrupt.[3] Ultimately, those most vulnerable to this kind of attack on the civil service were Black workers. Trump was just the latest contributor to a long history of delegitimizing and obscuring the work of African Americans in the nation's service.[4]

American politicians have been associating Black public workers with government corruption and waste since the Reconstruction era following the Civil War, when formerly enslaved Black men first won a place in American democracy and entered government service. To understand racialized notions of public work, we must examine this earlier era of patronage. White Southern "redeemers" in the 1870s attacked interracial Reconstruction governments in Southern states as "swamps" of corruption in need of draining. That swamp, they insisted, stretched all the way up to the Republican-dominated federal government in Washington, DC, where thousands of Black Southerners had fled for work and federal protection only to infect the entire democracy with their political depravity. This spurious story of Black political corruption was a tale that white politicians and historians told and retold over the next fifty years, until "Reconstruction" became a byword for corruption and Black public workers the ultimate symbol of bad government.[5]

In the mid-twentieth century, the threat of Black public work gained resonance once again as New Deal and Great Migration urban politics in the North pushed government to once again become the nation's leading fair practices employer.[6] Equal opportunity programs in the 1960s then brought even larger numbers of Black workers into government, just at the moment when Americans' faith in public institutions began to erode generally, thanks to economic stagnation, the Vietnam War, Watergate, and the rise of the modern conservative movement.[7] For many leading policy analysts in the 1980s, federal affirmative action programs became yet another sign of a persistent patronage scheme—a "spoils system"—infesting public offices unenlightened by meritocratic and efficient market solutions.[8] The nightmare of Reconstruction had recurred: a disproportionately Black federal service was, once again, a corrupt federal service. In the long history of Black public work, a focus on periods when politics and patronage were used to accomplish what the U.S. labor market would not—with particular emphasis on the post–Reconstruction and post–civil rights movement eras—reveals the roots and continuity of delegitimizing Black public workers.

This entanglement of Americans' ideas about race, efficiency, and good government has obscured what Black workers were doing in the federal bureaucracy in the first place. Most important, lost are the ways in which African Americans have used public employment to cope with the economic and social costs of racism. In the last decade, scholars have done pioneering work on the price of racism, especially the federal government's active undermining of Black communities through racist housing and real estate policies.[9] White supremacy is an economic system as well as a social and cultural one, and it is a system in which the federal government has been historically a key player, with Black politicians sometimes providing cover for or even advancing disinvestment from Black communities.[10] But recognizing the state's complicity in institutional racism should not divert us from understanding how African Americans have strategically used state structures to secure stable work and economic survival.

A nuanced understanding of the history of Black public work complicates and enriches some key themes in American history: patronage politics, Black agency, workplace gender constructions, and class development. And no set of Black public employees illustrates these themes better than the first generation of civil servants in Washington after Reconstruction. Tracking their agency and struggles is a critical first step to a fuller understanding of the politics and utility of public work for Black Americans. Their smart political maneuvering, remarkable social mobility, preoccupation with manliness, and restrictive desire for elite status reveal both the democratic possibilities of patronage politics and the struggle to make those possibilities real and equitable. Despite the creation of the U.S. civil service system in the 1880s, merit has always mixed with politics in public employment.[11] This was not a system Black politicians and public workers created, but they did learn to play well by its rules. Blanket dismissals of Black politics as corrupt or ineffective, from both racists and progressives in the past and today, create a veil over a more telling history about the meaning of Black patronage and public employment.

This chapter seeks to pierce that veil. It argues that public work has been a misunderstood and too easily dismissed organizing tradition for African Americans. Public work has been a vital source of economic agency since Black men won their full citizenship in the 1860s and in every era in which Black women and men were able to enact their rights and privileges as citizens. The spoils—that is, public jobs obtained by a crucial combination of political loyalty and professional merit—have frequently been African Americans' best means of seeking reparations, some compensation, for the financial thievery of American racism.[12] Those reparations, in the form of stable pay for work in the service of the nation, could do more than put cash in individuals' pockets; they could also represent investment in a group of Americans for whom state-sanctioned slavery, robbery, and disinvestment had been the most common experience.

Patronage: Of Jobs and Politics

In February 1912, census clerk Ocea Taylor and Oliver M. Randolph, a clerk in the Office of the Fourth Assistant Postmaster General in Washington, DC, were accused of political activity in their work with a local newspaper, the *Washington American*, a violation of civil service conduct rules.[13] Taylor and Randolph had violated good governance regulations and revealed themselves to be the "spoilsmen" they really were. Census Director E. Dana Durand's defense of the men indicated the special nature of African American employment during Republican administrations at the turn of the twentieth century. Taylor had claimed that his work was "not 'political' but 'racial' in character."[14] Durand agreed: "Mr. Taylor is a negro, and the paper with which he was connected was evidently intended in good faith to be an organ for the benefit and uplifting of the negro race." Durand concluded: "To the average negro the support of the Republican Party appears as an essential result of his race."[15] Taylor and Randolph, active Republican operators, were somehow

38   THE POLITICS OF PUBLIC WORK

not political. They were just "negroes," and, given the white supremacist platform of the Democratic Party, supporting the GOP was as essential to Black "uplift" as education and philanthropy. And it is no wonder: the Democratic Party's return to power in the South after Reconstruction was the product of outright violence, murder, and political coups that demolished not just the theoretical idea of Black citizenship but the practical daily lives of African Americans as well.[16] The Republican Party was a refuge, if an imperfect one, in a time when little else provided African Americans with any measure of security in private or public life.

The specious distinction Durand made between security and politics lies at the heart of how we misunderstand the nexus formed by race and public work in U.S. history. History (and historians) has conditioned us to reflexively view political patronage not as a bureaucratic system tied to democracy (elected officials representing the people who elected them by appointing like-minded individuals) but as exclusively a fount of self-serving corruption and inefficiency—"the spoils." As Theda Skocpol argues in her landmark book *Protecting Soldiers and Mothers*, middle-class and elite progressives in the late nineteenth century became so obsessed with the corruption they saw in patronage politics that they actually choked off the development of robust social policy. "Rooting out" became more important than "building in" within American governance.[17]

Political commentators—from mugwumps like E. L. Godkin, to progressives like Woodrow Wilson, to entrepreneurship evangelists like David Osborne, to austerity objectivists like Paul Ryan—have long argued that waste is an inevitable outcome of the human relations inherent in politics.[18] American ambivalence about state power and fears that public employees can get a shortcut to policymaking without going through the legislative process only exacerbated the preoccupation with corruption and Black political agency. Sensational political scandals—for example, the Whiskey Ring, Teapot Dome, Watergate, Whitewater, the Trump administration—almost always involve political appointees and serve as not just indictments of individual wrongdoing but of political patronage as a system. And while the most famous scandals have involved white officials, historian Derek Musgrove has shown that more ordinary accusations of day-to-day waste and corruption have been disproportionately aimed at Black officeholders.[19]

Thus, the long-held understanding of patronage as corruption, combined with white Americans' suspicion of Black people's competence and probity in politics, has produced an incomplete understanding of the relationship between Black politics and Black agency. For Black federal employees, politics and economic mobility have been deeply connected since their entry into

The Spoils as Reparations   39

public work (as free people) during the Civil War.[20] In a system in which, as historian Jane Dailey puts it, "patronage power bound many men's political identity to their livelihood," the most economically vulnerable had no choice but to jump into the game.[21] Bringing African Americans into the patronage system introduced them to the myriad ways party politics and mobility had become linked in the late nineteenth century. Politicians hoped to form reliable electorates by offering ways to help voters' direct economic well-being. "The chief kind of 'aid' that urban machines were geared up to provide (and, therefore, to make workers *want* more than any other kind of public help) was jobs," explain social scientists Theda Skocpol and John Ikenberry.[22]

Indeed, the so-called black-and-tan organizations of Black and white political operatives functioned primarily to run the patronage wheel. State-level politicians, at the behest of party bosses and often the president himself, made sure that jobs went to Black loyalists.[23] Those in politics understood that this system functioned not simply as graft or corruption: "If we admit that all the lower places are sought more for the money there is in them than for the glory of their possessions," remarked the *Washington Post* in 1897, "it does not by any means necessarily follow that the men who seek them are spoilsmen." The *Post* made no racial distinction here: patronage was a system for anyone who needed a decent job that would "help him to educate his boys and girls and give his family a better social position."[24]

As white Democratic Southerners removed African Americans from the electorate, Republican Party operatives continued to include them in their patronage machine. Though Abraham Lincoln first opened the spoils to Black citizens, it was Benjamin Harrison who modernized the Black patronage system after the civil service reforms of the early 1880s. Even more than just egalitarian neutrality, Harrison had proven himself to be "the black man's friend" by appointing more African Americans to office than any president before him.[25] In July 1891, the Treasury auditor for the Department of the Navy, John Roy Lynch, and former senator Blanche K. Bruce, whom Harrison had given the lucrative appointment of recorder of deeds in the District of Columbia, worked to make sure the White House understood the stakes of how it managed patronage in Mississippi, a state that was pioneering effective means for Black disfranchisement:[26] "We desire to say to you in confidence that, very important *political significance*, not known to the public, and to which we cannot allude in a letter, attaches to this appointment [emphasis added]." A federal judge had the power to determine how fairly, or unfairly, the law applied to Black Mississippians, and Lynch and Bruce worried that the leading candidate was a Republican in name only. They breathed a collective sigh of relief when Harrison appointed Black Republicans' favored candidate.[27]

40   THE POLITICS OF PUBLIC WORK

Party mechanics also mattered. So long as Republican leaders maintained a commitment to Black Republicans, or at least made no commitment to driving them out, then Southern delegations to national conventions would continue to be led by Black delegates. One could not earn the votes of enough delegates to win the presidential nomination at the Republican National Convention (RNC) without bringing in some of the Southern delegations, and that meant maintaining cordial relations with Black Republicans. Indeed, party leaders owed much of their power at nominating conventions to Black delegates from the South.[28] William Howard Taft, for example, desperately needed Black delegates loyal to the party regulars in order to hold off the resurgent Theodore Roosevelt at the 1912 RNC. Black delegates' maneuvers were not merely the products of conservatism or obsequiousness—Roosevelt had betrayed Black Americans throughout his second term, punctuated by his summary dismissal of Black troops in Brownsville, Texas, in 1906, and he would validate their wariness of him by appealing to "lily whites" in the South as the Bull Moose candidate. The actions of Black delegates reflected cold political calculations about how to protect the political relevance and economic security of themselves and the people they represented.

If these convention showings were merely tokenism (and in some important ways, they were), African Americans were nevertheless diligent in making the most of what they could get. "The *[Washington] Bee* intends to thoroughly investigate all the rumors in circulation concerning the conditions in the Census office, as they effect the colored employees therein," the capital's leading Black paper declared in 1907, "and if the investigation proves as rumor has it, the letters written to Senators and Congressmen concerning these matters will prove interesting reading and serve as red-hot campaign matter for the colored press in its fight against administration delegates to the next Republican National Convention."[29] Nominees and presidents responded. William McKinley's patronage machinations were the scourge of the National Civil Service Reform League because not only did he reward his allies, but he also actively removed thousands of federal jobs from civil service rules.[30] Black political operatives were not merely playing a game: this was about jobs and economic security in a country where both were scarce for African Americans. Patronage ruled even outside the safer confines of DC. Field positions, most notably some 60,000 postmasterships, were exempt entirely from civil service regulations.[31] Thus, even after Southern disfranchisement, 244 Black men and 36 Black women held appointments as local postmasters in 1907.[32]

The means of ending such Black power, reducing the proportion of delegate votes given to the South or seating lily-white delegations from rump conventions, were rejected by Republican leaders into the 1920s.[33] Washington, DC's paper of record, the *Evening Star*, maintained that the Republican Party would never surrender to the lily whites: "For the party of Abraham Lincoln, while still cherishing his memory and conjuring with his name, to turn its back in any section of the country upon a man solely because of his color would be to invite and deserve defeat," the paper declared in 1902 after Black votership in the South had already been driven to nil. "The republican party as a party will never do such a thing."[34]

It was not as if there was no racism among white Republicans. Rather, there had yet to develop unanimity about the correct approach to African Americans or how to deal with the South.[35] In the 1890s there were not enough African Americans in the North who could have punished the party as a whole with their ballots, and yet anti-Black racists could not quite purge the Grand Old Party. Many still argued that the party—and the nation—owed something to Black men. "Can we forget [that] in the darkest hour of the night of our trial," asked Pennsylvania Republican Marriott Brosius in 1890, "we made our covenant with him, sealed with his blood and ours and witnessed by heaven, that when the war was over and the nation saved that he should enter into the enjoyment of the blessings and glories of citizenship?"[36] As the nation retreated from Black equality, political patronage formed the Republican Party's last connection to that covenant.[37]

This tenuous balance was carefully watched and managed by Black politicians and civil servants. Black politicians appointed by McKinley and Roosevelt were the links between sympathetic white politicians and Black men and women seeking federal jobs. Racial violence continued unabated, of course. At least 520 Black men and women were lynched during McKinley's presidency, including a federal official, Postmaster Frazier Baker, and his infant daughter in Lake City, South Carolina, in 1898.[38] African American Republicans from the South could do little but retreat to Washington, DC, and into the federal government. Republican presidents after 1896 were at least willing to support an affirmative action system in federal offices.[39] Middle-class and even a few wealthy Black Americans were dependent on government work, so those known as the "representative" Black men and women paid close attention to patronage and partisanship—and not just for fellow elites. Laborer positions were frequently excluded from or managed informally beyond civil service regulations, providing something of a hidden patronage freeway to government employment. Laborers could even be given pay raises (up to a certain point) and assigned clerical work without going through the competitive system. As late as 1922, analyst Lewis Mayers of the Institute for Government Research complained that "the spoils system clings to labor positions with a tenacity almost equal to its hold on the higher executive positions."[40]

For African Americans, such slack brought opportunity. For example, President Harrison had failed to extend civil service appointment rules to the U.S. Census Bureau, a favorite patronage spot for Congress, and McKinley had refused to bow to growing pressure to cover the bureau when he came to office. Though examinations were still required for eligibility, census clerks were appointed according to the wishes of Congressmen.[41] Patronage made Charles E. Hall's extraordinary career in the Census Bureau possible. A trained and talented statistician, Hall was responsible for much of the serious census data we have today on African Americans at the turn of the twentieth century.[42] But it was connections that put Hall in the position to collect that data. Once Hall demonstrated his skills by passing the civil service exam, U.S. representative Albert J. Hopkins of Illinois ensured that Hall would be appointed in January 1900.[43] Public officials were regularly invited to comment on an applicant's "character and community standing," and the power of the purse in congressional appropriations made it very difficult to limit the role played by Congress and the parties.[44]

To protect against the whims of supervisors, government workers often found it useful to engage the help of powerful friends. This networking was by no means specific to Black government workers; it was a defining aspect of labor in modern America. With the rise of large institutional bureaucracies made up of white-collar workers after the Civil War, notes historian Karen Halttunen, the expression of American ambition changed, marking the "replacement of an earlier entrepreneurial pattern of success" with advancement through more systematized careers that required connections and "references."[45] Instead of seeking social mobility solely through property and independence, white-collar workers sought promotion up through the ranks. The "white-collar pattern" did not yield the rational meritocracy many hoped for but instead a realm of relationships and politics that could produce a series of "affirmative actions" in public work for veterans, white men, Black Republicans, and even some women, depending on the job and the predilections of individual supervisors.[46] Black public sector workers were not merely beneficiaries of a rationalized, color-blind system. Rather, Republicans had adapted Black patronage to the new system.

Spoils Men

Not all benefited equally. The differential between Black men and women in public work is notable, if not surprising. Evelyn Brooks Higginbotham, Glenda Gilmore, Michele Mitchell, and other scholars have shown how Black women in the South broadened their leadership roles in social activism and churches as public displays of Black male power and authority became in-

The Spoils as Reparations   43

Figure 2.1. One of the three collages of photographs of African American civil servants assembled by W. E. B. Du Bois for the "Exhibit of American Negroes" at the Paris Exposition of 1900. The bearing and dress of the "government clerks" were intended to show the dignity and progress of African Americans after emancipation. Only two women were included in the collages. (Courtesy of the Library of Congress Prints and Photographs Division, LC-DIG-ppmsca-33934.)

creasingly dangerous in the 1890s.[47] But as Elsa Barkley Brown has shown, the entry of Black men into American democracy under the Fifteenth Amendment created a gendered hierarchy in politics that did not reflect the power Black women held in their families and communities.[48] Black women, though certainly present in federal offices, were profoundly marginalized by the respectability politics that elevated the ambitions of Black men over Black women. Even as white women flooded into white-collar jobs in federal offices at the turn of the twentieth century, Black women continued to be relegated mostly to cleaning and laboring positions.[49] Thus, patronage politics was one example of what Kathleen Clark has called "a vocabulary that stressed, above all, the ascent of Black men to their right place as citizens enjoying all the prerogatives of American manhood."[50] Those prerogatives were reflected in patriarchal civil service management, which in most departments erected a glass ceiling over women's promotions.[51]

Moreover, for all of its opportunity, egalitarianism, and utility among the bourgeoisie of the nation's capital, patronage politics was nonetheless a far less democratic system than had been promised by the Reconstruction amendments. Though hundreds of Black men, and some women, earned good livings in Washington, the political system turned male leaders like Frederick Douglass, Blanche K. Bruce, Robert Terrell, and James Napier into the unofficial representatives of "the Race."[52] These men were earnest and often stunningly brave, but they were also typically privileged and conservative. Not only did they not fully challenge the Republican Party's acquiescence to disfranchisement, but they also heartily endorsed its increasingly conservative economic policies, thereby standing against the needs, and often the demands, of the huge mass of Black farmers and laborers for whom they claimed to speak. Patronage politics could turn these "great men" into the weak supplicants of white leaders, who carefully managed loyalties in order to confine Black politics. Recorder of Deeds Henry Cheatham, no doubt, tried to add some "manhood" to his prostrate position as a Black Republican by personally shooting and stringing a "toothsome delicacy" of birds for President and First Lady McKinley in 1897.[53] But as the gifting implies, patronage was always a carefully managed and unequal relationship.

New Machines

By the 1930s, this relationship within the Republican Party had fallen apart. It had shown strains earlier. William Monroe Trotter's National Independent Political League, for example, had argued that the GOP took Black voters for granted and endorsed Democratic presidential candidate Woodrow Wilson in 1912.[54] But Wilson's segregation of the federal government and the vicious racism of Southern Democrats stalled the drift of African Americans into the Democratic Party, despite white Republicans' embrace of segregation.[55] It was only with Franklin Roosevelt's reelection campaign in 1936, and African Americans' support of the New Deal's economic interventions, that the majority of Black voters pulled the lever for a Democratic president. By then, Black political organizing in Northern cities and the New Deal's expansive state—despite its exclusion of Black Southerners—had constructed a viable public-work patronage network within the Democratic Party, especially because Northern Black votes could be critical in competitive states.[56]

The arrival of hundreds of thousands of Black migrants to Northern cities in the 1940s added more Black voters and Black political connections to urban machines, which, coupled with wartime civilian labor needs, dramatically expanded the number of Black women and men in public work in Washington, New York, Detroit, and other cities. Roosevelt's 1941 Executive Order 8802 establishing the temporary Fair Employment Practices Committee (FEPC) and its subsequent iterations once again placed the government, by no means free of discrimination, ahead of the private sector in terms of opportunities for Black workers.[57] Nearly a million Black workers were employed by local, state, and civilian federal agencies by 1960, and beginning in the late 1950s, these workers were increasingly organized in public employee unions allied with the Democratic Party.[58]

In 1967 political scientist Samuel Krislov noted, "The federal equal employment program—whether consciously so or not—suggests that the governmental sector is not merely the instrument for induction of change, 'the vanguard of equality,' but the means of change itself."[59] In the midst of the Great Society, Krislov saw how equal employment practices in Lyndon Johnson's administration might create spaces in which Black women and men "could move up socially in a manner otherwise almost universally denied to those who had not had specialized or professional training."[60] The results were economic and political: a Black middle class bloomed in and around DC in the 1970s, and African Americans finally found the utility in their connection to the Democratic Party that they had hoped for since the 1930s.[61]

* * *

From the 1880s through the 1960s, then, Black patronage operators in both parties sought to blunt the economic marginalization of state-sanctioned Jim Crow with state-based employment. Often they failed, as when the Wilson administration shredded opportunities in federal offices or when Roosevelt's FEPC proved inadequate in terms of ensuring that Black workers were treated fairly and promoted for merit. Fittingly, racist lawmakers pointed to the disproportionate presence of Black workers in federal offices as evidence that the FEPC—and fair employment practices generally—were too effective, feeding government inefficiency. "The only conclusion I can reach is that these people would never have been employed if the FEPC had not insisted and, in fact, directed that there should be discrimination in favor of appointing these people instead of appointing more capable and efficient white persons in their place," railed South Carolina congressman B. B. Hare in 1944.[62] Two decades later, internal contradictions and failures of the Great Society, from its essential conservatism to the construction of the carceral state, revealed that the inclusion of African Americans in the promise of equal employment was always partial.[63] And as historian Frederick W. Gooding Jr. has shown, African Americans in government continued to face limitations, harassment, and exclusion throughout the postwar period.[64] Once Black public work was undermined by racist and unfounded narratives of Black incompetence, inefficiency, and political corruption, African Americans could be routinely denied positions and pay they had earned, even in eras of progress.[65] But that progress for many could also be genuine and, crucially, the result of careful, serious political work. Manufactured questions of legitimacy in the history of Black patronage seek to invalidate the broad, creative, and active efforts by Black women and men to access livable wages within a state that was denying them full citizenship.

The Ghosts of Reconstruction

The complexity of this historical patronage system has become shrouded, particularly by analyses of Black politics after the Voting Rights Act re-enfranchised African Americans in the mid-1960s. Scholars such as Adolph Reed, Robert C. Smith, J. Philip Thompson III, and many others have long noted that post–civil rights Black politics has often (if not always) been a disappointing affair. Redlining, job discrimination, white flight, and plenty of remaining interpersonal as well as structural racism all constrained Black politicians, who were under enormous pressure to make up for lost time during the disenfranchisement years. Reed notes that once strong and outspoken, civil rights activists in the 1970s "were gradually being absorbed into a developing apparatus of race relations management, as either public officials or quasi-public functionaries." They were a new kind of patronage politician whose "legitimacy as representatives of neighborhood or community interests simultaneously biase[d] them toward accommodation to the governing elite's agendas."[66] Again and again, students of post-1965 Black politics note,

The Spoils as Reparations   47

in the words of Ronald Walters, a "conservative doctrine that favors financial reward, materialist preoccupation with large institutional structures, and a fundamentalist interpretation of social life that affects their political identity and behavior." That is to say, many African American leaders have not only been seduced by the vestiges of official political power, but they have also been institutionally numbed to or disconnected from the needs of their less advantaged constituencies. Not nearly as capable of enacting real change as they had hoped, some became enamored with elite white allies and their neoliberal policies.[67]

I note these critiques not to tangle with or contest their claims about the limits of the political transition Reed and others describe. It is inarguable that Black ghettoization and incarceration accelerated in the same era that Black politicians took hold of new perches made possible by the Voting Rights Act. Rather, my point is less normative and oriented on a different perspective: that of the question of the place of African Americans in public work in U.S. history. For just as elite politicians were emerging from the more grassroots movements of the 1960s "from protest to politics," so too were ordinary folks emerging in the federal bureaucracy.[68] Reed and others have been, understandably, most interested in who was excluded from these structures.[69] For majority-Black cities—or cities that elected Black mayors—in the 1970s and 1980s, Black political relevancy or even power was not the same as effectiveness or coherence, especially in the midst of federal disinvestment in America's Black communities.[70] But as historian Julian Hayter notes, it is also true that some in the Black electorate did indeed benefit from Black leadership and public work, and not all leaders were self-serving "ward men." Municipal governments and schools became key sites of Black employment in postwar cities, even as declining tax bases limited the social mobility city work could guarantee.[71]

Moreover, an unfortunate and largely unintended result of important and valid critiques of American politics has been a reinscribing by scholars and pundits of the corruption taint around Black public employment that has clung to Black politics—and Black power—since Reconstruction. Because the results were partial in terms of racial equity, this argument goes, political patronage was an especially dirty game for Black politicians. Congressmen from the 1860s, civil servants from the 1910s, "Black Cabinet" members from the 1930s, mayors from the 1970s—they have all been cast as "spoilsmen," operators for graft, not public workers. The symbolic corrupt Black public servant (actual or imagined)—e.g., Blanche K. Bruce, Robert Smalls, Coleman Young, Marion Barry, Shirley Sherrod—has been integral to the study of Black politics, especially among political scientists trying to imagine new political avenues for Black agency after the civil rights movement. In the 1970s political scientist Martin Kilson notably dismissed patronage, or what he called "clientage," as serving only the status of the Black bourgeoisie rather than broader political rights. Kilson recognized the relationship between Black well-being and party politics, but he insisted that the beneficiaries were too few (and too exclusive) to really matter. But legal historian Risa Goluboff has encouraged us to be slower to dismiss the rights potential of patronage.[72] Far more ordinary African Americans made patronage systems work for them than Kilson's depiction allows. From newly freed people's pleas to Lincoln to the evolving political and legal strategies of the NAACP, political connections and public work proved more available and more useful to desperate people throughout post-emancipation U.S. history than the "spoils" appellation indicates.[73]

If we take seriously the relationship of public employment to the emergence of a Black middle class in the 1970s, warts and all, we cannot simply dismiss patronage, or even racial symbolism, as merely fraudulent. We are too tempted to read limitations or ineffectiveness as indicators of corruption, just as racist historians portrayed Reconstruction as debauched in order to delegitimize Black politics.[74] The promise of Black public employment never matched the lived reality, but that should not preclude considering the lived reality on its own terms. How else to explain that Black public servants have been better off and better organized than most other Black American workers? Should we really ignore the fact that the wages of Black public workers, even today, are far more likely to approach the prevailing wage rates for white workers than Black private sector workers? Put another way, working for the government is one of the few ways Black workers can mitigate the racial wage differential that persists in American workplaces.[75] Black leaders born in families supported by public workers—whether the cultural pioneers of the Harlem Renaissance in the 1920s, or Michelle Obama's generation of "firsts," or today's liberal millennials—are numerous and important. Their limitations should be put in the context of the white supremacist structures within which they worked.

Thus, stories from the Jim Crow era remind us to take care to honor historical and contextual distinctions. To be sure, the anticommunist, liberal Black leaders of the late twentieth century, those capable of earning election after 1965, were in different positions than the post-Reconstruction and Jim Crow patronage politicians. Both groups could be labeled as, in N. D. B. Connolly's phrase, "racial centrists," struggling to gain power in American institutions and represent the mass of Black Americans who were oppressed by those institutions.[76] But while the post-1965 cohort's capitalism and urban renewal

The Spoils as Reparations   49

entrepreneurialism often spoke of a class-driven betrayal, the earlier generation had fewer options—fewer ways to betray their constituents. No Black Power movement, almost no enfranchisement, nor any majority-minority districts existed to challenge them to represent the complex Black community with fidelity. Jim Crow–era patronage politicians were seizing the only levers of power available to any American politician (Black or white) and representing "Black interests" in a way that seemed to best fit a much more suppressed Black (non)electorate. Accusations of corruption emerging in this era and persisting ever since have rested, therefore, on a foundational belief that Black people need to be superhuman (far purer and far more capable of overcoming truly existential threats than their white counterparts) in order to avoid criticism.[77] This magical thinking around Black politics—and its politicians and ordinary public workers—is old and persistent, distorting how we understand the tools Black Americans have used to seek economic security.

Conclusion

That similar corruption allegations from the Reconstruction and Jim Crow eras rose again with the return of significant numbers of Black elected officials in the 1970s is a function of the way racism and historical memory merge with long-standing anti-statism in American politics.[78] White supremacists were, in all cases, expressing fear of Black citizenship and of a strong federal government capable of protecting it. The way the historical record reveals the lie in corruption accusations in the earlier periods should give us pause when examining Black public work generally. What does "corruption" mean in public work? Who gets labeled "corrupt"?[79] To what ends and to whose benefit? Finally, what is there to be gained by patronage in a specific context? For Black Americans in the Jim Crow era, patronage meant a decent livelihood in an era defined by disenfranchisement, violence, and hunger. The 1970s did not materialize into the proverbial mountaintop that Martin Luther King Jr. so famously envisioned before his death in 1968; African Americans continued to face a range of discriminatory forces during and after the civil rights era. But a rising Black middle class, affirmative action programs, and a legitimate Black electorate that could pull patronage strings were all aspects of eras, then and earlier, in which African Americans were permitted to act as citizens, public workers, and government officials.[80] An analysis of Black patronage free of the post-Reconstruction accusations of illegitimacy reveals the contextual agency of African Americans, the power of white supremacy in the United States, and the meaning of integration into the nation's public institutions. What has often been labeled "spoils," "corruption," or even "clientage," begins to look a lot more like compromise, agency, and survival—even an attempt at reparations—when these experiences are placed in the proper historical context. These words are not necessarily exculpatory of bad acts or poor policy decisions, but they are more accurate and less loaded with racist assumptions about the (il)legitimacy of Black citizenship and Black public work.

Further Reading

Masur, Kate. *An Example for All the Land: Emancipation and the Struggle over Equality in Washington, D.C.* Chapel Hill: University of North Carolina Press, 2010.

Musgrove, George Derek. *Rumor, Repression, and Racial Politics: How the Harassment of Black Elected Officials Shaped Post–Civil Rights America.* Athens: University of Georgia Press, 2012.

Reed, Adolph L., Jr. *Stirrings in the Jug: Black Politics in the Post-Segregation Era.* Minneapolis: University of Minnesota Press, 1999.

Rubio, Philip F. *There's Always Work at the Post Office: African American Postal Workers and the Fight for Jobs, Justice, and Equality.* Chapel Hill: University of North Carolina Press, 2010.

Yellin, Eric S. *Racism in the Nation's Service: Government Workers and the Color Line in Woodrow Wilson's America.* Chapel Hill: University of North Carolina Press, 2013.

Notes

1. Donald J. Trump, "State of the Union Address," February 5, 2019, https://trump whitehouse.archives.gov/briefings-statements/remarks-president-trump-state-union -address-2/.

2. On Trump's obsession with the "deep state," see James B. Stewart, *Deep State: Trump, the FBI, and the Rule of Law* (New York: Penguin, 2019); David Rohde, *In Deep: The FBI, the CIA, and the Truth about America's "Deep State"* (New York: W. W. Norton, 2020).

3. In 2018, African Americans held about 18 percent of federal civilian jobs while being 13 percent of the U.S. population. In Washington, DC, 32 percent of federal employees are African American. Historian Frederick Gooding Jr. notes that "blacks are understood to have become 'the face' of government employment in the modern era." For current federal employment numbers, see U.S. Office of Personnel Management, "FedScope," available at http://www.fedscope.opm.gov/, accessed January 2019; Frederick Gooding Jr., *American Dream Deferred: Black Federal Workers in Washington, D.C., 1941–1981* (Pittsburgh: University of Pittsburgh Press, 2018), 177.

4. Charles D. Ellison, "Trump's Federal-Workforce Plans Will Blow Up the Black Middle Class . . . and a Lot More," TheRoot.com, November 23, 2016; Eric S. Yellin,

"The Corrupt, Racist Proposal from the State of the Union Address That Everyone Missed," *Washington Post,* February 5, 2018. For a study of the ways in which Republicans have undermined Black participation in American democracy, see Jesse H. Rhodes, *Ballot Blocked: The Political Erosion of the Voting Rights Act* (Stanford, CA: Stanford University Press, 2017).

5. On Black Washington and corruption, see Chris Myers Asch and George Derek Musgrove, *Chocolate City: A History of Race and Democracy in the Nation's Capital* (Chapel Hill: University of North Carolina Press, 2017), 163, 176–78, 417–19, 423–24; Eric Foner, *Reconstruction: America's Unfinished Revolution, 1863–1877* (New York: Harper and Row, 1988), xvii–xviii; Kate Masur, *An Example for All the Land: Emancipation and the Struggle over Equality in Washington, DC* (Chapel Hill: University of North Carolina Press, 2010), 237.

6. This was particularly true in Northern municipal administrations and the U.S. Post Office. Robert H. Zieger, *For Jobs and Freedom: Race and Labor in America since 1865* (Lexington: University Press of Kentucky, 2001), 54; Thomas J. Sugrue, "'The Largest Civil Rights Organization Today': Title VII and the Transformation of the Public Sector," *Labor: Studies in Working-Class History of the Americas* 11, no. 3 (2014): 25–29. On opportunities in postal work, see Philip F. Rubio, *There's Always Work at the Post Office: African American Postal Workers and the Fight for Jobs, Justice, and Equality* (Chapel Hill: University of North Carolina Press, 2010).

7. Nancy MacLean, *Freedom Is Not Enough: The Opening of the American Workplace* (Cambridge, MA: Harvard University Press, 2007); Kevin M. Kruse and Julian E. Zelizer, *Fault Lines: A History of the United States since 1974* (New York: W. W. Norton, 2019), 17.

8. Right-wing pundit Pat Buchanan provides the most evocative version of this racist view of federal employment. Patrick J. Buchanan, "Obama's Race-Based Spoils System," *Human Events*, August 26, 2011, https://archive.humanevents.com/2011/08/26/obamas-racebased-spoils-system/. For a discussion of the relationship between "affirmative action" and "merit" during the Reagan administration's austerity push, see Sar A. Levitan and Alexandra B. Noden, *Working for the Sovereign: Employee Relations in the Federal Government* (Baltimore: Johns Hopkins University Press, 1983), 112–15.

9. For example, see Ta-Nehisi Coates, "The Case for Reparations," *The Atlantic* (June 2014); William A. Darity and Samuel L. Myers Jr., *Persistent Disparity: Race and Economic Inequality in the United States since 1945* (Cheltenham, UK: Edward Elgar, 1999); Thomas M. Shapiro, *The Hidden Cost of Being African American: How Wealth Perpetuates Inequality* (New York: Oxford University Press, 2005); Beryl Satter, *Family Properties: How the Struggle over Race and Real Estate Transformed Chicago and Urban America* (New York: Picador, 2010); David Freund, *Colored Property: State Policy and White Racial Politics in Suburban America* (Chicago: University of Chicago Press, 2010).

10. N.D.B. Connolly, *A World More Concrete: Real Estate and the Remaking of Jim Crow South Florida* (Chicago: University of Chicago Press, 2014).

11. Francis E. Leupp, *How to Prepare for a Civil-Service Examination* (New York: Hinds and Noble, 1898), 325–50; El Bie K. Foltz, *The Federal Civil Service as a Career: A Manual for Applicants for Positions and Those in the Civil Service of the Nation* (New York: G. P. Putnam's Sons, 1909), 45; Herbert Kaufman, "The Growth of the Federal Personnel System," in *The Federal Government Service*, ed. Wallace S. Sayre (Englewood Cliffs, NJ: Prentice-Hall, 1965), 40–43; Carl Russell Fish, *The Civil Service and the Patronage* (Cambridge, MA: Harvard University Press, 1904), 238; Stephen Skowronek, *Building a New American State: The Expansion of National Administrative Capacities, 1877–1920* (Cambridge: Cambridge University Press, 1982), 81; Lewis Mayers, *The Federal Service: A Study of the System of Personnel Administration of the United States Government* (New York: D. Appleton, 1922), 52.

12. For a sharp and brief discussion of the meaning and history of "reparations," see Ana Lucia Araujo, *Reparations for Slavery and the Slave Trade: A Transnational and Comparative History* (London: Bloomsbury, 2017), 1–6.

13. Taylor had come to Washington from Tuscaloosa, Alabama, to attend Howard University around 1900. President of the college literary society, he received his BA degree in 1906 and his LLB degree in 1908. Randolph was a Howard graduate from Mississippi's Gulf Coast. Randolph and Taylor had, in fact, sold the paper in January. H. A. Hesse and G. W. Hall to U.S. Civil Service Commission, February 9, 1912, employee folder no. BU016338, National Archives and Records Administration, National Personnel Records Center, St. Louis, MO (hereafter, NPRC). The same letter appears in Randolph's file, employee folder no. BU028751, NPRC; "The Editor of the Bee Removed," *Washington Bee*, May 2, 1885, 2; "Puts Ban on Politics," *Washington Post*, February 8, 1912, 3; "Would Classify District Clerks," *Washington Herald*, February 8, 1912, 3.

14. Ocea Taylor defended himself against the charges in a statement to the Civil Service Commission. The statement is undated and attached to a letter from Civil Service Commission president John C. Black. John C. Black to Secretary of Commerce and Labor, February 17, 1912, employee folder no. BU016338, NPRC.

15. E. Dana Durand to Secretary of Commerce and Labor, March 19, 1912, employee folder no. BU016338, NPRC. For Randolph's defense, which, in part, matches verbatim that of Durand, see Chief Clerk to United States Civil Service Commission, August 6, 1912, employee folder no. BU028751, NPRC.

16. The most vivid example of the violence that came with Democratic rule in the South came in the 1898 coup d'etat in Wilmington, North Carolina. See David S. Cecelski and Timothy B. Tyson, *Democracy Betrayed: The Wilmington Race Riot of 1898 and Its Legacy* (Chapel Hill: University of North Carolina Press, 2000).

17. Theda Skocpol, *Protecting Soldiers and Mothers: The Political Origins of Social Policy in the United States* (Cambridge, MA: Harvard University Press, 1992), 310.

18. Osborne was the efficiency guru behind Vice President Al Gore's "National Performance Review" in 1993. Osborne's *Reinventing Government*, written with Ted Gaebler, became a best seller, adding policy and liberal credence to modern anti-

The Spoils as Reparations   53

statism and suspicion of the public sector. David Osborne and Ted Gaebler, *Reinventing Government: How the Entrepreneurial Spirit Is Transforming the Public Sector* (Reading, MA: Addison-Wesley Publishing, 1992).

19. George Derek Musgrove, *Rumor, Repression, and Racial Politics: How the Harassment of Black Elected Officials Shaped Post–Civil Rights America* (Athens: University of Georgia Press, 2012), 5, 217–19.

20. Theda Skocpol, "African Americans in U.S. Social Policy," in *Classifying by Race*, ed. Paul E. Peterson (Princeton, NJ: Princeton University Press, 1995), 131, 137.

21. Jane Dailey, *Before Jim Crow: The Politics of Race in Postemancipation Virginia* (Chapel Hill: University of North Carolina Press, 2000), 56–57.

22. Theda Skocpol and John Ikenberry, "The Political Formation of the American Welfare State in Historical and Comparative Perspective," *Comparative Social Research* 6 (Greenwich, CT: JAI Press), 94–95. For more on the connection between politics, policy, and economic development in the nineteenth century, see Richard L. McCormick's classic text, *The Party Period and Public Policy: American Politics from the Age of Jackson to the Progressive Era* (New York: Oxford University Press, 1988).

23. Steven Hahn, *A Nation under Our Feet: Black Political Struggles in the Rural South from Slavery to the Great Migration* (Cambridge, MA: Harvard University Press, 2003), 385–87; Paul D. Casdorph, *Republicans, Negroes, and Progressives in the South, 1912–1916* (Tuscaloosa: University of Alabama Press, 1981), 55–56. For the term "black-and-tan" and a Black Republican state leader, see Hanes Walton Jr., *Black Republicans: The Politics of the Black and Tans* (Metuchen, NJ: Scarecrow Press, 1975), 45–46, 170–76.

24. "'Spoilsmen,'" *Washington Post*, March 17, 1897, 6. The *Bee* reprinted portions of the *Post*'s editorial approvingly in its edition: "'Spoilsmen,'" *Washington Bee*, March 20, 1897, 4.

25. "President Harrison," *Washington Bee*, November 22, 1890, 2; Maud Cuney-Hare, *Norris Wright Cuney: A Tribune of the Black People* (1913; New York: G. K. Hall, 1995), 105–126.

26. Mississippi was a forerunner in the South in finding ways to remove Blacks from the electorate, first by violence, intimidation, and, in 1890, by constitutional law. Neil R. McMillen, *Dark Journey: Black Mississippians in the Age of Jim Crow* (Urbana: University of Illinois Press, 1989), 36–43; Michael Perman, *Struggle for Mastery: Disfranchisement in the South, 1888–1908* (Chapel Hill: University of North Carolina Press, 2001), 70–71.

27. See the series of letters between John R. Lynch, Blanche K. Bruce, and Elijah Walker Halford, July 28, 1891–August 15, 1891, series 2, reel 77, Benjamin Harrison Papers, Library of Congress.

28. Casdorph, *Republicans, Negroes, and Progressives*, 11, 111; McMillen, *Dark Journey*, 58; Richard B. Sherman, *Republican Party and Black America from McKinley to Hoover, 1896–1933* (Charlottesville: University Press of Virginia, 1973), 19–20, 119–20; Walton, *Black Republicans*, 43. For more on Black party leaders in Southern states, see Margaret Law Callcott, *The Negro in Maryland Politics, 1870–1912* (Baltimore:

Johns Hopkins University Press, 1969); Andrew Bunie, *The Negro in Virginia Politics, 1902–1965* (Charlottesville: University Press of Virginia, 1967); Lester C. Lamon, *Black Tennesseans 1900–1930* (Knoxville: University of Tennessee Press, 1977); Thomas Holt, *Black over White: Negro Political Leadership in South Carolina during Reconstruction* (Urbana: University of Illinois Press, 1979).

29. Nominating power could be double-edged, of course, and Black Republicans were expected to toe the correct line as carefully as any party operative. For example, the powerful head of the Texas Republicans, Norris Wright Cuney, lost control of his delegation when he failed to back William McKinley in 1896. Still, Cuney was replaced by another Black Republican. "Call a Halt Mr. Director," *Washington Bee*, March 23, 1907, 1; Paul D. Casdorph, "Norris Wright Cuney and Texas Republican Politics, 1883–1896," *Southwestern Historical Quarterly* 68, no. 4 (1965): 461–63. See also Tera W. Hunter's introduction to Cuney-Hare, *Cuney*, xxii–xxiv.

30. Ari Hoogenboom, *Outlawing the Spoils: A History of the Civil Service Reform Movement, 1865–1883* (Urbana: University of Illinois Press, 1961), 264.

31. Skowronek, *Building*, 69–71.

32. U.S. Bureau of the Census, *Bulletin 94: Statistics of Employees: Executive Civil Service of the United States, 1907*, ed. Lewis Merriam (Washington, DC: Government Printing Office, 1908), table 90, p. 139.

33. Norris Wright Cuney, the powerful Black Republican in Texas in the 1880s, coined the term "lily-white" for Republican organizations that refused to accept Black members. Sherman, *Republican Party and Black America*, 1, 18–20, 119–20; Casdorph, *Republicans, Negroes, and Progressives*, 11.

34. "Editorial: The Southern Republicans," *Washington Star*, December 9, 1902, 4.

35. After Reconstruction, the party was split between the Stalwarts, those who stood by a national party with Black representation, and the Half-Breeds or liberals, those willing to look at an alternative set of strategies for keeping the party competitive in national politics. Skowronek, *Building*, 59; Mark Wahlgren Summers, *Rum, Romanism, and Rebellion: The Making of a President, 1884* (Chapel Hill: University of North Carolina Press, 2000), 64.

36. Brosius quoted in J. Morgan Kousser, *The Shaping of Southern Politics: Suffrage Restriction and the Establishment of the One-Party South, 1880–1910* (New Haven, CT: Yale University Press, 1974), 21–22.

37. Ibid., 38, 224. For the ways in which Republicans included African Americans in their efforts to be a national party, see Richard M. Valelly, "National Parties and Racial Disenfranchisement," in *Classifying by Race*, ed. Paul E. Peterson, 189–92 (Princeton, NJ: Princeton University Press, 1995).

38. Ever connected to tragedy in the South, Black Washingtonians took up a collection for the care of Baker's family, but neither McKinley nor congressional Republicans did much to respond. Baker's murder and the president's silence led Calvin Chase to wonder how the United States could expect Black Americans to support its occupation of Cuba. Nell Irvin Painter, *Standing at Armageddon: United States,*

1877–1919 (New York: W. W. Norton, 1987), 146–47; Crystal N. Feimster, *Southern Horrors: Women and the Politics of Rape and Lynching* (Cambridge, MA: Harvard University Press, 2009), 223; "The Week in Society," *Washington Bee*, March 12, 1898, 5; "False Patriotism," editorial, *Washington Bee*, March 19, 1898, 4.

39. Fish, *Civil Service and the Patronage*, 226; Bernard S. Silberman, *Cages of Reason: The Rise of the Rational State in France, Japan, the United States, and Great Britain* (Chicago: University of Chicago Press, 1993), 264; "Not In It," *Washington Bee*, May 1, 1897, 4.

40. Most significant among the appointive loopholes was the "rule of three." By regulation, the Civil Service Commission certified three people for every open position. On behalf of the department secretary, an appointing officer could choose to take the person with the highest exam score or the person with the most impressive résumé. He could choose to interview the candidates or he could flip a coin. Furthermore, he had the right to exclude a candidate for "unfitness," an admittedly vague designation that the commission interpreted loosely. The vast majority of the time, the top scorer was appointed. But that this was not true, for example, in a quarter of all cases in 1900, suggests that there was play in the system. Mayers, *Federal Service*, 465, 430–32; Foltz, *Federal Civil Service*, 126.

41. Fish, *Civil Service and the Patronage*, 224, 228.

42. Francille R. Wilson, *The Segregated Scholars: Black Social Scientists and the Creation of Black Labor Studies, 1890–1950* (Charlottesville: University of Virginia Press, 2006), 131.

43. Census director to Rep. A. J. Hopkins, January 26, 1900. All records relating to Charles E. Hall come from a collection maintained by Rodney A. Ross, archivist at the National Archives Building, Washington, DC.

44. Silberman, *Cages of Reason*, 260; Mayers, *Federal Service*, 20–22, 145–48.

45. Karen Halttunen, *Confidence Men and Painted Women: A Study of Middle-Class Culture in America, 1830–1870* (New Haven, CT: Yale University Press, 1982), 206–210.

46. For ways in which these groups benefited from targeted hiring and political connections, see Ira Katznelson, *When Affirmative Action Was White: An Untold History of Racial Inequality in Twentieth-Century America* (New York: W. W. Norton, 2006); Donald R. Shaffer, *After the Glory: The Struggles of Civil War Veterans* (Lawrence: University of Kansas Press, 2004); Jessica Ziparo, *This Grand Experiment: When Women Entered the Federal Workforce in Civil War–Era Washington, DC* (Chapel Hill: University of North Carolina Press, 2017).

47. Historian Lisa Materson notes that Black women entered the political arena at the same time as Black men, even if they were not allowed to vote formally. Moreover, in Northern states, like Illinois, they exercised even more political power, especially in the 1920s. Lisa G. Materson, *For the Freedom of Her Race: Black Women and Electoral Politics in Illinois, 1877–1932* (Chapel Hill: University of North Carolina, 2009), 4–9.

48. Elsa Barkley Brown, "Negotiating and Transforming the Public Sphere: African

American Political Life in the Transition from Slavery to Freedom," *Public Culture* 7 (1994): 107–146.

49. On Black women in federal offices, see Mary Elizabeth Murphy, *Jim Crow Capital: Women and Black Freedom Struggles in Washington, D.C., 1920–1945* (Chapel Hill: University of North Carolina Press, 2018), 28–29, 110, 135–39; Eric S. Yellin, *Racism in the Nation's Service: Government Workers and the Color Line in Woodrow Wilson's Washington* (Chapel Hill: University of North Carolina Press, 2013), 28–29, 59–60; Ziparo, *This Grand Experiment*, 29–32.

50. Kathleen Ann Clark, *Defining Moments: African American Commemoration and Political Culture in the South, 1863–1913* (Chapel Hill: University of North Carolina Press, 2008), 81.

51. Mayers, *Federal Service*, 356.

52. Adolph A. Reed Jr., "The Study of Black Politics and the Practice of Black Politics: Their Historical Relation and Evolution," in *Problems and Methods in the Study of Politics*, ed. Ian Shapiro, Rogers M. Smith, and Tarek E. Masoud (Cambridge: Cambridge University Press, 2004), 111.

53. McKinley's secretary acknowledged the gift, noting its "proof of [Cheatham's] sportsmanlike skill." John A. Porter to Henry P. Cheatham, November 13, 1897, series 2, reel 23, William McKinley Papers, Library of Congress.

54. Kerri Greenidge, *Black Radical: The Life and Times of William Monroe Trotter* (New York: Liveright Publishing, 2020), 181–86.

55. Yellin, *Racism in the Nation's Service*, 175–203.

56. Nancy J. Weiss, *Farewell to the Party of Lincoln: Black Politics in the Age of FDR* (Princeton, NJ: Princeton University Press, 1983); Anthony S. Chen, *The Fifth Freedom: Jobs, Politics, and Civil Rights in the United States, 1941–1972* (Princeton, NJ: Princeton University Press, 2009), 86.

57. Margaret C. Rung, *Servants of the State: Managing Diversity and Democracy in the Federal Workforce, 1933–1953* (Athens: University of Georgia Press, 2002), 69–75; Desmond King, *Separate and Unequal: African Americans and the U.S. Federal Government*, rev. ed. (Oxford: Oxford University Press, 2007), 32–35. For the way the FEPC spawned other policies and mechanisms for fair employment, however constrained, see Chen, *Fifth Freedom*.

58. Zieger, *For Jobs and Freedom*, 123–24, 141, 191.

59. Samuel Krislov, *The Negro in Federal Employment: The Quest for Equal Opportunity* (Minneapolis: University of Minnesota Press, 1967), 144.

60. Ibid., 12.

61. In 1935 political scientist Harold Gosnell attempted to account for the importance of government jobs for African Americans in the Jim Crow era. It shouldn't be surprising that Gosnell's work was republished in the mid-1960s. Harold F. Gosnell, *Negro Politicians: The Rise of Negro Politics in Chicago* (1935; Chicago: University of Chicago Press, 1967).

62. Rung, *Servants of the State*, 168–76; Hare quoted in Chen, *Fifth Freedom*, 68–69.

63. See Ira Katznelson, "Was the Great Society a Lost Opportunity?," in *The Rise and Fall of the New Deal Order, 1930–1980*, ed. Steve Fraser and Gary Gerstle (Princeton, NJ: Princeton University Press, 1989), 185–205; Elizabeth Hinton, *From the War on Poverty to the War on Crime: The Making of Mass Incarceration in America* (Cambridge, MA: Harvard University Press 2016); Julian Maxwell Hayter, *The Dream Is Lost: Voting Rights and the Politics of Race in Richmond, Virginia* (Lexington: University Press of Kentucky, 2017).

64. See chapter 3 as well as Gooding, *American Dream Deferred*, 10–11, 24.

65. Gooding, *American Dream Deferred*, 119, 148.

66. Reed notes in reviewing his earlier work that some of the criticism leveled in the 1970s was reactive and too dismissive of "the gains of the 1960s." Adolph A. Reed Jr., *Stirrings in the Jug: Black Politics in the Post-Segregation Era* (Minneapolis: University of Minnesota Press, 1999), 1, 4, 11.

67. Ronald W. Walters, *Freedom Is Not Enough: Black Voters, Black Candidates, and American Presidential Politics* (Lanham, MD: Rowman and Littlefield, 2005), 203. See also Robert C. Smith, *We Have No Leaders: African Americans in the Post–Civil Rights Era* (Albany: SUNY Press, 1996), 137; J. Philip Thompson III, *Double Trouble: Black Mayors, Black Communities, and the Call for Deep Democracy* (New York: Oxford University Press, 2006). On ideological elements of the "capitulation" in Black politics after 1965, see Cedric Johnson, *Revolutionaries to Race Leaders: Black Power and the Making of African American Politics* (Minneapolis: University of Minnesota Press, 2007).

68. Bayard Rustin, "From Protest to Politics: The Future of the Civil Rights Movement," *Commentary* 39, no. 2 (1965): 64–66.

69. Reed, "Study of Black Politics and the Practice of Black Politics," 136.

70. Black majority city councils and mayors were elected into political, racial, and economic circumstances that made broad-based development exceedingly difficult, and some simply "sold out," either because the headwinds were too stiff or because blackness offers no immunity to political corruption. See Hayter, *Dream Is Lost*, 198–99; Tom Adam Davies, *Mainstreaming Black Power* (Berkeley: University of California Press, 2017), 170. For useful case studies, see David R. Colburn and Jeffrey S. Adler, eds., *African American Mayors: Race, Politics, and the American City* (Urbana: University of Illinois Press, 2001).

71. See a discussion of Richmond politicians Alma Barlow and Willie Dell in Hayter, *Dream Is Lost*. On the importance of electoral politics and municipal jobs for African Americans, see Thomas J. Sugrue, *Sweet Land of Liberty: The Forgotten Struggle for Civil Rights in the North* (New York: Random House, 2009), 113; Colburn and Adler, *African American Mayors*, 14; Peter K. Eisinger, "Black Employment in Municipal Jobs: The Impact of Black Political Power," *American Political Science Review* 76, no. 2 (1982): 380–92.

72. Martin Kilson, "Political Change in the Negro Ghetto, 1900–1940s," in *Key Issues in the Afro-American Experience*, vol. 2, ed. Nathan I. Huggins, Martin Kilson, and Daniel M. Fox, 167–92 (New York: Harcourt Brace Jovanovich, 1971); Risa L.

Goluboff, "'Won't You Please Help Me Get My Son Home': Peonage, Patronage, and Protest in the World War II Urban South," *Law and Society Inquiry* 24, no. 4 (1999): 781.

73. Kate Masur, "Patronage and Protest in Kate Brown's Washington," *Journal of American History* 99, no. 4 (2013): 1047–71.

74. William A. Dunning, *Reconstruction, Political and Economic, 1856–1877* (New York: Harper & Bros., 1907). For context, see John David Smith and J. Vincent Lowery, *The Dunning School Historians, Race, and the Meaning of Reconstruction* (Lexington: University of Kentucky Press, 2013).

75. At the turn of the twentieth century, Black civil servants earned nearly double the pay of private sector workers. Yellin, *Racism in the Nation's Service*, 35. For recent data on the importance of the public sector in Black labor, see Steven Pitts, "Research Brief: Black Workers and the Public Sector," University of California, Berkeley Center for Labor Research and Education, April 4, 2011, http://laborcenter.berkeley.edu/pdf/2011/blacks_public_sector11.pdf/.

76. N.D.B. Connolly, "Black Appointees, Political Legitimacy, and the American Presidency," in *Recapturing the Oval Office: New Historical Approaches to the American Presidency*, ed. Brian Balogh and Bruce J. Schulman (Ithaca, NY: Cornell University Press, 2015), 130.

77. I share Adolph Reed's point that "thinking of past political figures as operating, as we do, within contingent history also muddies the issue of the accuracy of their views regarding the limits of possibility." But I cannot accept Reed's normative claim that "recognizing how tightly constrained Black options were and how powerful the white supremacist tide was does not justify the conclusion that nothing could have been at all different." Given the complexity of the contingencies Reed himself acknowledges, I haven't a clue how we begin to imagine what could have been done differently in general terms (leaving aside the occasional truly malevolent figure) without ascribing too much power to Black Americans in the midst of the Jim Crow era. Reed, *Stirrings in the Jug*, 22–23.

78. See Musgrove, *Rumor, Repression, and Racial Politics*.

79. Watergate and the Wilbur Mills "Fannie Fox" episode in the 1970s certainly contributed to long-standing ideas about corruption in politics, but they did not result in an assumption that every white man is incompetent or immoral. Kruse and Zelizer, *Fault Lines*, 12; Joseph A. McCartin, "Turnabout Years: Public Sector Unionism and the Fiscal Crisis," in *Rightward Bound: Making America Conservative in the 1970s*, ed. Bruce J. Schulman and Julian E. Zelizer, 210–26 (Cambridge, MA: Harvard University Press, 2008).

80. Marion Barry's best years in Washington, DC, were marked by both economic stabilization and massive patronage—a fact not to be overshadowed by the cocaine and crack epidemic that followed and destroyed Barry (personally and politically). The racist limits placed on participatory democracy in DC are manifest, and the blame shift of the "crack boom" denies a clear-eyed sense of both the limits and potential of Black politics. Asch and Musgrove, *Chocolate City*, 399.

PART II

Good Government Jobs for Whom?

African American and white women, along with African American men, have all made indelible and immeasurable contributions to the machinery operating what Alexis de Tocqueville referred to as the great experiment.[1] Still, it is an open question how these contributions are properly valued and measured.

In these two chapters, Frederick W. Gooding Jr. and Katherine Turk delve deeper into the tensions behind the constant and continual negotiations these three groups engaged as they "labored" for their citizenship. Even though they each invested directly into the federal government with the faithful contribution of an honest day's work, their corresponding pay and promotion rates did not reflect a reciprocally balanced relationship. Enduring racial and gender discrimination often frustrated and shrouded the promising allure of the American Dream—an opportunity that would, arguably, be all the more attainable when working for one of the greatest democracies on earth. Blatant racism more common from earlier years gave way to more subtle patterns of marginalization, which were no less pernicious in obstructing the federal workforce from operating at optimal capacity.

Together, Gooding and Turk ask us to consider what is the comparable worth of such labor that often goes undervalued and overlooked. For the labor is no less dispensable; the contributions of Black and white women and Black men are vital to the country's daily operation. These writings remind readers how the public benefits immensely from such individuals who keep their commitment to their country and work paramount, even if their own federal government has not delivered upon its promised ideals.

Note

1. Alexis de Tocqueville, *Democracy in America,* vol. 1, 3rd ed. (Cambridge: Sever & Francis, 1863), 30.

CHAPTER 3

Dead End Job?

Black Public Workers Struggle to See Light of Day

FREDERICK W. GOODING JR.

"I Was Hurting"

In 1977 National Institutes of Health (NIH) gardener Hoover Rowel finally obtained resolution of an antidiscrimination case he had initiated more than twenty years before. Rowel celebrated his victory publicly among such dignitaries as Senator Edward Kennedy, Congressman Don Edwards, and Walter E. Fauntroy as the American Civil Liberties Union honored his remarkable patience and persistence. Rowel settled his case out of court for $170,000, but he, twelve other men, and the widows of three more received individual checks less than $10,000 apiece.[1] This amounted to less than $500 for every year of discrimination—a paltry sum in view of the thousands of dollars Rowel would have earned had he received his timely promotion more than two decades earlier. One supervisor admitted that, based on his industriousness and craftsmanship, Rowel had qualified for a GS-9 promotion as early as 1958, but this would have meant advancing six slots at once from his GS-3 grade and was disallowed. As Pulitzer Prize–winning columnist William Raspberry of the *Washington Post* put it, Rowel "couldn't be promoted because he hadn't been promoted."[2]

Rowel testified about the roadblocks he faced in obtaining promotions as a Black federal worker:

> In order to really advance at NIH you either have to know someone or you just didn't make it. It was just impossible for a black man to get a promotion. The jobs were not posted, it wasn't posted on the bulletin board and although we knew that the job was available through the grapevine, as

they say, we would go and apply for the job and the job was either taken or it wasn't available.[3]

The NIH gardener did find ways to preserve his dignity on the job. Rowel recalled, "I remember once they put out a rule that if a heavy equipment operator wanted to go to the bathroom, he had to get permission from a supervisor. If there was no supervisor around, he had to leave a note on the machine indicating where he was gone and why." That rule was changed after "word got around that [Rowel] intended to park his machine right in front of the administration building with a huge cardboard sign saying: 'GONE TO S---.'"[4]

After Rowel began his quest for justice in 1956, seven plaintiffs had either retired or resigned and three had passed away. Undeterred, Rowel declared, "Frankly, I'm not a well-educated person, but I know what's right and what's wrong, and if I see something wrong, I'll speak up about it."[5] The two decades he spent seeking justice did take a toll on him, however: "Everyone comes to me and says, 'you never got angry.' Believe me, I was angry . . . I was hurting."[6]

Black federal workers like Hoover Rowel have labored diligently to keep America's operating machinery alive and well, particularly since the Second World War. Yet, pure altruism is not the nexus of this relationship; African Americans joined the federal service primarily because they had few other private sector options to pursue the American Dream. While this federal workforce development was undoubtedly beneficial for many African Americans, what must remain central is that many of these employees first entered the federal ranks under *economic duress* on two counts: (1) the federal system was stressed for labor supply and resorted to Black laborers as a substitute alternative to favored white workers, and (2) many Black workers were desperate to escape neo-slavery working conditions in the South. Black public workers have always sought such work because it can provide both security and mobility not available elsewhere. In exchange for this increased long-term stability against recessions and economic downturns (as in they will theoretically always be "in business" because there will always be an American public to serve), public sector employees nonetheless sacrifice more immediate financial gains. This forced choice of accepting stability at the cost of wealth building has had long-term consequences for African Americans in and out of public work.

Federal Financial Freedom Forbidden?

Generally speaking, federal employment is unique: what was once beleaguered and bemoaned as a cesspool of cronyism and nepotism for small groups of propertied and well-connected political allies of white male patriarchy in the nineteenth century has now grown to one of the country's largest employers and most elaborate fair practices bureaucracies.[7] The federal government as a comprehensive employer has its workforce now distributed among more than four hundred individual, smaller agencies, helping it to collectively represent the single-largest group of employees globally (as they theoretically all labor for one sole employer—"Uncle Sam").[8] As of 2019 there were 2.7 million total federal employees, most located outside of Washington, DC, with roughly $215 billion spent to compensate all federal employees in 2016.[9]

However, much of this compensation pales in comparison to comparable positions within the private sector.[10] In the United States the private sector routinely outpaces the public sector with open-ended compensation packages and bonuses that place a premium on experience as well as potential for future success. While federal employment offers increased job security over private sector firms who can terminate employees "at will," many federal employees must now accept that they may be forever financially limited in their earning capacity, even if promoted fluidly to the highest levels within the federal system.

According to the Congressional Budget Office, federally employed workers with high school diplomas (or less) do earn 53 percent more than similarly situated private sector workers. However, although federal employees with only a high school education are compensated at a higher rate in relation to comparable private sector jobs, a large disparity begins to emerge when contrasting top-earning salaries in the private sector to the highest-ranking salaries within the public sector. Upper-management positions within the federal public sector are consistently underpaid in contrast to comparable private sector positions.[11] For example, compensation packages for private sector employees holding doctorates or professional degrees were 18 percent higher than comparable workers in the federal public sector.[12]

Further, due to fixed compensation schemes that are rigidly followed for all government employees in the name of uniformity, there is less room for negotiation and for recognizing individualized value within the public sector among large groups of public employees. Salaries are slotted and fixed within the GS, or General Schedule, scale, starting at GS-1 with a maximum of GS-16. This publicly available information reveals that each grade level contains ten incremental steps between promotional grades, with salaries at the GS-9 or above ranking as upper-level pay.[13] To better retain top-level employees, the highest-ranking SES, or Senior Executive Service, package consists of both high salary and performance-based awards, although such

SES compensation packages often do not match similar job descriptions within the private sector.[14]

While people's reasons for joining the federal service vary (freedom of schedule, income security, or meaningful work), becoming economically wealthy beyond measure is likely not one of them. Nowhere has this implicit agreement to sacrifice open-ended financial gains been more apparent than with Black federal public sector workers—a sacrifice made by people who, historically, have had fewer other choices for pursuing pathways of prosperity. It is an open question whether African Americans would have chosen the federal government if other, more lucrative options were simultaneously available. The federal government thus may not have been the best choice financially but perhaps was the *only choice* economically for African Americans to pursue survival, as dearth often develops desperation.[15] African Americans are overrepresented within the federal sector at 18 percent of the federal workforce, despite constituting 12 percent of the nation's population.[16]

The Unique Case of Black Federal Workers

The federal government was not always a global leader, nor did it always demonstrate progressive politics when it came to race and employment. In fact, the federal government was segregated in 1913 upon Postmaster General Alfred Burleson's progressivist appeal to President Woodrow Wilson for more efficient processes.[17] Yet, a workforce that was once predominantly white and male at the turn of the twentieth century rapidly transformed into one that was significantly more diverse in gender and ethnicity just half a century later—particularly within densely populated urban metropolitan areas after World War II.[18] Nationwide, out of 232,000 total federal employees listed for the year 1900, only 868 (0.4 percent) were African American. By the time World War II was concluding, 273,971 Black employees constituted 11.9 percent of the total federal workforce of 2,295,614 employees.[19]

As a resounding rebuttal to Wilsonian segregationists, simple supply/demand dynamics during the Second World War essentially dictated that it was inefficient to maintain a segregated workforce less than half a century later, especially in view of the pressing need to expand the wartime workforce.[20] Black workers, once unwanted during the Wilsonian progressive era in upper-level or mid-management positions (but not in the lower ranks, as Wilson loved having Black servants), suddenly morphed into desirable replacement parts to keep the great American war machine in motion.[21] When many white servicemen left to fight abroad, African

Figure 3.1. Black federal worker Jewal Mazique seen performing cataloging duties inside the Library of Congress, Washington, DC. (Photo by John Collier Jr. Courtesy of the Library of Congress Prints and Photographs Division, LC-USW3-000381-C [P&P] LOT 296.)

Americans (both male and female) and white women became desirable targets of employment.

While Black populations increased during the Great Migration of World War I, they only continued to skyrocket during the second wave in the 1940s. (In Washington, DC, "there were less than 10,000 Negro workers in the Federal government in 1938; in 1944, there were 41,566.")[22] As a result, many African Americans were pulled away from their economically depressed Southern enclaves in hopes of escaping racially segmented, backbreaking domestic or agricultural work.

Hence, federal jobs were considered by many African Americans to be better than the types of jobs typically available in the South, despite continued racial frictions. Federal employment quickly earned the reputation among Blacks as being a "good government job" and was highly coveted given its groundbreaking benefits, stability, and generally higher pay than comparable jobs in the private sector—especially when highly trained and educated African American employees encountered increased difficulty landing white-collar work.[23] Ironically, many African American federal workers found jobs that were very similar to those they would have held in the private sector South (operating press machines for the Government Printing Office or mowing lawns for the Department of Interior), but they were now "protected" under the umbrella of federal employment, with the added benefits of health care and stable employment.

Once Black workers settled into federal jobs, their collective progress was merely the beginning of a new type of segregation—albeit economic in nature—that would make it exceedingly difficult for faithful Black federal workers to have their "American Dreams" see the light of day. In analyzing the federal government's GS wage system, data show that African Americans were systematically denied opportunities to access the highest wage-scale levels within federal employment after World War II. Further, Black workers continued to face tensions working alongside white laborers, despite theoretically working within "neutral" federal workspaces.

With the war effort spurring the steady stream of newfound Black laborers arriving in droves within a formerly mostly white federal workforce, adjustments had to be made. White workers were not yet accustomed to working side by side with people who were segregated from whites in all other walks of life outside of work. "Hate strikes" erupted in which white workers withheld their labor to protest sharing the same space with Black workers or, worse, having to work under an African American manager.[24]

Therefore, the fate of a hardworking Hoover Rowel having to economically grovel patiently in the shadows, with no clear light cast on a path of prosperity, could be described as a type of abstract, economically restrictive positionality that many Black workers simply had little choice but to accept. This restrictive positionality of Black bodies within the federal workspace helped to foster a new classification: *Black-collar workers*, or African American laborers who suffer from lower wages in contrast to whites with similar educational backgrounds.[25] Black-collar workers also significantly suffer from slower rates for promotional raises than their similarly situated white counterparts, against the larger backdrop of bureaucratically imposed and finite limits upon one's federal salary. Practically speaking, there were few alternatives, let alone improved alternatives, within the unabashedly more racially hostile private sector for Black laborers—most especially during the Jim Crow era.[26]

Black federal workers, perhaps from the start but certainly since the Wilson era, suffered from lower wages and slower raises both within federal offices and comparatively across private markets. This dynamic has remained largely consistent since the decades after 1940, despite changes in education and policies allowing for more purposeful and strategic placement of Blacks in mid- to high-level management positions.[27] If anything, changes in strategy to confront and defeat racial discrimination have only been met with equally sophisticated responses in resistance.[28] In other words, discrimination, much like water, can take on the shape of its container. Meaning, as grievance protocols became more developed and sophisticated, the protections afforded and accorded the accused also became more robust, thereby protracting the process even further. Moreover, as mechanisms have been developed to protect workplace civil rights over time, they have not necessarily been adopted wholesale or accepted unopposed, as they still remain under political threat.[29]

In the 1940s racially discriminatory conduct might have included a Black employee complaining about hearing the n-word bandied about "playfully" in front of the employee.[30] Yet, over time, it became more difficult to establish and prove racial discrimination absent concrete, incontrovertible evidence of somebody "in the act" of being racially insensitive as overt, obvious and offensive acts of racism became less en vogue in the aftermath of the civil rights movement. What often ensued was a high-stakes "cat and mouse" interplay where it was incumbent upon Black employees to undertake the increasingly difficult task of establishing their racial grievances absent increasingly rare "smoking gun" evidence, even though they may have suffered from equally as damaging and pernicious racial microaggressions.[31] Also, as grievance mechanisms grew more sophisticated over time, it simply was not practical to ask a new employee to retroactively record every single instance of disrespect they encountered in hopes of building up a future case. Ultimately, many Black-collar workers were left without adequate outlets for substantively addressing their grievances for discriminatory actions after the fact, even though they were making progress in getting administrative systems to acknowledge that they occurred.

A Painstaking Process

The difference between addressing Black federal workers' grievances and merely acknowledging them became especially stark after the Equal Employment Opportunity Act of 1972 brought federal employers and government agencies under Title VII of the 1964 Civil Rights Act. When the 1964 act was signed, it originally did not include federal workers within its purview, nor did its groundbreaking employment policies apply to any private business with less than twenty-five employees—a telling number, as, historically, 90 percent of American businesses have held fewer than twenty employees.[32] Thus, the 1972 policy change theoretically provided Black workers with additional options to resolve and reconcile their grievances. But as John E. Womack's lengthy—albeit successful—fight for a promotion demonstrates, the grievance process could still be tortuous.

As a Black employee at the Federal Housing Administration (FHA) central office in Washington, DC, Womack fought for six years to rectify racial discrimination on the job within his division at the Department of Housing and Urban Development (HUD). After clearing a series of administrative hurdles, Womack won a challenge in the United States Court of Appeals, District of Columbia Circuit in 1974. Instead of dismissal, the appeals court remanded Womack's case to federal district court for a new trial.[33] In the years preceding the appellate court's decision, Womack's claim of racial discrimination at the federal workplace was never in dispute. The only subject at issue was the adequacy of addressing the remedy for the already acknowledged discrimination. Meanwhile, the financial relief for which he sued had to wait while the judicial process took its course.

Womack's main legal fight centered on his remedy for racial discrimination suffered while on the job rather than proving the racial discrimination itself. Womack's saga began in 1968 when a white coworker with a lower pay grade and less experience obtained a supervisory position over him—a position for which Womack had also applied. In response, Womack pursued a grievance through the proper channels within both his governing department at the HUD and with the Civil Service Commission. To Womack's relief, a claims hearing officer substantiated his claims early in the process and found that his supervisors had wrongfully passed him over in violation of President Lyndon Johnson's Executive Order 11246, which prohibited discrimination by federal contractors.

Yet acknowledgment did not mean reward. In 1969 the assistant secretary for Equal Employment Opportunity at HUD, Samuel J. Simmons, ordered Womack's promotion. Simmons, however, declined to award him either the seniority or the back pay he should have received.[34] Thus, Womack's claim remained unaddressed financially. Despite a successful grievance process, Womack received no direct economic compensation. He then decided to take his case to court outside of existing federal administrative channels. In 1970 HUD made very slight concessions to Womack on the issues of back pay and the denial of seniority. When Womack appealed this decision, the Civil Service Commission's Board of Appeals and Review denied him again. The following year, in 1971, Womack filed suit in federal district court under a creative cocktail of several different federal laws. In 1972, when the Equal Employment Opportunity Act gave federal workers the right to sue the government for Title VII violations, Womack tried revising his pending action. The district court rejected Womack's revision request outright and dismissed his case that same day.

Although Womack's 1974 appeal was successful at last, the extent of his reward was still undetermined. Tellingly, the court ruled in Womack's favor and found that the FHA wrongfully passed over Womack for another white employee with less experience. Womack nonetheless waited years for an increase in salary while he waited for the official grievance process to "take its course." The difficulty for Womack became in knowing what else to do. A formal process to protect him from discrimination existed, had been followed, and concluded successfully with a finding in his favor. But he still had not won the financial compensation he was owed. Now, in starting a new trial, Womack had the unenviable task of proving his case yet again. Finally, in 1978 he emerged victorious—with an award of one hundred thousand dollars—a full decade after lodging his initial complaint.[35]

Desired Diversity Up to a Point

Whereas public awareness of the Black freedom movement and civil rights movement made open expressions of racial vitriol less acceptable, the ironic by-product was that fewer Black employees had "smoking guns" to produce in support of their grievances alleging disparate and discriminatory conduct on the job. The painful result was even more protracted scenarios endured by Rowel, Womack, and others. In Womack's case, with the federal government being his primary source of income, he was essentially frozen within a financially restrictive state during his pursuit of economic justice, accounting for potential opportunity costs that may ultimately prove incalculable.

Moreover, even when the government intentionally sought to be equitable through its processes and procedures, inequities nonetheless resulted for Black workers. On this point, the example of Ruth Bates Harris is equally instructive: In the early seventies, the National Aeronautics and Space Administration (NASA) hired a specialist to improve Black employment at the higher grade levels since there was just "one minority person at the GS 16–18 level, out of 640 positions."[36] That "one minority person," Harris, was also one of the few Black female employees at NASA overall. But Harris's unique status was short-lived.

Dead End Job? Black Public Workers Struggle   71

Harris, a proud graduate from Historically Black College and University Florida A&M University, was "a self-described 'Harlem Princess' whose first marriage had been to a [former] Tuskegee Airman."[37] In 1971 NASA hired Harris as NASA's first woman deputy assistant administrator for equal opportunity. Ominously, her bosses at NASA demoted her before she had even begun her job. One week after announcing her hire, and before she officially left her previous position as director of human relations with Montgomery County Public Schools, NASA administrator Dr. James C. Fletcher rehired her as an assistant deputy director rather than the promised post as director of the department. Harris started her new job that October and immediately encountered resistance from white colleagues who viewed her guardedly as a civil rights activist with a political agenda.

NASA administrators were well aware that their hiring rate for Blacks was low. However, while NASA leadership felt they did as well as the private sector in hiring only 3.5 percent of minorities in technical positions, they lacked an effective answer for why NASA hired only 6 percent of minorities in all nontechnical positions. Administrators blamed poor education for the gap. But during the mid-1970s, the proportion of Blacks and whites attending college was roughly equal based on demographic share, although the total population of students was not equal.[38]

In 1973, following two years of constant conflict with administrators, NASA terminated Harris shortly after she and two aides had just issued a hard-hitting, forty-page report titled "NASA's Equal Opportunity Program Is a Near-Total Failure." The report detailed how the agency was "dragging its feet in hiring minority and women workers."[39] Dr. Fletcher claimed that Harris was "not dismissed because of the critical report" but rather insisted that, since most of the data cited was already on the public record, "the time they spent preparing it should have been devoted to more positive kinds of things." Another NASA spokesperson said that the agency's termination decision was free from racial motivation since the direct agency official who recommended Harris's dismissal was himself Black—in fact, "physically blacker" than Harris.[40]

Harris had earned a master's degree in business administration and was NASA's highest-ranking Black female at the time of her dismissal, earning an annual salary of thirty-two thousand dollars. Yet, she seemingly bore punishment for merely publicizing the truthful facts about low minority participation. Harris's firing symbolized the confounding frustrations Black federal workers endured while working for the space agency. Black workers contended blatant racism in both hiring and promotion methods within the agency and in protest formed MEAN, or Minority Employees at NASA. Although MEAN sent its first formal communication to NASA chief Fletcher in the spring of 1974, the Harris firing during the previous fall had probably contributed to galvanizing the workers into action. The complaints MEAN raised in its letter to Fletcher formed the basis of a class action lawsuit filed later that same year.

Harris took her employment battle to the local district court as well. The NAACP Legal Defense Fund took up her case and almost immediately had her salary reinstated while her status was under review. The major legal question concerned whether she was a political appointee eligible for firing at will. Meanwhile, NASA administrators searched in vain for evidence that Harris was a radical who intended to disrupt daily operations, hoping to rebut the negative publicity they were receiving. By filing her suit and garnering press attention, Harris and her lawyers successfully highlighted how few women and Blacks of both genders participated in the space program.

Eight months after her initial dismissal, NAACP lawyers sat down with NASA attorneys to negotiate a settlement. While NASA administrators conceded the need for additional hiring of minorities and better anti-bias training of current employees, they resisted centralizing such oversight, claiming that the agency operated more efficiently without it. As with other nationally funded programs that disbursed funds locally, decentralization allowed NASA regional centers to continue with established racist practices—most especially in the South.

Harris returned to NASA in August 1974 as the deputy assistant administrator of public affairs for community and human relations. However, Ruth Bates Harris was still just a solitary individual with limited power and resources to alter hiring patterns and practices. Not to mention, Harris's legal fight and the continued frustrations of her job caused her much psychological pain. In 1976 Harris suffered a nervous breakdown caused by these pressures, as well as dealing with a failed marriage while caring for a morbidly ill son. Harris left her job at NASA soon after.[41]

It is difficult to accurately measure the emotional and spiritual "costs" of such treatment to a Hoover Rowels, a John Womack, or a Ruth Bates Harris as they experienced negation of agency while supposedly having access to a free, open, and equitable public sector marketplace. The agonizing and protracted cycle of being so close to a solution in theory but yet so far from a resolution is telling. These Black federal workers became swallowed up and lost within administrative processes that proclaimed fairness but could not produce fair outcomes.

John Henry Goes to Washington

At best, the federal government's GS wage system may represent a neutral incentivization model, whereby even if one attains the highest agency salary after navigating the predetermined steps, there is still little chance that such an employee can ultimately compete with similar private sector jobs. This limitation creates a fatalistic dynamic for the employee who values the open-ended potential of capitalistic gains. A worker who seeks unbridled profit might seek that profit in a less restricted labor market than public work. But the twist on Black Americans is that those profit-seeking opportunities are limited by persistent racism in the private sector, racism that the public sector has also pledged to root out. Black public workers are therefore directed to seek dignity, fairness, and social mobility in public work but wind up in a double bind: cut off from the private profit-seeking model so ingrained in American culture but also trapped in a public workplace that will not live up to its claims of fairness either.

Within this bind, Black-collar workers also have the additional disadvantage of battling narratives suggesting that they must work twice as hard for half as much pay in the form of John Henryism. Coined by epidemiologist Sherman James, the term "John Henryism" suggests that some African Americans "are routinely exposed to psychosocial stressors (chronic financial strain, job insecurity, and subtle or perhaps not so subtle social insults linked to social class) that require them to use considerable energy each day to manage the psychological stress generated by these conditions."[42] The term "John Henry" comes from an American folktale that recognized the legendary working prowess of many African American railroad laborers, with John Henry being the exceptional case who was so widely respected that he was nominated to compete against a railroad machine.[43] To no one's surprise and to everyone's delight, Henry bested the machine, but it cost him his life, as he exerted and literally exhausted himself to death.

Hence, African Americans exhibiting John Henryism are those individuals who tend to respond to those psychosocial stressors by working harder to achieve their desired goal—even if that goal is effectively elusive. The hypothesis contends that the sustained, persistent effort to cope even in the face of difficult conditions (and especially when there are insufficient economic resources) increases the risk of individuals suffering negative health outcomes. The conundrum then manifests whereby, ironically, the more one attempts to help themselves through work and effort, the more that individual runs the risk of hurting themselves through increased and undue burdens.

With respect to the harmful physical effects of an imbalanced work ethic, testing shows that individuals who display high levels of John Henryism also have higher blood pressure (and hypertension) than those who score lower and have more economic resources.[44] More importantly, these and other, more recent studies suggest that this driven, ambitious approach to achieving goals in the face of adversity seems to have a more detrimental effect on physical health to those of lower socioeconomic status than it does on those of higher socioeconomic status.[45] It appears that only when or where one has enough physical and psychological resources, the pressures of high-effect coping may in fact be adaptive, and John Henryism may actually have a positive effect on mental health.[46] If the stories of Rowel, Womack, or Harris are any indication of other similar experiences, then John Henryism may have proven to be quite costly to many a Black-collar worker.

Captive Capital

Based on public sector salaries alone, African Americans appear resigned to eke out a collectively captive capitalistic existence. Although many federal salaries (especially those without higher education requirements) are significant and stable, many Black federal workers are merely receiving higher pay for performing duties similar to tough industrial or domestic jobs that pay less within the private sector, with the majority of African American federal workers still slotted in the lower grades of GS 1–8. Such a calculation engages a perverse theory of relativity whereby, compared to cleaning toilets in the private sector, the Black worker is "better off" if allowed or afforded the opportunity to do so within the public sector with the added benefit of health care. The data serves as a damning referendum, for African Americans are doubly constrained if saddled with internally depressed federal wages that already pale in comparison to more externally lucrative private sector jobs, despite the presence of a seemingly more transparent federal wage system.

If African Americans have been consistently restricted from participating fully within the free market, private sector economy, the federal employment structure for African Americans may not be that functionally different. The sobering reality is that many African Americans have been unable to liberally participate in the free market economy at a collective, lucrative level ever since the first recorded contingent of enslaved African slaves arrived on American shores at Jamestown, Virginia, in 1619.[47] Thus, the tenuous position of Black-collar workers is in stark contrast to many similarly situated white federal workers, who, despite imperfect working conditions, are more likely to find comparable (if not higher) pay within the private sector unbridled by the friction of racial discrimination and constrained only by more general market forces.

For instance, the thirty-four-day government shutdown that occurred in late 2018 and early 2019 helped expose the peculiarly precarious economic position of African American federal workers. While the federal government ground to a halt in many areas, some functions still continued (the travel of congresspersons to and from their constituents). The shutdown resulted in many workers placed on furlough, with over eight hundred thousand employees not receiving two paychecks.

While *all* federal workers were affected, Black-collar workers were disparately affected during the shutdown because not only are Black workers overrepresented in the federal workforce, but they are also overrepresented in the lower wage scales.[48] Thus, one curious development was the "expectation" that some essential (mostly Black) federal government employees would still report to work without pay—but, ironically, not the highest-paid (mostly white) workers.[49] Mostly African Americans and their disembodied economic prospects once again bore the financial brunt of the federal government's processes and protocols designed to be equitable to all. Perhaps the indomitable shadow of John Henry was there to make sure the government—or, rather, Black federal workers—kept going, even if it cost them their (financial) life.

When Good Enough Is Not Good Enough

When it comes to Black-collar workers, the promising economic relationship many could have had with government work has been frustrated by a lingering, self-deprecating logic: although such public sector jobs were not financially lucrative, at least these positions were better than the dirtiest and most dangerous jobs typically awaiting Black workers in windowless factories or in dubious domestic private sector jobs. In other words, the traditional relationship of exploited Black labor created an uneven bargaining table, predisposing Blacks to be "happy" or content with "something" as it was better than "nothing" (beggars cannot be choosers).

If anything, the heightened appeal of "good government jobs" to African Americans reflects a telling commentary on just how bleak and dismal job prospects truly were within the larger private sector, which make public sector pay rates appear greater in value than what they actually are. For as America's democratic republic allows for free enterprise unrivaled and marveled the world over, serving as a beacon or a "shining city on a hill" and attracting numerous businesses and individuals alike to form one of the world's largest economies, what remains lesser known is to what extent its federal public sector workers directly reap the fruits of their labors to keep America free and open for business.[50]

As many African Americans are now cloaked with "good government jobs," or stable and secure jobs in contrast to the private sector, perhaps many Black-collar workers can legitimately claim that they are indeed closer to financial freedom (the "American Dream"). Yet, the more that African Americans become mired in "good government jobs" that cannot provide great pay and promotional opportunities, the more such jobs can, ironically, facilitate stagnation rather than the progress they appear to foster.

The federal government did more than recover from its inauspicious beginning as an initially impartial bystander on equity issues, complete with federal workforce segregation in 1913. Since then, the federal government can legitimately be viewed as an eventual leader of the private sector on diversity matters, especially with the advent of Title VII of the 1964 Civil Rights Act, which forever changed the way both private and public sectors conduct business when it came to any type of workplace discrimination. Not only could successful racially discriminatory grievances possibly trigger monetary penalties for the first time, but also the Equal Employment Opportunity Commission (EEOC), established in 1965, was held forward as likely the most comprehensive grievance-reporting mechanism for employees of all types.

Yet, while Title VII was designed to address and punish documented examples of racial discrimination within the workplace, a workplace can conceivably hire a homogeneous group of people and not be in violation of any law as long as no racial animus is established. For example, according to the U.S. Commission on Civil Rights, "Word-of-mouth recruitment that produces a largely homogenous work force is not illegal discrimination."[51] In looking at the larger picture, harrowing economic prospects historically facing Black Americans in the private sector likely made public sector work appear as a more appealing means to access the "American Dream," relatively speaking. Upon further analysis, these "good government jobs" were perhaps over-esteemed. Such jobs were called "good" only insofar as they presented sensible options over the limited pathways available. What is required is further analysis of whether these jobs were objectively better than comparable alternatives.

Dead-End Job?

Black federal workers' economically restrictive status coupled with a lack of alternate choices recalls another era of unfreedom endured by Black bodies. Writing of the Era of Enslavement, historians such as Edward Baptist use the word "torture" to more accurately describe the hidden spark that kept the ever-expanding machinery of cotton production in operation in the dusty backwoods of Louisiana. Baptist's argument is that euphemisms such as "discipline," "punishment," or even "correction" do not adequately convey or capture the chief impetus used to drive cotton production totals up consistently, which was torture.[52] Hence, the enslaved African Americans were reduced to a state akin to that of barely existing as capitalistic *zombies*, the Haitian word for half-dead Black bodies who feared their souls would remain trapped if they died an unsavory life here on earth (via suicide). These undead were condemned to labor in perpetuity and in constant fear that their daily work product would not measure up to the weighing scale at the end of a grueling day's work.

In reflecting upon Black federal workers within a contemporary context, invoking a metaphor dating back to the Era of Enslavement may indeed appear to be crude. After all, so much time has passed and so much change has occurred over time. We should take care not to simplistically project enslavement as a metaphor onto the lives of paid federal workers in the modern era whose lives were far less violent and coercive, so as not to diminish the harsh realities of enslavement. Yet, it is time to challenge the historiographical resistance to drawing such connections among people who share a lineage and legacy as linked through time. While it may indeed be overbroad to blanketly state that all current problems within the African American community are directly attributable to the Era of Enslavement, at the same time it would be equally as irresponsible not to analyze and appreciate its historical connection to, as well as its impact and influence on, present-day economic conditions, even after some clear markers of progress.

If anything, the concept of a disembodied capitalistic zombie is quite prescient, as it appears that in agreeing to work for the federal government, Black federal employees also sacrifice the full realization of their earning potential—at least within the open-ended private sector—in exchange for a salary that is more stable and secure, albeit more stultified economically. Unfortunately for Black federal workers, the data demonstrate that despite numerous groundbreaking, encouraging policy changes over the decades, African Americans' collectively restrictive economic condition within federal employment has remained relatively constant.[53] Numerous studies have shown a remarkably disturbing consistency with respect to many African Americans being unable to escape their Black-collar condition, no matter how high up the GS scale they were promoted.[54]

While African Americans are no longer enslaved, a fair question exists as to whether they still are economically restricted within an abstract, capitalistic way—meaning, African Americans as Black-collar workers may still labor diligently daily to produce for a larger American machinery, but they may not fully benefit from the fruits of such labor. In extending the enslavement allegory, this scenario speaks to states of both torture and freedom: Black workers have had little choice in escaping economic and social segregation (and, by extension, economic suffocation) but to accept Uncle Sam's half-a-loaf offer of imperfect working conditions and pay within a federal employment structure that is quite alluring and aspirational in character.

The ultimate irony is that America would not be what it is without the manifold contributions of its federal public sector workers, and the country might still be on her deathbed if Black federal workers did not come in during the Second World War as a triage move to help stop the labor supply from bleeding dry. However, several decades after the Second World War, the EEOC continues to discover that "unconscious biases and perceptions about African Americans still play a significant role in employment decisions in the federal sector."[55] If such disparities stubbornly persist along racial lines within the more transparent public sector, such reports serve as a sobering referendum as to what African American prospects are truly like within the private sector, as federal incomes may not adequately compare to those salaries commanded within Silicon Valley.

Analyzing data surrounding the financial prospects of African Americans within the federal public sector is instrumental insofar as such information serves as a litmus test to reflect the true accessibility of wealth within our free market economy. Romantic racialist misconceptions of highly compensated African American sports figures and entertainers should not distract from the rugged reality many African Americans still face in gaining a foothold on the American Dream. Continued economic frustrations within the public sector coupled with private sector data that shows as of 2019, no Fortune 500 company is Black owned, with only a handful of African Americans serving as CEOs, give us the clues necessary to bring to a halt this economically torturous equation.

Otherwise, African American federal workers especially run the risk of merely keeping alive a capitalistic zombie campaign, whereby all of their earnings directly invested in their half-dead state into their country will merely continue to be distributed to others after they are fully dead and long gone.

It remains to be seen whether the federal government will make good on its fiduciary promises to "put its money where its mouth is," with respect to honoring and respecting the lifeblood of its employees who help to keep its capitalistic machinery in fluid operation. For if Black-collar workers struggle financially at virtually all levels of federal employment, we must also ask, What does such systemic discrimination say about the overall American economy, which includes both the private and public sectors? Such comprehensive analysis—or a full picture of the labor market in which Black workers operate across lines of both "public" and "private"—puts into perspective the supreme difficulty of keeping an open-ended and highly lucrative financial career for Black workers from becoming trapped within a half-dead state, where lively growth is unlikely to be based on federal salaries alone.

In sum, if a racially inhospitable private sector pushed many Blacks toward finding jobs within the public sector, and if as Black-collar workers such public sector employees were essentially cut off from realizing the American Dream within a democratic apparatus that was unfair to its own laborers, then the conclusion is that many Black federal workers continue to suffer through an economically torturous condition that systemically restricts collective economic progress within both the public and private sectors.

While many financial goals can be stymied due to happenstance or circumstance, systemic and institutionalized racial discrimination have historically served as barriers to African American economic progress. The deeply traumatizing Era of Enslavement, followed by failed Reconstruction, Jim Crow, and neoliberal racism periods, have all contributed to objectively challenging periods whereby daily African American existence was subject to economic duress (in addition to psychological trauma). Fortunately, the United States federal government in theory guarantees certain basic minimums (life, liberty, and the pursuit of happiness) to every citizen and means well to enforce these minimums. In practice, though, working for the federal government can possibly mean an economic existence in which one does not necessarily financially thrive but merely survives—especially if one is a Black federal worker struggling to merely see the light of day.

Further Reading

Bowser, Benjamin P. *The Black Middle Class: Social Mobility—and Vulnerability*. Boulder, CO: Lynne Rienner Publishers, 2006.

Oliver, Melvin, and Thomas M. Shapiro. *Black Wealth, White Wealth: A New Perspective on Racial Inequality*. New York: Routledge, 2006.

Pattillo-McCoy, Mary. *Black Picket Fences: Privilege and Peril among the Black Middle Class*. Chicago: University of Chicago Press, 1999.

Rothstein, Richard. *The Color of Law: A Forgotten History of How Our Government Segregated America*. New York: Liveright Publishing, 2017.

Shapiro, Thomas M. *The Hidden Cost of Being African American: How Wealth Perpetuates Inequality*. New York: Oxford University Press, 2004.

Notes

1. "ACLU Cites Gardener," *Afro American*, December 9, 1978; Nancy Ferris, "A Long Discrimination Fight Finally," *Washington Star*, November 20, 1977.

2. William Raspberry, "Lawyer Says NIH Words, Deeds Don't Jibe on Job Equality," *Washington Post*, October 12, 1969.

3. Rowel quoted in William Raspberry, "Can't Make Reparations, NIH Claims," *Washington Post*, October 13, 1969.

4. Ibid.

5. William Raspberry, "Discrimination at NIH: Winning and Waiting," *Washington Post*, October 24, 1975.

6. Ferris, "Long Discrimination Fight."

7. Historian Eric Yellin makes the cogent point that progressive politics, which essentially resulted in the whitening of government rolls, was presented as a simple and rational choice, rather than a racist one, due to many casting aspersions at the time about Blacks in public sector work as associated with dirty politics. See Eric S. Yellin, *Racism in the Nation's Service: Government Workers and the Color Line in Woodrow Wilson's America* (Chapel Hill: University of North Carolina Press, 2013), 8; Michael B. Sauter and Grant Suneson, "Who Is the Largest Employer in Your State? Walmart Top in Nation with Amazon Second," *USA Today*, March 30, 2019.

8. As of February 7, 2019, 445 agencies were listed under the *Federal Register*; see "Agencies Found," *Federal Register: The Daily Journal of the United States Government*, n.d., https://www.federalregister.gov/agencies/, accessed February 7, 2019.

9. The U.S. federal government also holds the distinction of being the world's largest employer, with more than 2.7 million employees. Walmart is next, with 2.2 million (1.3 million of whom are actually in the United States). See Joyce Chepkemoi, "The Largest Employers in the United States," *World Atlas*, June 6, 2017, https://www.worldatlas.com/articles/the-largest-private-employers-in-the-united-states.html/, accessed February 7, 2019. Note that the 2.7 million does not include military employees nor employees of the U.S. Postal Service, which is a quasi-governmental agency with approximately 600,000 employees. See "Federal Employees by State," *Governing*, January 25, 2019, http://www.governing.com/gov-data/federal-employees-workforce-numbers-by-state.html/, accessed February 7, 2019; Congressional Budget Office, "Comparing the Compensation of Federal and Private-Sector Employees, 2011 to 2015," April 25, 2017, https://www.cbo.gov/publication/52637/, accessed February 7, 2019.

10. Eric Yoder, "Federal Employees Lag behind Private Sector Workers in Salaries by 32 Percent on Average, Report Says," *Washington Post*, April 11, 2018.

11. Congressional Budget Office, "Comparing the Compensation."

12. Nicole Ogrysko, "Latest Study on Federal Compensation Puts Public, Private Pay Gap at Widest Margin Yet," *Federal News Network*, September 25, 2017, https://federalnewsnetwork.com/all-news/2017/09/latest-study-on-federal-compensation-puts-public-private-pay-gap-at-widest-margin-yet/.

13. Office of Personnel Management, "Salary Table 2019-GS," January 2019, https://www.opm.gov/policy-data-oversight/pay-leave/salaries-wages/salary-tables/pdf/2019/GS.pdf/, accessed February 7, 2019.

14. Office of Personnel Management, "Senior Executive Service," n.d., https://www.opm.gov/policy-data-oversight/senior-executive-service/compensation/, accessed February 7, 2019.

15. See Frederick Gooding Jr., *American Dream Deferred: Black Federal Workers in Washington, DC, 1941–1981* (Pittsburgh: University of Pittsburgh Press, 2018), 188.

16. James Lartey, "Barely above Water: US Shutdown Hits Black Federal Workers Hardest," *The Guardian*, January 11, 2019.

17. Gooding, *American Dream Deferred*, 12.

18. Mitra Toossi, "A Century of Change: The U.S. Labor Force, 1950–2050," *Monthly Labor Review* (May 2002): 15–28.

19. Gooding, *American Dream Deferred*, 29.

20. See Derrick A. Bell. "*Brown v. Board of Education* and the Interest-Convergence Dilemma," *Harvard Law Review* 93, no. 3 (1980): 518–33.

21. Yellin, *Racism in the Nation's Service*, 7–8.

22. Isabel Wilkerson, *The Warmth of Other Suns: The Epic Story of America's Great Migration* (New York: Vintage Books, 2010), 243–44; Gooding, *American Dream Deferred*, 29.

23. Gooding, *American Dream Deferred*, 85.

24. Aaron Brenner, Benjamin Day, and Immanuel Ness, eds., *The Encyclopedia of Strikes in American History* (New York: Routledge, 2009), 127.

25. Gooding, *American Dream Deferred*, 14.

26. The Jim Crow era can possibly be said to have concluded with the 1954 *Brown v. Board* Supreme Court decision that officially ended school segregation—albeit with "all deliberate speed." Another possible date to formally mark the declension of the Jim Crow period is 1964, with the official signing into law of the 1964 Civil Rights Act.

27. "Unconscious biases and perceptions about African Americans still play a significant role in employment decisions in the federal sector." U.S. Equal Employment Opportunity Commission, "EEOC African American Workgroup Report," January 2010, https://www.eeoc.gov/federal/reports/aawg.cfm/, accessed October 21, 2017.

28. Philip Kennicott, "Revisiting King's Metaphor about a Nation's Debt," *Washington Post*, August 24, 2011.

29. Laura Meckler and Devlin Barrett, "Trump Administration Considers Rollback of Anti-Discrimination Rules," *Washington Post*, January 3, 2019.

30. Gooding, *American Dream Deferred*, 58–59.

31. See, generally, Frederick Gooding Jr. and Mikio Akagi, "Microaggressions and Objectivity: Experimental Measures and Lived Experience," *Philosophy of Science* 88, no. 5 (2021): 1090–1100.

32. Gooding, *American Dream Deferred*, 130.

33. *Womack v. Lynn*, 504 F.2d 267 (D.C. Cir. 1974).

34. "Samuel Simmons Appointed President of Black Aged," *Jet Magazine* 62, no. 5 (1982), 6.

35. Simeon Booker, "Ticker Tape U.S.A.," *Jet Magazine* 54, no. 24 (1978), 11.

36. U.S. Commission on Civil Rights, *The Federal Civil Rights Enforcement Effort: A Reassessment* (Washington, DC: Government Printing Office, 1973), 42–43.

37. Ruth Bates Harris, *Harlem Princess: The Story of Harry Delaney's Daughter* (New York: Vantage Press, 1999), 4.

38. Robert M. Hauser, "Trends in College Entry among Whites, Blacks, and Hispanics," in *Studies of Supply and Demand in Higher Education*, ed. Charles T. Clotfelter and Michael Rothschild (Chicago: University of Chicago Press, 1993), 70.

39. Mark Lawrence, "At GPO, 15-Year Job Bias Fight Ends; $2.4 Million Settlement Reached in Black Workers' Suit," *Washington Post*, August 12, 1987.

40. Kim McQuaid, "'Racism, Sexism, and Space Ventures': Civil Rights at NASA in the Nixon Era and Beyond," in *Societal Impact of Spaceflight*, ed. Steven J. Dick and Roger D. Launius (Washington, DC: NASA Office of External Relations, History Division, 2007), 427.

41. Ibid., 442.

42. S. A. James, "John Henryism and the Health of African Americans," *Culture, Medicine, and Psychiatry* 18 (1994): 163–82.

43. J. Bicknell, "Reflections on 'John Henry': Ethical Issues in Singing Performance," *Journal of Aesthetics and Art Criticism* 67, no. 2 (2009): 173—80.

44. Ibid.

45. V. Bonham, S. L. Sellers, and H. Neighbors, "John Henryism and Physical Health among High SES African American Men," *American Journal of Public Health* 94 (2004): 737–38.

46. S. L. Sellers, H. W. Neighbors, and V. L. Bonham, "Goal-Striving Stress and the Mental Health of College-Educated Black American Men: The Protective Effects of System-Blame," *American Journal of Orthopsychiatry* 81, no. 4 (2001): 507–518.

47. See, for example, "The 1619 Project," which "aims to reframe the country's history by placing the consequences of slavery and the contributions of black Americans at the very center of our national narrative." Nikole Hannah-Jones, "The 1619 Project," *New York Times*, August 14, 2019, https://www.nytimes.com/interactive/2019/08/14/magazine/1619-america-slavery.html/.

48. Jason Johnson, "No Check, Snowed In, and No End in Sight: How Black D.C. Is Surviving Trump's Government Shutdown," *The Root*, January 14, 2019, https://www.theroot.com/no-check-snowed-in-and-no-end-in-sight-how-black-d-c-1831735993/, accessed February 7, 2019.

49. Amanda Sakuma, "TSA Agents Are Calling in Sick Rather Than Work without Pay

during the Shutdown," *Vox*, January 5, 2019, https://www.vox.com/2019/1/5/18169683/tsa-agents-skip-work-government-shutdown-pay/, accessed February 7, 2019.

50. Daniel T. Rodgers, *As a City on a Hill: The Story of America's Most Famous Lay Sermon* (Princeton, NJ: Princeton University Press, 2018), 244.

51. U.S. Commission on Civil Rights, "Racial and Ethnic Tensions in American Communities: Poverty, Inequality, and Discrimination," vol. 6 (December 1999), 50.

52. See, generally, Edward E. Baptist, *The Half Has Never Been Told: Slavery and the Making of American Capitalism* (New York: Basic Books, 2016).

53. Joe Davidson, "Latest Federal Diversity Report from OPM Shows Little or No Progress and Some Regression," *Washington Post*, April 2, 2018, https://www.washingtonpost.com/news/powerpost/wp/2018/04/02/latest-federal-diversity-report-from-opm-shows-little-or-no-progress-and-some-regression/, accessed February 7, 2019.

54. For example, "The percentage of minorities in the Senior Executive Service (SES) remained the same in FY 2016 as it was in FY 2015 at 21.2 percent. The SES is 11.0 percent Black." U.S. Office of Personnel Management, "Federal Equal Opportunity Recruitment Program (FEORP) Report to Congress," February 2018, https://www.opm.gov/policy-data-oversight/diversity-and-inclusion/reports/feorp-2016.pdf/, 2.

55. EEOC, "African American Workgroup Report," 2010, https://www.eeoc.gov/federal/reports/aawg.cfm/, accessed February 7, 2019.

CHAPTER 4

"We're the Backbone of This City"

Women and Gender in Public Work

KATHERINE TURK

"We are responsible for life and death matters," Frances Honeggar testified in 1982 on behalf of two dozen nurses suing the city of Madison, Wisconsin, for wage discrimination. They earned between $60 and $125 less per month than the sanitarians—all men—who inspected the city's bars and restaurants. The two jobs were not identical, the nurses' lawsuit acknowledged, but they had comparable levels of responsibility, skill, and effort, and they were equally essential to the public good. The nurses argued that creating workplace equality meant raising the wages for their "necessary, valuable and satisfying" jobs rather than making them "feel they should have to become carpenters or plumbers to be paid equitably." By framing their demands for equal pay in terms of their work's inherent worth rather than its similarity to "male-typed" work, the nurses tapped into a long history of public workers offering expansive rights claims by defining the state as a unique kind of employer. Sometimes aided by the law but always buoyed by their resilience and creativity, their struggle continues.[1]

The Madison nurses helped define a dramatic chapter in the history of public work and the gendered and racialized norms that have shaped it since the mid-nineteenth century. The swelling post–Civil War federal bureaucracy opened clerical work to white women, who helped forge a new mixed-sex middle class. African American men gained access to these clerical jobs a few decades later, creating a Black bourgeoisie in Washington that was an example for the nation. But Black men were largely purged from upper-level government jobs as part of Progressive Era reforms.[2] Married women met the same fate during the 1930s, as federal officials fired them by the scores to blunt the Great Depression's effects on male breadwinners. Reflecting Cold War–era fears of Washington's cosmopolitanism, gay and lesbian civil servants were targeted for dismissal as "gender deviants" and, thus, security risks, and in the 1960s public workers drew energy and inspiration from the civil rights movement in their emboldened demands. Prevailing race and gender hierarchies shaped public work from its origins until the mid-twentieth century.

But public workers' distinct points of leverage—the nature of their work and having the state as their employer—positioned them to attack structured inequalities across the labor force toward the end of the twentieth century. Expanded workplace rights laws, a robust feminist movement, and the growth and feminization of government jobs made public work the testing ground for a radical redefinition of gendered rights in the 1970s and early 1980s. In the name of equality, these advocates argued, public officials should not only cease distinguishing between the sexes at work but also recalculate the wages paid to every state employee based on the value and the skills they brought to their jobs. Historic sex discrimination and gendered ideas about work's value, they said, explained why female-dominated jobs paid so much less than jobs performed mostly by men. Like the Madison nurses, they claimed that only sexist stereotypes could justify the lower wages paid to a preschool teacher than a zookeeper, or to a clerical worker than a truck driver, for example. This theory, called "comparable worth," had significant momentum in the public sector by the early 1980s. Comparable worth's potential to reshape employment law and ripple into the private sector drew a massive conservative response that all but crushed its legal viability by the end of the decade.[3]

Since then, public workers have mostly come to share the fate of their private sector counterparts, reflecting conservatives' resistance to gender equality and any kind of labor rights. Women have struggled to cross the public sector's gendered division of labor into the uniformed jobs of firefighter, police officer, and sanitation worker, and public workers' long-fought job security, decent wages, and benefits have eroded. But public workers— most recently, teachers—continue to highlight how their labor is essential yet undervalued as they push the state to become a fair employer.

Gender and Race Define Public Work

Public work was mostly invisible in the mid-nineteenth century. In local areas, public and private workers toiled side by side, and fewer than thirteen hundred men worked for the federal government before the Civil War. The first women entered federal employment at the start of that conflict, when the U.S. Treasury introduced paper currency to help finance the conflict. Workers printed new bills on large sheets that had to be broken down, and worn-out bills had to be recycled. The new U.S. treasurer, Francis Spinner, had drafted his wife and daughter for those tasks in his previous career as a New York banker, and he was disappointed to find two dozen "hale and hearty young men, armed with small shears, busy clipping bank notes" at the Treasury Department. Such men "should have muskets instead of shears placed in their hands and should be sent to the front," he declared, and replaced by women, "who would do more and better work, at half the pay that was given to these 'men milliners.'" To Spinner, processing currency was women's work, and men's labors were better applied to more valuable tasks. Indeed, the Treasury Department hired women to cut currency at a wage of six hundred dollars per year, which was half the salary the lowest-paid male cutter had drawn. Within a year of women becoming bill trimmers, the department began using machines to cut sheets of money. Some women lost their jobs, but others took up the new work of counting machine-cut currency.[4]

The federal bureaucracy more than doubled between 1860 and 1900 as it provided more services to the American population. Women and men soon began working together in federal office jobs with decent wages, hours, and benefits, violating the predominant separate spheres ideology that disdained both women's wage earning and mixed-sex environments. This work appealed to downwardly mobile men battered by the economic instabilities left in the war's wake and newly delivered by Gilded Age capitalism. Taking on clerical work and answering to a boss required men to make a "substantial psychological sacrifice" because government employment "seemed, to many, to signal an eclipse of independence," writes historian Cindy Sondik Aron. The women who took these jobs—mostly white and native born—also challenged gender norms with their new independence. By the turn of the century, there were more than twenty-five thousand federal civil servants, nearly seven thousand of whom were women.[5]

As Republican officials built the federal employment sector, they created a temporary new opening for African American civil servants, most of whom were men. The Pendleton Civil Service Act of 1883 required many federal job applicants to take an entrance exam. More than one million people took the test in its first sixteen years, and it curtailed officials' ability to deny jobs to Black applicants outright, although some discriminatory provisions and practices remained. White-collar government workers then earned nearly double the average American salary, which made government jobs especially attractive to African Americans who endured a racist labor market. Whites tended to see clerical jobs as women's work, and Black women struggled to enter it, but to African American men these positions offered upward mobility, a professional setting, and clear rules for pay, promotions, and protection from arbitrary firing. Some of these Black male civil servants earned enough to keep their wives and children outside of the labor force. For example, postal clerk Henry Hood earned eleven hundred dollars annually, a typical wage for full-time civil servants, and he and his wife, Emma, a homemaker, rented a comfortable home in the District of Columbia. This new male-led Black middle class, albeit fledgling, was a powerful magnet for African Americans nationwide.[6]

Black men began to lose their tenuous foothold in the civil service in the 1910s as white women gained more prominence. Wilsonian Progressives attacked African American civil servants and racial mixing in Washington as evidence of social or moral corruption, setting out "to transform clean government into white government," writes historian Eric S. Yellin. The Progressives' emphasis on professionalism and expanding bureaucracy opened important new space for white women, a handful of whom won top government posts. The Women's Bureau of the U.S. Department of Labor, established during World War I, offered women social scientists and reformers an important, albeit weak, platform. The bureau's officials were effectively "Outsiders as Insiders," historian Judith Sealander writes, and they produced detailed studies of women's working conditions but could not enforce their recommendations. President Franklin Delano Roosevelt appointed longtime labor reformer Frances Perkins as the U.S. secretary of labor in 1933. The first woman to serve in any president's cabinet, "Ma Perkins" fashioned herself as a caring grandmother to highlight workers' vulnerability and their need for a strong and wide social safety net.[7]

Rigid gender norms also shaped public work in American cities as public sector unions emerged to attack political machines and corporate influence in urban government. Boston police officers struck in 1919 to protest low wages and long hours that deprived the all-male officer corps of "enjoying the comforts of their home and family," the union president claimed. The officers especially resented their lack of independence when they were forced into the feminized role of running supervisors' personal errands. Two decades later, male sanitation workers in Philadelphia protested their filthy and dangerous conditions and low wages, which were 50 percent below the minimum rate that could support a wife and children. Their 1938 strike became a family affair. The men's wives heckled police officers and strikebreakers, and their children used metal nails to puncture the tires of police vehicles. The Philadelphia strikers won key concessions and formed a male-led chapter of the American Federation of State, County, and Municipal Employees (AFSCME) union. Women began moving into more city jobs at mid-century as AFSCME grew stronger, but the men at the top embraced masculine priorities, neglecting to incorporate a group of seven hundred women crossing guards who organized in 1954 or to fight for a formalized maternity leave policy until women began to sue the city on their own decades later.[8]

Other public sector workers had broader notions of gender and racial solidarity in the early twentieth century. The Building Service Employees International Union (BSEIU) was formed in 1912 by private sector janitors in Chicago, but it also recruited public school janitors. From its inception, the BSEIU had many people of color and white women in leadership roles. A few of the union's locals were comprised entirely of women, and most had a high female membership. These locals often demanded equal pay between the sexes and sometimes won it. A 1929 article in the union's national journal, *Public Safety*, declared that women's wages, far from supplemental "pin money," were "often . . . the only means of holding the family together."' Seattle teachers formed a local of the American Federation of Teachers in 1927, and three-fifths of the officers were women. Reflecting the group's heavily female membership, their demands included an end to unequal treatment of married teachers—a policy that especially harmed women—as well as discrimination on the basis of race, religion, and political beliefs. The state supreme court upheld in 1930 the city school board's right to force teachers to sign "yellow dog" contracts, which prevented them from joining or forming unions, but the school board, shamed by public appeals, voted unanimously to drop the policy the following month.[9]

The federal civil service began to recruit a more democratic membership in these years, but the Great Depression curtailed these efforts and exposed officials' sexist prejudices. Section 213 of the Appropriations Act of 1932 included the "Married Persons Clause," which stated that two civil servants could not be married to each other. The clause did not indicate which spouse should be laid off, but women were 16 percent of the federal workforce from 1932 to 1935 and 78 percent of workers dismissed under the law, while many other women resigned preemptively rather than waiting to be let go. Section 213 was repealed in 1937, but new social science theories compounded women's subordination in federal employment by defining unmarried or gender-nonconforming women as unsuitable for the civil service. Supervisors in the Agricultural Adjustment Agency targeted fifty-five-year-old Emma Youngman for dismissal in 1936, for example. When she appealed the decision, officials enlisted a psychologist who deemed her a "psychopathic spinster" with "a tense, suspicious type of emotional make-up with rather strong paranoid trends." Through the 1940s, officials abandoned the Depression-era argument that women worked only to supplement their families' income and embraced this new "objectivity."[10]

The boundary between public and private sector work collapsed during World War II as the nation's industrial demands increased while men left by the millions for military service. Five million women entered the workforce between 1940 and 1944, and many others gained better-paying and more prestigious war jobs. Under pressure from Black workers—especially the threat by Brotherhood of Sleeping Car Porters leader A. Philip Randolph and others to hold a massive March on Washington—FDR created the Fair Employment Practices Commission (FEPC) in 1941, which was empowered to receive and investigate claims of discrimination in war work. In their FEPC claims, African American women in particular framed their grievances in terms of shared sacrifice and their right to equal citizenship, which included fair treatment at work. "If we can fight abroad for justice[,] surely we can have justice here at home," Gary, Indiana, resident Merle Stokes Dunston reasoned with an FEPC official in 1942. Dunston worked at the Kingsbury ordnance plant, which drew twenty thousand workers from northern Indiana's urban African American and rural white communities. Black women were especially segregated and vulnerable to poor treatment there because gendered notions of Black men's strength opened up many more jobs to them. "The officials there are inclined to be what you may call hard boiled," Ruth Strickland wrote to the FEPC. "They do not seem to realize that the [Negro] employees are there for the one and same cause that they are." Black women's FEPC appeals made little headway due to both the agency's lack of clout and the complexity of their rights claims, which reflected their layered experiences of discrimination.[11]

Gender norms contracted further during the Cold War as Washington police and federal officials alike sought to purge gay men and lesbians from federal employment as part of a "lavender scare" that reinforced the McCarthyist hunt for Communists. A State Department official claimed in early 1950 that ninety-one homosexuals had been dismissed from the department, and the firings soon expanded. From mid-1953 to mid-1955, over eight hundred federal workers resigned or were dismissed because of their suspected "sex perversion." The purge represented a conservative effort to undermine the New Deal, which critics framed as Socialist and even Communist, and it also reflected deeper anxieties about Washington's recent growth. Only two of the ninety-one initially purged workers were women, but the Cold War military ousted suspected lesbians at higher rates than suspected gay men on account of the women's "queerness" for choosing a military career over marriage.[12]

However, the civil service soon became the front line for fighting workplace discrimination against gay people. Fifteen-year NASA veteran Clifford Norton was fired in 1963 for "immoral, indecent and disgraceful conduct" after DC police discovered him at a popular gay trysting place. Norton fought back through the Mattachine Society of Washington, a gay rights group, nearly half of whose members held a government security clearance. In *Norton v. Macy*, the U.S. Court of Appeals for the District of Columbia Circuit found in Norton's behalf, ruling that the civil service had not established a link between his after-hours behavior and his job performance. In the 1970s the Civil Service Commission consistently lost similar challenges by fired gay and lesbian workers, and the service removed a de facto ban on openly gay federal workers in 1975, although agencies' practices varied and barriers remained.[13]

New Rights Claims and Leverage Points

The public sector expanded significantly in the 1960s as public workers' rights, union density, and determination all swelled. President John F. Kennedy established Executive Order 10988, a 1962 provision that permitted public workers to form unions and bargain collectively. Later in the decade, President Lyndon Johnson's Great Society programs created government jobs in states and cities, many of which were female-dominated clerical and service jobs. The Equal Employment Opportunity Act of 1972 further boosted public workers' rights by granting many of them new protection under Title VII of the Civil Rights Act. These workers flocked to public sector unions like AFSCME, whose leadership and ideologies were thoroughly masculine. There were 3.9 million unionized public sector workers in 1968 and 6.1 million a decade later as the service sector itself expanded and those workers gained new protections for collective bargaining. Public workers, including schoolteachers, struck with new frequency in these years, and their militancy affected nonunionized public workers as well. Nearly thirteen hundred African American male sanitation workers struck in Memphis in early 1968, protesting their low pay and explicitly racist and dangerous treatment. Martin Luther King Jr. joined these workers, who coined and disseminated the slogan "I *Am* a Man." One striker explained that "I *Am* a Man" meant "We ain't gonna take that shit no more." Memphis laundry worker Hazel McGhee struck alongside her sanitation-worker husband. She told him, "Stand up and be [a] man. If you can be a man, I can be a woman. If you can be strong, I can be strong."[14]

Women and Gender in Public Work   91

When McGhee spoke, women's own entry into the public sector was outpacing their entry into waged work. Their labor force representation rose from 29 percent in 1950 to 40 percent in 1975, a proportion that more than doubled in public work. As women gained ground within public sector unions, they pressured for more attention to their concerns. In particular, they began advocating that their wages be recalculated using the principle of comparable worth. This theory contends that the wage gap between male- and female-dominated jobs stems from the family wage ideology, which defined men as breadwinners and women as their dependents. "There was historical discrimination against women going back to the 1930s, when it was legal," explained labor lawyer Winn Newman, "and even though the pay scales were relabeled after sex discrimination became illegal, in many cases, the same basic pay structure was kept." Thus, sexist presumptions, not an impartial market, determined workers' wages. "Adam Smith never taught us that the market sought out the sex of the worker before deciding wages," declared Equal Employment Opportunity Commission chairperson Eleanor Holmes Norton in 1980.[15]

Comparable worth advocates argued that to create meaningful equality between the sexes, entire pay schemes should be transformed to reflect a job's value rather than its going rate. "You can compare apples and oranges if you compare their nutritional qualities rather than the superficial appearance," explained advocate Nancy Pearlman. "It's the same with jobs." They especially targeted the public sector, where states and localities employed many different types of workers whose job descriptions and wage rates were public information and where bargaining practices and civil service regulations typically referenced equitable wages. Women of color found comparable worth especially attractive because they more often lacked the professional training that could help them leave feminized jobs, and their proportion of the public sector workforce rose from 5.1 percent in 1977 to 6.9 percent in 1980.[16]

Labor feminists had nearly managed to get comparable worth included in the 1963 Equal Pay Act, but conservative legislators narrowed the bill's language so that the law required equal pay for work with "equal skill, effort and responsibility" that was "performed under similar working conditions." Even as lawmakers declined to endorse comparable worth, AFSCME embraced it. The union had around one hundred thousand members in 1955, and in 1978 it reached one million members, a rise propelled by the growth of feminized workforce sectors such as clerical and health work. AFSCME began to build a strong program on women's rights in the early 1970s. The twenty-four members of the Interim Committee on Sex Discrimination it established, chaired by fifty-year-old Detroit juvenile court worker Mozell

McNorriell, began attacking the problems of gender disparity and unequal pay in the public sector. Men were more than 96 percent of state full-time skilled craft workers and earned a median salary of $11,761; women earned $9,904 for jobs in these male-dominated jobs. Women were more than 86 percent of state-employed clerical workers, but they earned around $1,000 less per year than men in these feminized jobs. Beyond the problem of unequal pay in the same job categories, AFSCME determined that wages in feminized public sector positions in the early 1980s were between 15 and 35 percent below the pay for comparable male-dominated jobs.[17]

AFSCME began to pressure cities and states to investigate their wage rates and work with the union to restructure them. Some outposts of the union took their own initiative. Washington state's chapter of AFSCME accused the state's governor, Daniel Evans, of wage discrimination in 1973, claiming that female- and male-dominated jobs were unequally paid where workers produced equal value for the state. They argued that the state was especially well suited to revisit its pay practices because it employed people in a wide range of jobs and determined salaries using standardized criteria such as education and training, length of service, and supervisory responsibilities. State officials took the charge seriously, creating a system to compare jobs in terms of skill and other requirements. They determined that the male-dominated jobs earned around 20 percent more than equivalent female-dominated positions and that correcting the inequity would cost between $27 million and $37 million. Evans did not do much with the information and the state's next governor tried to quash the project in 1977.[18]

AFSCME also looked beyond the law, promoting transformative gender justice within the union, at the bargaining table, and in confronting employers. The Washington state workers inspired San Jose, California, clericals in AFSCME Local 101, who held a nine-day strike in 1981 that yielded raises of between 5 and 15 percent. That same year in Los Angeles, AFSCME helped win raises rooted in comparable worth for nearly four thousand clerical workers. A union official called the contract's guarantee of monthly salary increases of one hundred dollars or 10 percent, whichever was higher, "a genuine breakthrough." California governor Jerry Brown adjusted the state labor code to set salaries for feminized jobs "on the basis of comparability of the value of the work." "We're not just coffeemakers anymore," claimed San Jose union clerical Jan White. "We're the backbone of this city."[19]

The San Jose clericals won comparable worth raises in a dramatic standoff, but changes in the law also held out broader promise for the theory in the courts. Advocates looked especially to Title VII of the Civil Rights Act of 1964, whose open-ended ban on sex discrimination seemed to have more

Women and Gender in Public Work   93

Figure 4.1. In 1981, Local 101 of the American Federation of State, County, and Municipal Employees struck in San Jose, California. Those members' strike for gendered pay equity, which was the nation's first, compelled city officials to address the gap between women's and men's pay for work of equal value. (Photo by Lou Dematteis. Courtesy of Walter P. Reuther Library, Archives of Labor and Urban Affairs, Wayne State University.)

potential than the Equal Pay Act. Prior to passing the Civil Rights Act, conservative senators tried to extinguish this possibility by attaching the "Bennett Amendment," proposed by Utah senator Wallace Foster Bennett, which intended to keep Title VII's sex equality measure from extending beyond the Equal Pay Act's standard of "substantially similar" work. Some federal courts interpreted the Equal Pay Act more broadly, and the U.S. Supreme Court affirmed a weakened interpretation of the Bennett Amendment in the 1981 case *County of Washington v. Gunther*. In a 5–4 decision, the Court ruled that female prison guards in Oregon, who earned an average of two hundred dollars per week less than male guards, could pursue wages equal to those of male guards even though their work was substantially different. This ruling seemed to encourage equal pay claims when work was not identical and thus open the possibility for comparable worth to be written into federal law. AFSCME and other comparable worth advocates began to broaden their strategy and emphasize litigation. "It is time to move comparable worth from the conference room to the court room," Newman declared.[20]

AFSCME sued Washington state officials in federal court in 1980 when they neglected the comparable worth issue. The union won class certification for the over ten thousand women working for the state in job categories where women were more than 70 percent of workers. The plaintiffs, who included secretaries, school counselors and nurses, librarians, and food service workers, alleged that their jobs demanded "the same skill, effort and responsibility as predominately male jobs which are paid at a higher salary." Union officials estimated that state workers could win up to $1 billion in back pay and raises. At trial, AFSCME's witnesses, who included EEOC chairperson Eleanor Holmes Norton, testified that comparable worth was essential to achieving meaningful sex equality and accused the state of negligence for maintaining sexist pay structures. The state's experts denied that conforming with sex equality laws meant overhauling state workers' wages. "To my knowledge we have never recruited for employment with the state for what is termed 'male' or 'female' employment," testified state personnel officer Roger Sanford; nor had anyone "ever intentionally discriminated against women in state employment." Another state expert mocked AFSCME's argument for undermining fundamental market principles. "Arguments over the 'just price' were in vogue in the days of St. Thomas Aquinas," retorted economist June O'Neill.[21]

Judge Jack Tanner ruled in AFSCME's favor in 1983 and ordered the state to start implementing robust comparable worth raises. AFSCME's president Gerald McEntee jubilantly predicted that comparable worth would soon lose its controversial status. "Every time employers are forced to provide more fairness and justice in their employment practices, the corporate Chicken Littles predict economic collapse," he noted. But there had been no emergency when the Fair Labor Standards Act and Equal Pay Act were established, "and there won't be when employers start paying their female employees a full salary." Eleanor Holmes Norton had already committed the EEOC to fighting for comparable worth, conducting research, broadening the agency's equal pay policies to reflect the *Gunther* opinion, and holding public hearings to overcome the problem that "the average woman hasn't heard of" comparable worth. AFSCME advanced the struggle in the press and at the bargaining table; it and other advocates were campaigning for comparable worth in more than 140 states, cities, and other localities in 1983.[22]

Comparable worth's momentum emboldened conservatives to amplify their arguments that the market determined wages fairly. They repackaged the theory as an infringement upon citizens' right to low taxes rather than a matter of equality for state workers. In federal courts, business groups attacked comparable worth as an illegal expansion of the judiciary's power. They targeted the states as well. In Florida, for example, business lobbyists defeated a state-funded comparable worth wage study by claiming that it would require raises for state workers that would raise each resident's taxes by nearly nine hundred dollars. Conservatives in federal agencies and courts began to attack comparable worth as well. The U.S. Commission on Civil Rights voted 5–2 in 1985 to condemn it as a remedy for sex discrimination, with commission chairman Clarence Pendleton calling the theory "the looniest idea since Loony Tunes" and "a radical departure from the policies underlying our market economy."[23]

The legal setbacks continued. The EEOC, led by conservative chairman Clarence Thomas, rejected comparable worth that same year. There was some irony in these officials' position that "job evaluation systems are inherently subjective and unreliable," observed comparable worth advocate Eileen Stein, because "its own staff, like most of the federal sector, is paid according to just such a 'subjective' system—i.e. The G.S. rating." The judiciary became less hospitable as well. The Ninth Circuit Court of Appeals reversed the lower court's opinion in *AFSCME v. State of Washington* in 1985, ruling that the state was not required "to eliminate an economic inequality which it did not create." The Seventh Circuit Court of Appeals similarly decided against a group of Illinois nurses and several nurse associations the following year, finding that their failure to receive comparable worth pay raises did not violate Title VII.[24]

Courts extinguished sex equality law as a route to comparable worth in the mid-1980s, but public sector unions pursued the theory along other avenues. Washington state eventually approved raises for its public workers. "Yeah, we lost in court" there, said AFSCME official Cathy Collette "but then we turned around and won $101 million and 23 percent increases for nurses and secretaries" from the state legislature, "so is that really losing?" From 1983 to 1994, states spent over $527 million raising the wages of more than 335,000 workers. Twelve states completely transformed their wage practices to reflect the theory, with typists, nurses, librarians, and clerks as the strongest benefactors. In Minnesota, for example, officials found that women's wages lagged behind men's by 20 percent. In 1982 the state began a four-year campaign to upgrade women's pay, which expanded the state's total payroll by 3.7 percent. In 1984 all Minnesota school districts, counties, and cities were required to change their pay practices to ensure that women's jobs were not undervalued. AFSCME lost its last big pay equity class action suit in 1992, but public sector workers continued to win narrower pay equity gains through their unions. AFSCME continues to advocate comparable worth alongside other labor feminist priorities, but the union's own list of its major comparable worth victories ends in the late 1990s, and efforts to write comparable worth into law, through the Fair Pay Act of 1996, for example, have stalled.[25]

Gendered Boundaries Remain

While AFSCME was fighting for comparable worth, more conservative public sector unions supported new limits to sex equality, especially in the male-dominated uniformed services. When Title VII was extended to the public sector in 1972, women could no longer be prevented from applying for male-dominated jobs in firefighting, policing, corrections, and sanitation. Some public employers built, and unions supported, less obvious barriers. These often included new minimum height and weight requirements and physical ability tests that were not closely related to job performance and could help men of color while keeping most women out. Alabama prisons, for example, established a new policy that corrections officers had to be at least 5'2" tall and weigh at least 120 pounds, guidelines that would disqualify more than 40 percent of women but less than 1 percent of men. The U.S. Supreme Court found these requirements illegal in the 1977 case *Dothard v. Rawlinson* because the Department of Corrections failed to demonstrate that they corresponded to one's ability to do the job. The Court held that the state could limit "contact positions" to men, ruling that women in jobs that required close proximity to male inmates would be personally vulnerable to attack and render prisons less secure.[26]

Women and Gender in Public Work   97

Public sector unions in male-dominated fields also endorsed sexist notions of women's unsuitability for physically demanding and stressful jobs. Women were prevented from taking New York City's examination for firefighters until 1972. Over the next six years, 389 out of 410 women earned a passing score on the written test, but none could pass the newly intensified physical test. A city official described it as "the most arduous test [the city has] ever given for anything" and "substantially different from the last physical test," which was replaced in 1971. The women filed a class action lawsuit in 1982, challenging the physical test as sexist. The Uniformed Firefighters Association defended the exam, with its president, Nicholas Mancuso, describing it as well suited to screen for a "physically demanding job, a hazardous job and a dirty job." Mancuso explained, "It's not that we're opposed to females coming on the job," but they wanted to prevent "a reduction in standards for entrance to the job" and make certain that "only those individuals able to perform the job are appointed to the position of firefighter."[27]

In this instance, the law delivered for workers. The women firefighters won in federal district court when a judge ordered the city to establish a new test and set aside forty-five spots for women, who became the first women to join the city's firefighting force of thirteen thousand. After several appeals and prolonged legal wrangling, city officials gained permission to emphasize speed more than stamina on the physical test, limiting all but a few women from earning a high enough combined score on both the written and physical exams to secure a job. Five women graduated from the fire academy in 2018, representing the highest total since the 1982 lawsuit. They brought the city's ranks of female firefighters to just seventy-two.[28]

Conclusion

Old-fashioned gender norms still shape public work as it shares growing similarities to the private sector. The hard-won comparable worth raises of the 1980s have eroded amid reduced public sector spending and in a legal climate hostile to public workers' rights. The 2018 U.S. Supreme Court opinion *Janus v. AFSCME*, for example, ruled that public workers may not be required to pay union fees to cover bargaining costs, lowering state and local government union membership by an estimated 8.2 percent and cutting public workers' wages by an average of 3.6 percent. The thirty-five-day federal government shutdown that started in late 2018 threatened much of the job security that public sector workers traded for higher private sector wages. Where women have broken into male-dominated public jobs, some have struggled to gain accommodations for their physical needs. Women prison workers have had to smuggle breast pumps into their workplaces, for example, and police officers have had to fight for clean, safe places to use them.[29]

Public sector unions have diverged when it comes to gendered workplace justice. Women are more than half of AFSCME members, and the union continues to focus on them in its policies and leadership. Its recent resolutions decry pay inequities and rollbacks to abortion rights and demand secure voting rights, quality health care, and racial justice for all. But blatant sexism persists even within some other public sector unions, where women have experienced hostile environments, disparate treatment, and retaliation for speaking out.[30]

In the meantime, policymakers continue to valorize and shield male-typed public work from the climate of austerity that has harmed its feminized forms. Crafting his assault on Wisconsin's public sector in the early 2010s, Governor Scott Walker sought to exempt police, firefighter, and state trooper unions. They were overwhelmingly white and male, unlike the rest of the state's public labor force, as well as the only three public sector unions in the state that endorsed his candidacy.[31] And despite budget troubles, officials in Chicago vowed in 2019 to move ahead with a controversial $95 million training center for the city's police and firefighters. Community groups have pushed for those public funds to go to schools, after-school programs, and mental health centers.[32] Men in male-typed public jobs thus have gendered advantages in today's conversations about the value of public labor.

But other public workers have flexed their own muscle. Public school teachers have recently made gains nationwide through public protests that emphasize the social value of their gendered work. "Our legislators must finally realize that an education system is the most critical component of a successful society," wrote Oklahoma public school teacher Jon Hazell amid a 2018 statewide strike. A similar strike in West Virginia that year yielded a 5 percent pay raise for teachers and the state's other public workers. Reading teacher Renita Benson stood near the state capitol when the strike was won there. "Teachers across the state came together for one goal," she said, echoing the Madison nurses who testified to their essential value to their city and its citizens more than three decades earlier. "It's not the raise as much as it is having the respect that we deserve from government."[33]

Further Reading

Acker, Joan. *Doing Comparable Worth: Gender, Class, and Pay Equity*. Philadelphia: Temple University Press, 1989.

Aron, Cindy Sodnik. *Ladies and Gentlemen of the Civil Service: Middle-Class Workers in Victorian America*. New York: Oxford University Press, 1987.

Johnson, David K. *The Lavender Scare: The Cold War Purge of Gays and Lesbians in the Federal Government*. Chicago: University of Chicago Press, 2006.

Riccucci, Norma. *Women, Minorities, and Unions in the Public Sector*. Westport, CT: Greenwood Press, 1990.

Rung, Margaret C. *Servants of the State: Managing Diversity and Democracy in the Federal Workforce, 1933–1953*. Athens: University of Georgia Press, 2002.

Shockley, Megan Taylor. *"We, Too, Are Americans": African American Women in Detroit and Richmond, 1940–1954*. Urbana: University of Illinois Press, 2004.

Notes

1. Marianne Taylor, "Seeking Pay for 'Comparable Worth': Nurses Open a Legal Front," *Chicago Tribune*, February 2, 1982, B1; *Briggs v. City of Madison*, 536 F. Supp. 435 (W.D. Wis. 1982), May 7, 1982. After a five-day trial, the nurses lost in federal district court for failing to prove that the pay disparity was the result of "intentional discrimination" by the city.

2. Eric S. Yellin, *Racism in the Nation's Service: Government Workers and the Color Line in Woodrow Wilson's America* (Chapel Hill: University of North Carolina Press, 2016).

3. On the comparable worth movement, see Joseph E. Hower, "'You've Come a Long Way—Maybe': Working Women, Comparable Worth, and the Transformation of the American Labor Movement, 1964–1989," *Journal of American History* 107 (December 2020): 658–84; Henry J. Aaron, *The Comparable Worth Controversy* (Washington, DC: Brookings Institution Press, 1986); Joan Acker, *Doing Comparable Worth: Gender, Class, and Pay Equity* (Philadelphia: Temple University Press, 1989); Linda M. Blum, *Between Feminism and Labor: The Significance of the Comparable Worth Movement* (Berkeley: University of California Press, 1991); Paula England, *Comparable Worth: Theories and Evidence* (Piscataway, NJ: Aldine Transaction, 1992); Sara M. Evans and Barbara J. Nelson, *Wage Justice: Comparable Worth and the Paradox of Technocratic Reform* (Chicago: University of Chicago Press, 1989); and Norma Riccucci, *Women, Minorities, and Unions in the Public Sector* (Westport, CT: Greenwood Press, 1990).

4. Cindy Sondik Aron, *Ladies and Gentlemen of the Civil Service: Middle-Class Workers in Victorian America* (New York: Oxford University Press, 1987), 70–71.

5. Ibid., 3–9, 25, 39–41, 65–71, 91.

6. Margaret C. Rung, *Servants of the State: Managing Diversity and Democracy in the Federal Workforce, 1933–1953* (Athens: University of Georgia Press, 2002), ix; Yellin, *Racism in the Nation's Service*, 22–23, 35.

7. Yellin, *Racism in the Nation's Service*, 82; Judith Sealander, *As Minority Becomes Majority: Federal Reactions to the Phenomenon of Women in the Work Force, 1920–1963* (Westport, CT: Praeger, 1983), 162; Kathleen A. Laughlin, *Women's Work and Public Policy: A History of the Women's Bureau, 1945–1970* (Boston: Northeastern University Press, 2000), esp. 6–9; Kirsten Downey, *The Woman behind the New Deal: The Life*

and Legacy of Frances Perkins (New York: Anchor, 2010), 114–25; Rung, *Servants of the State*, 24.

8. Joseph E. Slater, *Public Workers: Government Employee Unions, the Law, and the State, 1900–1962* (Ithaca, NY: ILR Press, 2004), 25; Francis Ryan, *AFSCME's Philadelphia Story: Municipal Workers and Urban Power in the Twentieth Century* (Philadelphia: Temple University Press, 2011), 19–20, 59–60, 75, 129.

9. Slater, *Public Workers*, 41–42, 46, 67; 98–99.

10. Rung, *Servants of the State*, 63–69, 137, 142–43, 152.

11. Alice Kessler-Harris, *Out to Work: A History of Wage-Earning Women in the United States* (Oxford: Oxford University Press, 1982), 273. On women war workers and their rights claims, see D'Ann Campbell, *Women at War with America: Private Lives in a Patriotic Era* (Cambridge, MA: Harvard University Press, 1984); Andrew Edmund Kersten, *Race, Jobs, and the War: The FEPC in the Midwest, 1941–1946* (Urbana: University of Illinois Press, 2000); Megan Taylor Shockley, *"We, Too, Are Americans": African American Women in Detroit and Richmond, 1940–1954* (Urbana: University of Illinois Press, 2004); Eileen Boris, "Fair Employment and the Origins of Affirmative Action in the 1940s," *NWSA Journal* 10 (Fall 1998): 142–51; and Katherine Turk, "'A Fair Chance to Do My Part of Work': African American Women, War Work, and Rights Claims at the Kingsbury Ordnance Plant," *Indiana Magazine of History* 108 (September 2012): 209–244; Merle Stokes Dunston to Robert Weaver, Executive Secretary of FEPC, February 18, 1942, La Porte, Indiana; Kingsbury Ordnance Plant folder 1, box 67, Active Cases, Records of the Committee on Fair Employment Practice, Region VI, Record Group 228, National Archives and Records Administration, Chicago, Illinois (hereafter, FEPC Papers) ; Willie Young to Fair Employment Practices Region VI Office, June 7, 1943, Gary, Indiana; Kingsbury Ordnance Plant folder 2, box 67, FEPC Papers. See Russell Jackson to FEPC (n.d.), Kingsbury, Indiana; Kingsbury Ordnance Plant folder 1, box 67, FEPC Papers; Ruth Strickland to President Franklin D. Roosevelt, August 27, 1943, Gary, Indiana; Kingsbury Ordnance Plant folder 1, box 67, FEPC Papers; and Max Parvin Cavnes, *The Hoosier Community at War* (Bloomington: Indiana University Press, 1961), 134.

12. David K. Johnson, "Homosexual Citizens: Washington's Gay Community Confronts the Civil Service," *Washington History* 6 (Fall/Winter 1994/1995): 50–53; Margot Canaday, *The Straight State: Sexuality and Citizenship in Twentieth-Century America* (Princeton, NJ: Princeton University Press, 2011), 175–78, 184.

13. Johnson, "Homosexual Citizens," 45–47, 58, 61; Gregory B. Lewis, "Lifting the Ban on Gays in the Civil Service: Federal Policy toward Gay and Lesbian Employees since the Cold War," *Public Administration Review* 57 (September/October 1997), 387. See also Margot Canaday, *Queer Career: Sexuality and Work in Modern America* (Princeton, NJ: Princeton University Press, 2023).

14. Hower, "'You've Come a Long Way—Maybe,'" 662–63; "Nixon Proclaims Day for Women's Equality," *Hartford (CT) Courant*, August 17, 1973, 2; Joseph A. McCartin, "Bringing the State's Workers In: Time to Rectify an Imbalanced US Labor Historiography," *Labor History* 47, no. 1 (2006), 78–81; Deborah Bell, "Unionized

Women in State and Local Government," in *Women, Work, and Protest: A Century of U.S. Women's Labor History*, ed. Ruth Milkman (New York: Routledge, 1987), 283, 285; Jon Shelton, *Teacher Strike!: Public Education and the Making of a New American Political Order* (Urbana: University of Illinois Press, 2017); Michael K. Honey, *Going Down Jericho Road: The Memphis Strike, Martin Luther King's Last Campaign* (New York: W. W. Norton, 2008), 99–100, 211–13.

15. Hower, "'You've Come a Long Way—Maybe,'" 664; Tamar Lewin, "Pay Equity for Women's Jobs Finds Success Outside Courts," *New York Times*, October 7, 1989, A1; Claudia Levy, "'Comparable Worth' May Be Rights Issue of '80s," *Washington Post*, October 13, 1980, WB3.

16. Bell, "Unionized Women in State and Local Government," 292; Acker, *Doing Comparable Worth*, 8–9; "A Fair Payday Is All They Ask," *San Diego Union*, December 3, 1982, D1; Norma Riccucci, *Women, Minorities, and Unions in the Public Sector* (Westport, CT: Greenwood Press, 1990), 14.

17. Cobble, *Other Women's Movement*, 98–99, 163–67; Heidi Hartmann and Stephanie Aaronson, "Pay Equity and Women's Wage Increases: Success in the States, a Model for the Nation," *Duke Journal of Gender Law and Policy* 69, no. 1 (1994): 72; Katherine Turk, *Equality on Trial: Gender and Rights in the Modern American Workplace* (Philadelphia: University of Pennsylvania Press, 2016); U.S. Equal Employment Opportunity Commission, *Minorities and Women in State and Local Government: Equal Employment Opportunity Report, 1978* (Washington, DC: Government Printing Office, 1980), 8, 9, 11; Winn Newman Statement before U.S. House of Representatives Subcommittee on Civil Rights, Subcommittee on Human Resources, Subcommittee on Compensation and Employee Benefits, p. 14, September 16, 1982, folder 26, box 4, Susan Holleran Papers, Walter Reuther Library, Wayne State University, Detroit, MI (hereafter, "Holleran Papers").

18. Douglas E. Sayan and Leonard Nord to Daniel J. Evans, folder 3, box 1, AFSCME Program Committee Records, Walter Reuther Library, Wayne State University, Detroit, MI (hereafter "AFSCME Program Committee Records"); Gerald W. McEntee, Statement before U.S. House of Representatives Subcommittee on Civil Rights, Subcommittee on Human Resources, Subcommittee on Compensation and Employee Benefits, September 21, 1982, p. 1, folder 20, box 4, Holleran Papers; "Affirmative Action in Washington State," July 1974, p. 2, folder 9, box 5, AFSCME Program Committee Records; Larry Goodman to Winn Newman, August 8, 1983, re: Basic History of Salary Setting in Washington State, folder 3, box 1, AFSCME Program Committee Records.

19. Hower, "'You've Come a Long Way—Maybe,'" 665–69; Lewin, "Pay Equity for Women's Jobs Finds Success," A1; Levy, "'Comparable Worth' May Be Rights Issue of '80s," WB3; " . . . It All Began with Council 28," *AFSCME Public Employee*, September 1981, folder 12, box 4, Holleran Papers; Norm Schut, Executive Director, Washington Federation of State Employees, to Daniel J. Evans, Governor of Washington, November 20, 1973, folder 2, box 1, AFSCME Program Committee Records; "Supervisors' Job Analysis Questionnaire, 1984," State of Wisconsin Task Force on Comparable Worth,

folder 14, box 2, Holleran Papers; "A 16% Hike in San Jose—And Maybe Much More on the Way," *AFSCME Public Employee*, 1980, folder 12, box 4, Holleran Papers; "San Jose Strike Gains," *Comparable Worth Project Newsletter*, December 1981, folder 2, box 382, Winn Newman Papers, Library of Congress, Washington, DC (hereafter, "Newman Papers"); Judy Baston, "L.A. Clericals: 'We're Not Just Coffeemakers Anymore,'" *AFSCME Public Employee*, 1980, folder 12, box 4, Holleran Papers.

20. Turk, *Equality on Trial*; George T. Floros, "The Comparable Worth Theory of Title VII Sex Discrimination in Compensation," *Missouri Law Review* 47 (Summer 1982): 499–500; Michael Evan Gold, "A Tale of Two Amendments: The Reasons Congress Added Sex to Title VII and Their Implication for the Issue of Comparable Worth," Faculty Publications–Collective Bargaining, Labor Law, and Labor History, Paper 11 (1981), http://digitalcommons.ilr.cornell.edu/cbpubs/11; *Schultz v. Wheaton Glass Company*, 421 F.2d 259 (3rd Cir. 1970); *Corning Glass v. Brennan*, 417 U.S. 188 (1974); *IUE v. Westinghouse*, 631 F.2d 1094 (3rd Cir. 1980); *Lemons v. City and County of Denver* (620 F.2d 228 (10th Cir.), cert. denied, 449 U.S. 888 (1980); *County of Washington v. Gunther*, 452 U.S. 161 (1891). Lewin, "Pay Equity for Women's Jobs Finds Success," A8; Julie A. Saltoun, "*County of Washington v. Gunther*: Sex-Based Wage Discrimination Extends beyond the Equal Pay Act," *Loyola of Los Angeles Law Review* 16 (1983): 151–71; Winn Newman Statement before U.S. House of Representatives Subcommittee on Civil Rights, Subcommittee on Human Resources, Subcommittee on Compensation and Employee Benefits, p. 22, September 16, 1982, Holleran Papers.

21. "Surrounding Info from the Case *AFSCME v. Washington*, Appeal No. 84-3569, Excerpt of Record v. 1," folder 1, box 28, Newman Papers; "Plaintiffs' Answers to Defendants' Interrogatories," folder 3, box 52, Newman Papers; *AFSCME v. Washington* Trial Transcript, folder 4, box 28, Newman Papers; Huntly Collins, "Public Workers Gaining 'Comparable Worth,'" *Washington Post*, August 28, 1986, F1; Affidavit of Roger Sanford, taken August 1983, folder 4, box 34, Newman Papers; Testimony of June O'Neill: Exhibit TTT, box 34, folder 12, Newman Papers.

22. "Washington State Told to Pay Women in Sex-Bias Lawsuit," *Wall Street Journal*, December 5, 1983; Gerald W. McEntee, Statement before U.S. House of Representatives Subcommittee on Civil Rights, Subcommittee on Human Resources, Subcommittee on Compensation and Employee Benefits, September 21, 1982, pp. 2–3, folder 20, box 4, Holleran Papers; Blum, *Between Feminism and Labor*, 49–50; Louise Ott, "Equal Pay for Work of Comparable Value: A Story of Dollars and Sense," *Matrix* (Spring 1980), 23, folder 19, box 52, Papers of Toni Carabillo and Judith Meuli, Schlesinger Library, Radcliffe Institute, Harvard University; "Notice Adopted by EEOC to Provide Interim Guidance to Field Offices on Identifying and Processing Sex-Based Wage Discrimination Charges under Title VII and the Equal Pay Act," August 25, 1981, reprinted in "The Comparable Worth Issue," *BNA* 1981, pp. 79–83; Acker, *Doing Comparable Worth*, 9.

23. Stephen Wermiel, "High Court Looks at Women's Pay in Dispute on 'Comparable Worth,'" *Wall Street Journal*, May 14, 1981, 29; Robert Pear, "U.S. Report Assails Idea of Job Worth Idea," *New York Times*, March 28, 1985, A29; *Chicago Daily Law*

Bulletin, April 11, 1985, folder 3, box 5, Holleran Papers; Beth Kivel, "Pay Equity Advocates Fight Back," *off our backs* 15 (January 31, 1985): 4; *Daily Herald* (Arlington Heights, Illinois), April 5, 1985, folder 2, box 5, Holleran Papers; Statement by EEOC Chairman Clarence Thomas, June 17, 1985, folder 5, box 382, Newman Papers.

24. Eileen Stein, "Draft Testimony before Civil Rights Commission," April 16, 1985, pp. 2–3, folder 10, box 80, Coalition of Labor Union Women Records, Walter Reuther Library, Wayne State University, Detroit, MI; Blum, *Between Feminism and Labor*, 24–25; Donna Blanton, "Business Lobby Successfully Stalls Comparable-Worth Bill," *Ft. Lauderdale News*, April 4, 1985, folder 1, box 5, Holleran Papers; *AFSCME v. Washington*, 770 F.2d 1401 (9th Cir., 1985); Collins, "Public Workers Gaining 'Comparable Worth,'" *Washington Post*, August 28, 1986, F1; *ANA v. Illinois* (7th Circuit Court of Appeals, 1985).

25. Hower, "'You've Come a Long Way—Maybe,'" 680–82, Heidi I. Hartmann and Stephanie Aaronson, "Pay Equity and Women's Wage Increases: Success in the States, a Model for the Nation," *Duke Journal of Gender Law and Policy* 1 (1994): 73; National Committee on Pay Equity Report, April 1986, folder 1, box 121, Newman Papers; National Committee on Pay Equity, "Survey of State Government-Level Pay Equity Activity," 1988, p. 2, folder 22, box 4, Holleran Papers; Collins, "Public Workers Gaining 'Comparable Worth,'" F1; Lewin, "Pay Equity for Women's Jobs Finds Success"; *AFSCME v. County of Nassau*, 799 F. Supp. 1370 (E.D. N.Y. 1992); National Committee for Pay Equity, "History of the Struggle for Fair Pay," https://www.pay-equity.org/info-history.html/, accessed January 14, 2019; "What Is AFSCME's Record on Pay Equity?" AFSCME, https://www.afscme.org/news/publications/working-for-government/were-worth-it-an-afscme-guide-to-understanding-and-implementing-pay-equity/what-is-afscmes-record-on-pay-equity/, accessed January 14, 2019.

26. *Dothard v. Rawlinson*, 433 U.S. 321 (1977); Riccucci, *Women, Minorities, and Unions*, 105; "Supreme Court Activities," *New York Times*, June 28, 1977, 15.

27. *Berkman v. City of New York* (705 F.2d 548); E. R. Shipp, "Ruling Could Curtail Hiring More Women in Fire Department," *New York Times*, April 14, 1987, 1; Riccucci, *Women, Minorities, and Unions in the Public Sector*, 110–11.

28. "FDNY Graduation Raises Number of Female Firefighters to Historic Level," April 20, 2018, https://www.firefighternation.com/articles/2018/04/fdny-graduation-raises-number-of-female-firefighters-to-historic-level.html/, accessed January 14, 2019.

29. Natalie Kitroeff, "The Plot to Pump in Prison," *New York Times*, January 6, 2019, BU1.

30. Hower, "'You've Come a Long Way—Maybe,'" 682; "AFSCME: Our Priorities, Our Issues," https://www.afscme.org/priorities/issues/, accessed December 14, 2020; Kathleen Stanley, "The Fairfax, Virginia Fire Department Is Sexist," May 25, 2018, ACLU, https://www.aclu.org/blog/womens-rights/womens-rights-workplace/fairfax-virginia-fire-department-sexist/, accessed December 14, 2020; Vin Gallo, "Female East Hartford Police Officer Claims Harassment, Discrimination," *Journal Inquirer* (CT), October 6, 2020, https://www.journalinquirer.com/towns/east_hartford/

female-east-hartford-police-officer-claims-harassment-discrimination/article_
b2332616-07e4-11eb-914e-bb6a038d8a44.html/, accessed December 14, 2020.

31. Alyssa Battistoni, "The Dirty Secret of Public-Sector Union Busting," *Salon.com*, February 24, 2011, https://www.salon.com/2011/02/24/battistoni_public_employees/, accessed December 14, 2020.

32. Kori Rumore, "Inside the City's Plans for a Controversial Police Training Center," *Chicago Tribune*, June 25, 2019, https://www.chicagotribune.com/news/ct-cb -joint-police-fire-training-academy-chicago-htmlstory.html/, accessed November 19, 2022.

33. *Janus v. AFSCME*; Alana Semuels, "Is This the End of Public-Sector Unions in America?" *The Atlantic*, June 27, 2018, https://www.theatlantic.com/politics/archive/ 2018/06/janus-afscme-public-sector-unions/563879/, accessed January 14, 2019; Jon Hazell, "The Oklahoma Teachers Strike Is 26 Years in the Making," *Huffington Post*, April 7, 2018, https://www.huffingtonpost.com/entry/opinion-hazell-oklahoma- teachers-strike_us_5ac7f017e4b0337ad1e821f3/; Jess Bidgood, "West Virginia's Teach- ers Get Pay Raise to End Statewide Strike," *New York Times*, March 7, 2018, A15.

PART III

Organizing Public Workers

How have public workers organized? For much of the history of public work, municipal workers have led the way in union organizing and labor actions. Uniformed workers (police and firefighters) and federal employees have been constrained by anti-organizing laws and harsh management suppression, despite nearly a century of unionizing in both fields of public sector work. The chapters in this section examine efforts by city employees to organize for better pay and working conditions as well as to seek recognition of their value from city officials, the wider public, and the national labor movement.

This story begins, explains legal scholar Joseph Slater in his chapter, with police officers and the 1919 Boston police strike that came to define both the promise and limits of public worker organizing. After World War II, as public sector workers in general earned new collective bargaining rights, however, police unions became a special entity within American labor law.

While the American Federation of State, County, and Municipal Employees (AFSCME) has emerged as the most prominent voice for nonfederal public workers today, chapters by William P. Jones and Francis Ryan reveal that AFSCME's recognition of blue-collar workers and its capacity to lead a national movement of public workers has been uncertain and unstable. With their lenses trained on municipal sanitation workers, Jones and Ryan reveal the complex politics of race and civil rights within public sector organizing. In the South, explains Jones, AFSCME's realization that the inclusion of Black workers could energize the public sector union movement laid the groundwork for the now famous 1968 sanitation strike in Memphis, Tennessee, in which the labor and civil rights movements finally learned to make common cause. But a few years later, reveals Ryan, the complexity of municipal politics, the specific terrain of increasingly Black Northern cities, and divisions within the civil rights movement could shatter the powerful unity on display in Memphis.

CHAPTER 5

Police Unions and Public Sector Labor Law and Policy

JOSEPH E. SLATER

For over a century, police unions have played an outsized role in the development of policy in the United States toward public sector unions generally. From the Boston police strike of 1919 to arguments over whether police unions contribute to abusive acts by police in current times, the unionization of this particular type of public worker has prompted heated debates. For much of the twentieth century, concerns about police unions drove legal rules and policy decisions that affected all public sector unions. In more recent times, a new set of concerns has led to moves to distinguish police unions from other public sector unions, raising difficult questions about protections and rights granted to police as other public workers are made more vulnerable.

The centrality of police unions to public sector union history is especially true in the area of public sector labor law. Notably, public sector labor law has always been a contested battlefield for unions. While private sector unions won the right to organize, bargain, and strike at the federal level with the National Labor Relations Act in 1935 (or for some, even earlier with the Railway Labor Act of 1926), public sector labor law has mostly been a matter of state law, and states did not begin granting government employees the rights to bargain and organize until the 1960s. Even today, while the majority of states grant collective bargaining rights to most of their public employees, a sizable minority grant no such rights or grant them to only one or two types of public employees (e.g., police). Even among the states that grant public sector unions collective bargaining rights, only about a dozen permit any public employees to strike (and none permit police to strike).[1] Further, basic public sector labor law rights remain unstable; a number of states have severely restricted or attempted to restrict public sector bargaining rights beginning in 2011, again with police unions holding a prominent place in political and legal debates.

This chapter traces the influence of police unions on public sector labor law over time, beginning with the Boston police strike of 1919. The strike had long-lasting effects on the legal rules facing public sector unions as well as policy and the evolution of unions themselves. For decades, the image of a police union affiliating with the American Federation of Labor (AFL) and striking contributed both to the inability of public sector unions of any kind to win collective bargaining rights and to bans on affiliating with the broader labor movement. This chapter also looks at why police unions mattered to judges in the mid-twentieth century, during the "pre–collective bargaining era" in the public sector, and explores how concerns over police unions affected the development of the first state public sector labor law in Wisconsin, finally enacted in 1959. Long after the breakthrough in Wisconsin, the role of police unions continued to be contested within public sector labor law. Today, criticisms of police unions come from the political left, as opposed to the antiunion right, in light of debates over police unions and police misconduct in the Black Lives Matter era. Throughout the past century, development of law and policy in the United States toward public sector unions generally has been shaped by the perceptions and actions of police unions.

The Boston Police Strike of 1919 and Its Enduring Influence

The Boston police strike of 1919 set back public sector labor union development and public sector labor law for decades.[2] When Boston police officers unionized that year, they did so for reasons similar to most unions of the era: they wanted better wages, hours, and working conditions. Unionists had traditionally been wary of police because they often broke strikes. Yet, beat cops were typically from working-class backgrounds, performed disciplined wage labor, and generally shared concerns with other workers. Indeed, the unionization in Boston was part of a national trend of police affiliation with the AFL, which in turn was part of a national boom in the organizing of a broad range of public employees around World War I. But the effort to unionize in Boston was preceded by an unprecedented job action strike. The strike led to days of lawlessness, property damage, assaults, and some deaths, mainly from state National Guard troops firing into the crowd. After the strike was successfully suppressed by Governor Calvin Coolidge, all 1,147 strikers were fired and never rehired. The event became a cautionary tale, leading to legal bans in many places not only on police unions but on all public sector unions, bans that courts enforced until the late 1960s. The strike also led to rules barring police from AFL affiliation, which had a long-term effect on public unions: even today the largest police union is not affiliated with the AFL-CIO.

Opposition to police affiliation with the labor movement caused the Boston strike, but beyond that, a central issue debated before, during, and after the strike was whether *any* public employees should be allowed to organize, especially into a body affiliated with the AFL. Government officials, business leaders, unionists, and socialists all predicted that public sector unions would shift the balance of power in all labor relations. The AFL maintained that government employees were members of the working class. Opponents, notably including a large number of private business interests, insisted that they had nothing in common with labor and that AFL organizing in the public sector would lead to union interests dominating the state. Union advocates and opponents sparred over the propriety of government workers organizing. After Postmaster General Albert Burleson argued that government employees should not be allowed to join an "outside organization," the AFL magazine the *American Federationist* replied that in "every kind of employment" workers needed a representative whom supervisors did not control. "Public employees must not be denied the right of organization . . . and collective bargaining."[3] In the months before the Boston strike, public and private employers attacked not only police unions but all types of public sector unions (18–19).

Around the time of World War I, public sector organizing was on the rise. The AFL chartered the American Federation of Teachers (AFT) in 1916, and in 1918 the AFT grew from 2,000 to 11,000 members. In 1917 the AFL established the National Federation of Federal Employees, and both the National Association of Letter Carriers and the Railway Mail Carriers affiliated with the AFL. In 1918 the AFL created the International Association of Fire Fighters (IAFF), and from 1918 to 1919 the number of IAFF locals increased from 82 to 262. In 1910 union density in the public sector was around 3.5 percent; from 1915 to 1921, it grew from 4.8 percent to 7.2 percent. Combined with an increase in the size of government, this meant that the number of unionized public workers nearly doubled in those years (17–18).

Until 1919 the AFL had refused to charter police locals. The 1897 AFL convention rejected an application from police in Cleveland. The AFL explained that it was "not within the province of the trade union movement to specially organize policemen, no more than to organize militiamen, as both . . . are too often controlled by forces inimical to the labor movement." But, in part due to repeated requests, in June 1919 the AFL switched positions. It soon had chartered thirty-seven police locals in at least twenty-one states, including a local in Boston (19–20).

Lurking in the background, however, was the question of police strikes. AFL leader Samuel Gompers, when asked about the possibility, simply objected that the AFL could not order strikes and that police could not join private sector unions that did strike. He did not, however, point to any rule in the labor movement or otherwise specifically barring police strikes (21). In addition to fears of police themselves striking, union opponents repeatedly expressed concerns about how police officers affiliated with the AFL would behave during strikes by other unions. Police union opponents predicted "divided loyalty" and "favoritism" in such contexts. Such concerns were raised by both business interests and public officials about the Boston police in the lead-up to the strike. On the other side, the socialist *New York Call* predicted that unionized police might not attack other employees who struck (22–23). Whether AFL police unions would refuse to break strikes or strike themselves were issues that came to a head in Boston.

The conflict in Boston began in 1918 when then–police commissioner Steven O'Meara learned that Boston police officers were considering AFL affiliation. Unsurprisingly, their complaints were typical of all workers seeking unionization: low wages, long hours, unhealthy conditions, and abusive supervisors. Police were voted a raise in 1898, but that was not put into effect until 1913. A small increase was granted in early 1919, but the cost of living had doubled since 1913; the inflation rate in 1919 was 14.57 percent. Working conditions were challenging: officers worked seventy-three to ninety hours a week, station houses were unsanitary, and supervisors required subordinates to run menial errands that were unrelated to work (25).

O'Meara sought to end the unionization before it began, issuing an order stating that even rumors of unionization were "likely to injure the discipline, efficiency and even the good name of the Force." If officers had obligations to an outside organization, he stated, they would be "justly suspected of abandoning their impartial attitude." While not disputing the "wisdom or even necessity" of unions in the private sector, O'Meara insisted that public sector unions generally were "of doubtful propriety," and police in particular should not be allowed to organize because they were responsible for impartial law enforcement. On July 29, 1919, in response to more talk of affiliation, new commissioner Edwin Curtis barred officer affiliation with the labor movement, stating that "a police officer cannot consistently belong to a union and perform his sworn duty" and that a police officer "should realize that his work is sharply differentiated from that of the worker in private employ" (25).

Undeterred, police officers in Boston affiliated with the AFL on August 9, 1919. Two days later, Curtis issued General Order 110, which barred officers from belonging to almost any organization with ties outside the police department. On August 20, Curtis summoned union leaders to his office and told them he would not permit affiliation with the AFL. Nonetheless, the next day, over eight hundred officers met and installed the officers of their AFL local. Curtis held disciplinary hearings for the leaders, and then, on September 7, suspended nineteen men for violating his antiunion policy. In response, the union voted to strike, 1,134 to 2. On September 9, more than eleven hundred officers walked out. Well after the event, Curtis maintained that the "sole issue" of the strike was police membership in the AFL (26).

Debate over this union turned on a central issue in U.S. labor history: the extent to which government employees, including police, could be a part of organized labor. Boston's AFL newspaper, the *Labor World*, consistently supported police and other public sector unions throughout the country, affirming that they were part of a larger struggle for workers' rights. In contrast, opponents of the police union made objections that applied to all public sector unions. The heads of many private businesses wrote to Curtis recommending that no government employee of any kind be allowed to join the AFL. A statement by the Boston Chamber of Commerce raised the specter of sympathy strikes by police to support other AFL locals. In contrast, the *Labor World* noted the history of police being used to attack strikers, sarcastically asking, "Did someone say 'neutral'?" Some union supporters explicitly identified why private sector employers were concerned about police unions: the *New York Call* published a cartoon boasting that "a union cop won't club another union worker" (27–30).

Still, neither side was prepared for an actual strike by police. During the Boston strike, local AFL leaders actually proposed a system that many police and other public sector unions use today: settling bargaining impasses by using a mutually selected arbitration board that would make binding decisions. Such a system, they suggested presciently, would eliminate the need for work stoppages. But with the strike raging, the door was closed to their suggestions (31–32). The Boston Central Labor Union considered but then rejected the idea of joining the police in a general strike. The recent defeats of general strikes in Seattle and Winnipeg were explicitly discussed during this decision-making. Local, state, and even out-of-state unions did provide some aid to the strikers. Labor papers stuck up for the union, if only verbally.

Police work "may be a sacred trust," the *Detroit Labor News* argued, "but the landlord will not accept it in lieu of . . . rent, nor does the grocer consider it as a medium of exchange" (33–34).

The strike was a failure. Intriguingly, afterward, Boston increased minimum pay for police from eleven hundred to fourteen hundred dollars per year. Police in many other jurisdictions that had been unionized received significant pay increases as well. But despite repeated efforts, none of the strikers were ever rehired. Police locals affiliated with the AFL across the country, including Boston's, were soon destroyed. Congress barred police and firefighters in the District of Columbia from striking or affiliating with the AFL, and a number of local governments and police departments followed suit. There would be no AFL-affiliated police locals until the 1930s and 1940s, and these too would meet strong opposition. In 1932 Philadelphia enacted an ordinance forbidding police to form any group other than a benefit society. A national AFL-CIO ("CIO" being the abbreviation for the Congress of Industrial Organizations) police union would not be created until 1979 (35–36).

The damage went far beyond police organizing. While other public sector unions tried to avoid association with the Boston disaster by emphasizing or adopting no-strike policies, many were still devastated. In the year after the Boston strike, the IAFF lost fifty locals, including its Boston affiliate. The AFT and other public sector unions lost membership after the strike. After years of increases, the number of unionized government employees fell from 172,000 in 1921 to 171,000 in 1922, despite an increase in total government employment from 2,397,000 to 2,455,000. The rate of unionization in the public sector, which had bolted up rapidly in the preceding years, now stagnated, hovering just below the 1921 rate of 7.2 percent for nearly all the 1920s (36). New antiunion rules were put in place in the wake of the strike, and such rules continued to be promulgated for decades. In 1942 Dallas passed a rule preventing city employees from forming a labor organization. Police organizing remained a major target too. After the American Federation of State, County, and Municipal Employees (AFSCME) began organizing police in the early 1940s, many more cities blocked this affiliation, including Chicago, Detroit, Los Angeles, Saint Louis, and Jackson, Mississippi (93–94).

Thus, the Boston strike inhibited the growth of public sector unions for decades. It was used in arguments against any public workers being allowed even the right to organize on the grounds that such rights would lead, literally, to death and destruction. In school board elections in Seattle in 1928 and 1930, opponents of candidates sympathetic to the AFT brought up the Boston police strike (56, 62). In 1957 a study of public sector labor relations observed that "even today, in the defense of their opposition to public employee unions, officials refer to [the Boston] strike as embodying all of the evils of unionism for government employees." Forty-three years after that event, South Dakota's court cited Coolidge on the Boston strike in upholding the ban on unionizing police, fire, and health departments.[4] In 1963 the Michigan Supreme Court upheld a bar on police unionizing, stressing the need for "undivided allegiance." President Ronald Reagan cited the Boston strike as precedent for firing striking members of the Professional Air Traffic Controllers Union (PATCO) in 1981, and the PATCO dispute also prompted the *Wall Street Journal* to publish a tribute to Coolidge's actions in Boston.[5]

Another lingering effect was that public employees were forced to organize outside the AFL. Indeed, even today some major public sector unions remain outside the AFL-CIO; most importantly here, the Fraternal Order of Police has long been by far the largest police union in the United States, and it has never been affiliated with the AFL, CIO, or AFL-CIO. Beyond police, though, the history of rules against public employees affiliating with the labor movement is a major reason why the largest teachers' union, the National Education Association (NEA), is not affiliated with the AFL-CIO despite being larger in size than the AFL-CIO-affiliated American Federation of Teachers.[6]

Police Unions and the Law in the Mid-Twentieth Century

Before the 1960s, state courts effectively made public sector labor law, even after the National Labor Relations Act. The law everywhere in the United States prohibited strikes and granted no right to bargain collectively in government employment. Because no state statute granted union rights to public employees, state courts endorsed whatever rules public employers imposed. Courts in this era upheld bans on union membership for all sorts of public employees. Two separate court decisions in the 1940s, from Texas and New York, used the same reasoning verbatim: "To tolerate or recognize any combination of . . . employees of the government as a labor organization or union is not only incompatible with the spirit of democracy but inconsistent with every principle upon which our Government is founded."[7] This "pre–collective bargaining era" for public workers in the United States lasted decades beyond when public workers in, for example, Britain and France won bargaining and related rights quite similar to those of private sector workers in those countries.[8]

Many of the cases upholding public employer bans on unionizing involved police. For example, *City of Jackson v. McLeod* overturned a jury verdict that had found the Mississippi city liable for firing police officers who had joined the AFSCME.[9] The local Civil Service Commission had upheld the removals, based on charges that AFSCME membership constituted insubordination and "acts tending to injure the public service."[10] In 1947 *King v. Priest* upheld a rule banning an AFSCME local that more than eight hundred police officers had joined in Missouri. The local's charter barred striking and bargaining; instead, the local would, "by publicity, direct public attention to conditions that need correcting, . . . seek legislative action, . . . represent individuals in administrative procedures, and prevent discriminatory and arbitrary practices."[11] Nevertheless, the Missouri Supreme Court, stating that "the court, of course, knows what a labor union is," took judicial notice of the "common knowledge" that "some of the most common methods used by labor unions . . . are strikes, threats to strike, [and] collective bargaining agreements."[12] Also in 1947, *Perez v. Board of Police Commissioners* upheld a ban on AFSCME membership by the Los Angeles Police Department.[13] Both *King* and *Perez* echoed the "disloyalty" charge of the Boston police strike era, taking as the *King* ruling stated, "judicial notice . . . of the fact that members of one union ordinarily refuse to cross the picket line of another union."[14] *Perez* approvingly quoted the city's argument that union membership could impair police "independence . . . where controversies exist between employers and employees; . . . a divided responsibility would occur."[15]

Without collective bargaining rights, public sector unions used various tactics to represent their members from the 1930s through the 1950s. They engaged in politics, represented workers in civil service hearings and other legal processes, and provided training and other resources for their members. Some even engaged in informal bargaining, which led to quasi collective agreements.[16] Indeed, a 1946 study found that ninety-seven cities had written agreements with employee organizations.[17] Of course such agreements were far short of modern, binding labor contracts, both in their narrow scope and their questionable enforceability. Employers had no obligation—and in some cases, arguably, no actual legal power—to enter into them.

The First State Public Sector Collective Bargaining Law in Wisconsin and Police

The end of the pre–collective bargaining era began with Wisconsin passing the first state statute permitting public sector collective bargaining, enacted in 1959 and amended in 1962. The law did not arise out of thin air. Proponents of the Wisconsin law, led by AFSCME, made their first attempt in 1951 and then did so in every legislative session (at that time, every other year), with bills in 1955 and 1957 explicitly excluding police. All failed to pass. As would be true in 2011 and beyond, many of the votes on these bills were along strict party lines, with Republicans opposing them and Democrats supporting them.[18]

Strikes, including the specter of police strikes, were a recurring issue in debates over Wisconsin's various bills. More generally, the Wisconsin law would not be passed until drafters developed alternatives to strikes for resolving bargaining impasses in the public sector.[19] The 1951 bill would have given Wisconsin public employees the right to organize unions and granted some limited quasi bargaining rights ("collective considerations"). As an alternative to strikes, the bill provided that if bargaining reached an impasse, a state agency, the Wisconsin Employment Relations Board (WERB) would offer conciliation services.[20] Nonetheless, Governor Walter Kohler Jr. vetoed the bill largely because opponents stressed the problems that strikes by police and other government employees could cause. It was not enough that proponents added a clause to the bill explicitly barring public sector strikes or that police had never struck in Wisconsin and police union constitutions barred strikes. For example, bill opponent Oliver Grootemaat, president of the Village of Whitefish Bay, wrote Kohler that the "mere elimination of one phrase could grant municipal employees the right to strike." Echoing opponents of the Boston police union, Grootemaat added that allowing police to organize "might place them in the anomalous position of being called upon to police a strike called by a brother union."[21] The Wisconsin League of Municipalities, a group of public employers, opposed the bill, explicitly citing the Boston police strike.[22] The shadow of the Boston police strike remained throughout the decade. In 1958 the International Association of Chiefs of Police bulletin, *Police Union*, mischaracterized the Boston police strike as having been over the question of whether police should have the right to strike.

The political environment in Wisconsin changed, however, after the 1958 elections. For the first time in decades, the state elected a Democratic governor, Gaylord Nelson, and a Democratic State Assembly. Nelson was friendly toward unions. AFSCME introduced another bill in 1959 that would, after modifications, become law on September 2, 1959. For the first time, most employees of county and municipal government in Wisconsin had a statutory right to organize and be represented by unions in negotiations over wages, hours, and working conditions. Not surprisingly, the law barred strikes, and it did exclude public safety workers.[23]

The new law provided no mechanisms for resolving bargaining impasses, so in 1962 it was amended to provide for fact-finding and arbitration, albeit on a voluntary and nonbinding basis. Later public sector labor laws (including

Wisconsin's) would use both, typically on a mandatory basis, with "interest" arbitrators issuing binding decisions. Also, the 1962 amendment added police to the statute's coverage.[24] Developing alternatives to strikes to handle bargaining impasses was a necessary prerequisite for public sector collective bargaining rights, given the impact of the 1919 Boston police strike.

The Rise of Public Sector Labor Laws and Public Sector Unions

The Wisconsin law was the first of many. Federal employees received limited collective bargaining rights for the first time just after the Wisconsin law was signed in 1962, when President John F. Kennedy issued Executive Order 10988. (A federal statute in 1978 would strengthen bargaining rights and provide for binding interest arbitration at impasse.) By 1966 sixteen states had enacted laws extending some bargaining rights to at least some public workers.[25]

Also significant for police and other public sector unions, in the late 1960s courts finally accepted an argument that unionists had urged for decades: that the First Amendment of the U.S. Constitution bars public employers from firing or otherwise discriminating against at least most public employees because of membership in or support of a union. Such arguments had been rejected through the mid-1960s. For example, *AFSCME Local 201 v. City of Muskegon* (1963) upheld a local ban on police union organizing, rejecting constitutional objections and citing a variety of cases from around the country with similar holdings.[26]

But beginning with *Garrity v. New Jersey* (1967), the U.S. Supreme Court began to hold that public employees could not have their employment subject to "unconstitutional conditions."[27] While *Garrity* involved the Fifth Amendment, the Supreme Court and lower courts began holding that public employees had constitutional rights generally in their employment, including the First Amendment right to support and join unions. For example, *Atkins v. City of Charlotte* (1969) held that a ban on firefighters joining a union violated the First Amendment.[28] Thus, while some public employees were and still are without a legal right to bargain (the constitutional right does not extend to a right to bargain or strike), all relevant public employees have a constitutional right to form unions.[29] This has an important practical impact in debates about police unions. Such unions exist in states where they do not have collective bargaining rights, and they are sometimes able to exercise significant political influence even without bargaining rights.

The later 1960s and 1970s saw a brief period of relative militance in the public sector. Teachers, sanitation workers, and even police engaged in job actions and (often illegal) strikes. In some cases unions won rights with those tactics; in other cases the actions caused a backlash. Beginning in the 1980s, however, the number of public sector strikes declined considerably.

By the twenty-first century, a clear majority of states provided for public sector collective bargaining, if not a right to strike. In 2007 twenty-eight states and the District of Columbia allowed collective bargaining for all major groups of public employees; thirteen states allowed only one to four types of public workers to bargain (e.g., police); and seven did not allow any public workers to bargain. Two had more limited "meet and confer" rights. Also in 2007, only twelve states allowed any public workers to strike; thirty-eight states and the District of Columbia provided alternative procedures to resolve bargaining impasses, generally involving some combination of mediation, fact-finding, or interest arbitration.[30]

Political fights over such rights continued, however. For example, the George W. Bush administration would not approve a bill creating the Department of Homeland Security (DHS) after the 9/11 attacks in 2001 unless administration officials were empowered to design a new personnel system that could vitiate collective bargaining rights for DHS workers. About forty-eight thousand of these workers had such rights in predecessor agencies. In 2004 the governors of Indiana and Missouri unilaterally withdrew executive orders permitting state employees to bargain collectively.[31] This retrenchment set the stage for battles in 2011 and beyond.

Political Fights over Public Sector Unions in 2011 and Beyond

The year 2011 saw an unprecedented wave of laws restricting and sometimes eliminating public sector bargaining rights, and the years after that added more antiunion laws to the total. In some of the most prominent examples of the move against unions, police unions played a prominent role. Unlike in previous eras, however, the second decade of the twenty-first century saw police unions more protected than most other unions in these fights. Successful police organizing no longer coincided with protecting or extending the rights of other public workers.

Most famously—and ironically, given its historical role as a leader in public sector unionization—Wisconsin passed Act 10 in 2011. The law gutted collective bargaining rights for all public workers other than those in "protective occupations," most notably police. By this time, Wisconsin had two fairly similar and robust public sector labor statutes: One covered local and county government employees, the result of those organizing and legal drives of the 1950s. The other covered state employees. While exempting police unions from all changes in public sector labor law, Act 10 eliminated collective bargaining rights entirely for some employees (e.g., University of Wisconsin employees and certain home care and child care providers). For others, it limited subjects of collective bargaining to total base wages only, and even there a proposed increase could be no greater than the relevant increase in the consumer price index. No other issues could be negotiated, including "fair share" clauses that obliged members of a union bargaining unit to pay the portion of their dues used to represent the bargaining unit. Such clauses would later be held unconstitutional in *Janus v. AFSCME* (2018), but at the time, making Wisconsin's public sector "right to work" was a radical step.[32] Further, Act 10 made it illegal for an employer to agree to automatic dues deduction, even for employees who voluntarily wished to pay dues.[33]

Act 10 did more than undermine unions' ability bargain collectively on behalf of public workers. For the unions it covers, Act 10 limits the duration of union contracts to one year, which is very unusual. It also requires an unprecedented mandatory recertification system under which every union must face a recertification election every year and will be recertified only if 51 percent of the employees in the bargaining unit—not merely those voting— vote for recertification. Under the prior system, and the one still applicable to police, a request from 30 percent of the bargaining unit was required to schedule a decertification election. Crucially, decertification elections could not take place during the terms of valid union contracts, except that there had to be a "window period" every three years allowing a decertification election. In any case, the majority of those actually voting determined the outcome, not the majority of those in the bargaining unit.[34]

Unions challenged Act 10 under the First Amendment and Equal Protection Clause of the Constitution. While a lower court agreed with the challenge regarding the recertification provision and the bar on dues check-off in *Wisconsin Educ. Ass'n Council v. Walker*, the Seventh Circuit reversed this decision and upheld Act 10 in full.[35] The Seventh Circuit did note the union's argument that all five unions that had endorsed Wisconsin governor Scott Walker were excluded from Act 10 as "public safety unions." But the court added that some of the other excluded unions had not endorsed Walker. It further explained that the distinctions Act 10 makes between protective service unions and other public sector unions survive "rational basis" scrutiny.[36] That basis was, in a historical twist, the state's claimed concern that if public safety officers were denied the rights Act 10 denies most public sector unions, public safety officers might strike.[37] In a mirror image of the debates over Wisconsin's labor law sixty years earlier, the fear of police strikes was now being used to maintain collective bargaining rights for police when they were being gutted for other public workers.

In Ohio a story with a different ending took place the same year Wisconsin's Act 10 was passed, and police probably made the difference. In 1983 Ohio had enacted a robust public sector labor law applicable to most government employees; the law even allowed most public workers to strike. But in 2011 Governor John Kasich signed Senate Bill (SB) 5, which would have gutted collective bargaining rights for public workers generally, including police. Among other things, SB-5 would have eliminated collective bargaining rights entirely for some employees, including at least most public university faculty and lower-level supervisors in police and fire departments. It would have eliminated both the right to strike, for those who had that right (all covered employees except police, fire, and a few other small categories), and the right to binding interest arbitration at impasse, for employees who could not strike, such as police. Instead, the parties would have been left to nonbinding mediation and fact-finding, and if those did not lead to an agreement, the governing legislative body could have, essentially, chosen to adopt the employer's final offer. SB-5 also would have imposed "right to work" rules limiting unions' organizing power and also would have greatly restricted their scope of bargaining.[38]

But SB-5 never went into effect. It was put on hold pending a voter referendum in November 2011, and in that referendum the voters overwhelmingly rejected SB-5.[39] It is impossible to know for certain why collective bargaining advocates succeeded in Ohio while they failed in Wisconsin. It seems safe to guess, however, that the political power of police unions, who were not affected by Wisconsin's new law but would have been in Ohio's, played a significant role in the latter state.

The stage had been set to make distinctions between police and other public sector unions, and unlike in previous eras, the distinction now favored police unions. Some of the dozen or so state laws passed in 2011 restricting the rights of public sector unions did affect police as well as other types of employees. But more often they did not. For example, also in 2011, Oklahoma excluded police and firefighters when repealing a law that required cities with populations of at least thirty-five thousand to bargain collectively with unions.[40] In 2017 Iowa enacted House File (HF) 291, which was largely modeled after Wisconsin Act 10. HF 291's severe restrictions apply to most public sector unions but not bargaining units whose membership contains at least

30 percent public safety employees. For the employees it covers, this law essentially limits bargaining to base wages and raises recertification hurdles.[41] In 2018 Missouri enacted House Bill (HB) 1413, which again excluded employees in public safety unions. The law required the public sector unions it covered to undergo a mandatory recertification election every three years, and it required unions to obtain annual permission from members before having dues or fees deducted from their paychecks. However, unlike in Iowa, where the state supreme court upheld the new law, the Missouri Supreme Court struck down HB 1413 on equal protection grounds.[42] If states were inconsistent in upholding new public sector union restrictions, they proved generally consistent in distinguishing between police and other public workers.

The Debate over Police Unions as an Obstacle to Reform

In addition to public sector labor law, police typically receive protections in discipline matters from civil service statutes and in what are often labeled Law Enforcement Officer Bill of Rights Laws (LEOBORs). Further, the political power of police, even where they lack the right to bargain, is significant, and the role and attitude of police management, in both negotiating and enforcing rules in labor contracts, is crucial.

In the years leading up to 2020, police unions came under new scrutiny. Critics argued that police unions interfere with disciplining officers who commit violent and racist acts. Disciplinary procedures that police unions negotiate, these critics argued, provide too much protection to "bad cops," making it too difficult to fire or discipline those guilty of serious misconduct. As one scholar noted discussing police labor arbitrations in 2017, "There is a growing sentiment that it is difficult or even impossible to fire a bad cop."[43]

While it is beyond the scope of this chapter to attempt to offer solutions to the problem of excessive force and racist acts in policing, this section will describe some complexities of the issue in terms of legal rules. Most radically, some critics of police unions (this time on the political left) have suggested that police should not be allowed to unionize at all or that the labor movement should expel such unions. "It wouldn't make any sort of strategic sense for police-affiliated unions to try and make nice with the rest of the movement," a *New Republic* article argued in 2020. "So that leaves one obvious, if tricky, option: abolishing police unions as part of the broader fight to defund, demilitarize, and ultimately dismantle the U.S. police force as it currently exists."[44]

The legal obstacle to the idea of "abolishing police unions" is the constitutional right to associate in unions, described at the beginning of this chapter.

One legal scholar has analogized the police to the military, noting that soldiers do not have the right to unionize.[45] One response to this argument is that viewing police as a type of military force is one cause of the problems in policing in the United States, and it would be better instead to make police departments less militarized. In any case, the constitutional right for public employees to organize, which has included police for over fifty years at this point, is not likely to be amended to exclude police.

A somewhat related argument is that the AFL-CIO should expel police unions because they are not part of what critics believe the labor movement should be. But recall that the legacy of the Boston police strike well into the 1960s included rules barring police from affiliating with the labor movement. Even today, the largest police union by far, the Fraternal Order of Police, is not affiliated with the AFL-CIO. The significantly smaller International Union of Police Associations is affiliated, but expelling that organization from the AFL-CIO would arguably be little more than symbolism. In other words, expelling police unions from the labor movement would be at best empty symbolism; at worst, it would create further practical obstacles for solidarity within the working class.

More commonly, police union collective bargaining is criticized for leading to unusually robust contract protections in the discipline context.[46] While police union contracts often do contain such protections, the question of the relationship between such protections and police misconduct is complex. First, not all police are unionized, and not all states give police officers the right to bargain collectively. Specifically, police have no collective bargaining rights in Alabama, Arizona, Arkansas, Colorado, Georgia, Idaho, Indiana, Louisiana, Mississippi, North Carolina, Oklahoma, South Carolina, Tennessee, Utah, Virginia, and Wyoming. In addition, North Dakota and West Virginia grant police significantly weaker "meet and confer" rights in lieu of collective bargaining rights.[47] That was true of Missouri until quite recently. And in states that do authorize such bargaining, not every department is organized.

The evidence that police without collective bargaining contracts better address race and excessive force issues is not conclusive. Comparisons of disciplinary protections between police departments with and without collective bargaining are possible because almost a third of all police officers are not covered by bargaining contracts.[48] The leading paper arguing that there is a significant negative effect of police union contracts found that introducing collective bargaining rights to sheriffs' departments in Florida corresponded with a statistically significant uptick in misconduct complaints about violence committed by sheriff department employees. The authors estimate that collective bargaining rights led to about a 40 percent increase in violent incidents by members of these departments.[49] But there are two criticisms of this study. First, it does not examine the effects of actual labor contracts but rather just notes a change after a certain group of employees were granted collective bargaining rights. Second, while a 40 percent increase in violent incidents seems significant and indeed alarming, as the authors explain, this number was so high because the original baseline rate of violent incidents before collective bargaining was so low. The study found that the estimated effect of bargaining rights would mean an increase of 0.2 violent incidents per agency year. The baseline was relative to a previous mean of about 0.5 violent incidents per year, thus the 40 percent figure. But as the article explains, its prediction would mean that the presence of collective bargaining rights would result in an additional one officer in an average sheriff's office of 290 officers being involved in one additional violent incident every five years. Further, this study cites another study that found an even smaller impact of collective bargaining rights.[50]

One could argue that it is intuitive that unions' bargaining disciplinary protections will make it more difficult to fire bad cops, especially given the relatively aggressive disciplinary protections that police unions often negotiate. There are two responses to that argument. First, even in the absence of collective bargaining rights or unionization, police officers typically receive just cause and related disciplinary protections from both civil service laws (which usually provide "just cause discharge" protections for the public employees they cover) and from LEOBOR statutes. Such statutes exist in states that do not grant any collective bargaining rights to police.[51] Second, those generally sympathetic to unions should take care to avoid the trap of assuming that employers, including police employers, want to fire bad employees for good reasons but that unions are the main obstacle stopping them. Union advocates would not want such an assumption to be made about, say, public school administrators who claim union protections work mainly to keep bad teachers on the job or, for that matter, employers in most other occupations. Police supervisors and managers (sergeants, lieutenants, and even chiefs) typically rise from the ranks, famous for their "thin blue line" and "us vs. them" culture. And while it is reasonable to think that some could sometimes be pressured to do the right thing through politics, political pressure can work both ways.

Critiquing police unions while upholding the rights of public sector labor unions in general requires nuance. Some protections in police union contracts do, in my opinion, go too far. For example, some feature overly long waiting periods before officers suspected of misconduct could be interviewed. Some bar anonymous complaints.[52] But some critics go further and decry

124   ORGANIZING PUBLIC WORKERS

the use of standard union grievance/arbitration clause provisions when applied to police. One article faults police union contracts for the common provision that allows the parties to choose arbitrators from lists supplied by, for example, the American Arbitration Association because of the supposed incentive for arbitrators to compromise.[53] That criticism could be applied to all union contracts. Also, some oppose provisions that provide for removing discipline from an officer's file after, say, three years if the officer has not had any further discipline. Yet, such provisions are common in union contracts and, arguably, create incentives for employees to correct their misbehaviors.[54]

Further, it is not clear that police union contracts lead to "too many" reinstatements of fired police officers. One recent article critical of union collective bargaining agreement protections showed that of the 1,881 officers fired for misconduct in the nation's largest police departments in the previous several years, the disciplinary appeals process reinstated the employment of just over 450 of these officers, or about 24 percent.[55] Further, this includes only cases that were litigated to arbitration. It does not include discipline that police unions chose not to contest at arbitration. In short, police unions lost more than three-quarters of the cases they thought were worth fighting to the end.

It is unclear the extent to which arguments against bargained discipline protections for police officers will prevail as a matter of legal rules or how changes based on them will work in practice. One recent, notable development should be mentioned, however. In 2020 the District of Columbia amended its public sector labor statute such that disciplining police officers became a management right not subject to negotiation. Specifically, the District of Columbia enacted the Comprehensive Policing and Justice Reform Second Emergency Amendment Act of 2020 in response to that summer's protests of "injustice, racism, and police brutality against Black people and other people of color." Section 116 amended the "Management rights; matters subject to collective bargaining" section of the district's Comprehensive Merit Personnel Act by adding the following: "(c)(1) All matters pertaining to the discipline of sworn law enforcement personnel shall be retained by management and not be negotiable." This rule became effective on September 30, 2020. A police union challenged the law, but the U.S. District Court for the District of Columbia upheld the law in November 2020.[56]

Massachusetts also recently made legal changes to try to address these problems, although the changes did not eliminate bargaining over discipline. In late December 2020, Massachusetts adopted rules under which police officers are required to be certified every three years and can lose their certification for violating policing standards. The law created Massachusetts Peace Officer Standards and Training Commission, a body that establishes policing standards, certifies police officers, investigates allegations of misconduct, and suspends or revokes the certification of officers who are found by clear and convincing evidence to have violated its standards. While the commission includes a police chief, a law enforcement officer below the rank of sergeant, and a law enforcement officer chosen from nominations by the Massachusetts Association of Minority Law Enforcement Officers, it is to be composed mostly of civilians. It also includes a retired superior court judge, a social worker, an attorney from the Civil Rights and Social Justice Section Council of the Massachusetts Bar Association, and three others, one of whom must be recommended by the Massachusetts Commission against Discrimination. The law also prohibits or restricts certain types of use of force, restricts the use of no-knock warrants, and contains other protections for civilians.[57]

Other states have taken the intermediate step of limiting who can act as an arbitrator in police discipline cases. For example, in 2021 the state of Washington enacted SB 5055, which, among other things, establishes a commission that will appoint a roster of between nine and eighteen people who are allowed to act as arbitrators in police discipline cases and sets minimum qualifications for such arbitrators. Minnesota Statute 626.892, enacted in 2020, limits arbitrators in police discipline cases even further: such arbitrators are not allowed to take other labor arbitration cases. As of this writing, how any of these laws will work in practice remains to be seen.[58]

In some ways, questions about police unions today are surprisingly similar to those voiced a century ago. First, are police unions primarily another example of workers organizing to further their workplace interests, or does the nature of the job of policing make these organizations something significantly different from other unions? Second, if one believes the latter and that this difference justifies fewer legal rights for police unions, how might that affect the rights of other public sector unions or even unions in general? Of course, the political valence of those questions has shifted. Further, in the present day there will be valuable opportunities for research and study. A variety of different types of police reform efforts currently under way—many inevitably involving police unions and their rights—will be fertile ground for determining what measures produce what results. Neither the analysis nor the implementation of policy will be easy. But it will be very important to police officers, the labor movement, and society as a whole.

Further Reading

Fisk, Catherine L., and L. Song Richardson. "Police Unions." 85 *Geo. Wash. L. Rev.* 712 (2017).

Gammage, Allen, and Stanley Sachs. *Police Unions*. Springfield, IL: Charles Thomas, 1972.

Harris, Seth, et al. *Modern Labor Law in the Private and Public Sectors: Cases and Materials*. 3rd ed. Durham, NC: Carolina Academic Press, 2020.

Kraftchick, Lee. "How Hard Is It to Fire a Police Officer?" 50 *Stetson L. Rev.* 491 (2021).

Levine, Martin J. "A Historical Overview of Police Unionization in the United States." *Police Journal: Theory, Practice and Principles* 61 (October 1988): 334–43.

Malin, Martin, et al. *Public Sector Employment: Cases and Materials*. 4th ed. Saint Paul, MN: West Academic Publishing, 2021.

Russell, Francis. *A City in Terror: Calvin Coolidge and the Boston Police Strike of 1919*. Boston: Beacon Press, 1975.

Slater, Joseph. *Public Workers: Government Employee Unions, the Law, and the State, 1900–62*. Ithaca, NY: Cornell University Press, 2004.

Notes

1. Richard Kearney and Patrice Mareschal, *Labor Relations in the Public Sector*, 5th ed. (Boca Raton, FL: CRC Press, 2014), 65–66, 245–46.

2. For more details on this event, see Joseph Slater, *Public Workers: Government Employee Unions, the Law, and the State, 1900–62* (Ithaca, NY: Cornell University Press, 2004), ch. 1, from which much of this section is taken.

3. Slater, *Public Workers*, 18. Hereafter, page numbers for this source are given parenthetically in the text.

4. *Levasseur v. Wheeldon*, 79 S.D. 442, 447 (1962).

5. Slater, *Public Workers*, 37.

6. See Slater, *Public Workers*, ch. 2, for an example of a ban on a teachers' union affiliating with the AFL in the 1920s–1930s.

7. *CIO v. City of Dallas*, 198 S.W.2d 143 (1946); *Railway Mail Ass'n v. Murphy*, 44 N.Y.S.2d 601, 607 (1943).

8. Slater, *Public Workers*, 92–93.

9. 24 So.2d 319, 321 (1946), *cert. den.*, 328 U.S. 863 (1946).

10. Slater, *Public Workers*, 76.

11. 357 Mo. 68, 82.

12. 357 Mo. at 83.

13. 78 Cal.App. 638.

14. 357 Mo. at 84.

15. 78 Cal.App. 640.

16. Slater, *Public Workers*, ch. 3.

17. Slater, *Public Workers*, 157.

18. Slater, *Public Workers*, 174–78.

19. For more details on the Wisconsin law and its development, see Slater, *Public Workers*, ch. 6.

20. Slater, *Public Workers*, 170.

21. Slater, *Public Workers*, 170–73.

22. Ibid.

23. Slater, *Public Workers*, 183.

24. Slater, *Public Workers*, 186–87. For more on fact-finding and interest arbitration in modern law, see Seth Harris, Joseph Slater, Anne Lofaso, Charlotte Garden, and Richard Griffin, *Modern Labor Law in the Private and Public Sectors: Cases and Materials*, 3rd ed. (Durham, NC: Carolina Academic Press, 2020), 928–78.

25. Harris et al., *Modern Labor Law*, 69–70.

26. 385 U.S. 493.

27. Ibid.

28. 296 F.Supp. 1068.

29. Harris et al., *Modern Labor Law*, 70–77.

30. Ibid., 78.

31. Ibid.

32. 138 S.Ct. 54.

33. Harris et al., *Modern Labor Law*, 79.

34. Ibid.

35. 824 F. Supp. 2d 856 (W.D. Wis. 2012); *Wisconsin Educ. Ass'n Council v. Walker*, 705 F.3d 640 (7th Cir. 2013).

36. 705 F.3d 640, 643.

37. Harris et al., *Modern Labor Law*, 80.

38. Harris et al., *Modern Labor Law*, 81.

39. Harris et al., *Modern Labor Law*, 81.

40. Harris et al., *Modern Labor Law*, 83.

41. Harris et al., *Modern Labor Law*, 83–84.

42. 928 N.W.2d 21 (2019); 623 S.W.3d 585 (Mo. 2021).

43. Tyler Adams, "Factors in Police Misconduct Arbitration Outcomes: What Does It Take to Fire a Bad Cop?" 32 *ABA J. Lab. & Emp. L.* 133, 134–35 (2017). See also Steven Rushin, "Police Disciplinary Appeals," 167 *U. Pa. L. Rev. 545* (2019) (arguing that police disciplinary appeals serve as an underappreciated barrier to officer accountability and organizational reform).

44. Kim Kelly, "No More Cop Unions," *New Republic*, May 29, 2020, https://newrepublic.com/article/157918/no-cop-unions/.

45. Gilbert Rivera, "Armed, Not Militarized: Achieving Real Police Militarization," 20 *Berkeley J. Crim. L.* 227 (2015).

46. Catherine L. Fisk and L. Song Richardson, "Police Unions," 85 *Geo. Wash. L. Rev.* 712 (2017) contains a good discussion of such provisions.

47. Kearney and Mareschal, *Labor Relations in the Public Sector*, 65–66.

48. Unions with formal collective bargaining agreements exist in about half of all local police departments, representing 71 percent of all officers. Samuel Walker, "Institutionalizing Police Accountability Reforms: The Problem of Making Police Reforms Endure," 32 *St. Louis U. Pub. L. Rev.* 57, 71–72 (2012).

49. Dhammika Dharmapala, Richard McAdams, John Rappaport, "Collective Bargaining Rights and Police Misconduct: Evidence from Florida," *University of Chicago Coase-Sandor Institute for Law and Economics Research Paper No. 831 U of Chicago, Public Law Working Paper No. 655* (January 5, 2018), https://papers.ssrn.com/sol3/papers.cfm?abstract_id=3095217/.

50. Felipe Goncalves, "Police Unions and Officer Misconduct," dissertation draft, Princeton University (2018), cited in Dharmapala, McAdams, Rappaport (2018 version).

51. See Kevin M. Keenan and Samuel Walker, "An Impediment to Police Accountability? An Analysis of Statutory Law Enforcement Officers' Bills of Rights," 14 *B.U. Pub. Int. L.J.* 185 (2005).

52. See Fisk and Richardson, "Police Unions," 741–44.

53. Rushin, "Police Disciplinary Appeals," 574–76.

54. For this and further skepticism that eliminating collective bargaining rights will improve policing, see Martin Malin and Joseph Slater, "In Defense of Police Collective Bargaining," *Chicago Sun-Times*, August 12, 2020, https://chicago.suntimes.com/2020/8/12/21365763/chicago-police-fop-collective-bargaining-rights/.

55. Rushin, "Police Disciplinary Appeals," 579–80.

56. *Fraternal Order of Police, Metropolitan Police Department Labor Committee, D.C. Police Union v. District of Columbia*, Civil Action no. 20-2130 (JEB) (D.D.C., Nov. 4, 2020).

57. Colin A. Young, "Gov. Baker Signs Landmark Policing Reform Law," *Berkshire (MA) Eagle,* December 31, 2020, https://www.berkshireeagle.com/news/local/gov-baker-signs-landmark-policing-reform-law/article_f3866408-4b9a-11eb-a90b-4f61cf655b32.html/.

58. More recently, Connecticut enacted a law nullifying the restrictions in the state trooper union's CBA on releasing disciplinary records. See *Connecticut State Police Union v. Rovella*, 36 F.4th 54 (2d Cir 2022). For a similar decision on a similar law in New York, see *Uniformed Fire Officers Association v. DeBlasio*, 846 F. App'x 45 (2d Cir. Feb. 16, 2021).

CHAPTER 6

The Road to Memphis

Southern Sanitation Workers and the Transformation of Public Employee Unionism in the Postwar United States

WILLIAM P. JONES

"Every one of those men fired themselves this morning by not appearing for work," the commissioner of public improvement in Birmingham, Alabama, told reporters after nearly four hundred African American garbage collectors, street sweepers, and janitors walked off their jobs on April 20, 1960. Earlier that year, the city commission had reduced labor costs by shortening the workweek for all city employees to forty hours. While salaried civil servants retained their previous income, Black men who were employed as day laborers saw a three-dollar cut in their weekly pay. Pointing out that sanitation workers were "essential to the health and welfare of all citizens of the community," a local union leader urged Commissioner J. T. Waggoner to raise their hourly rate "rather than discriminate against the day laborers." Waggoner refused and, citing a 1956 ordinance requiring city employees who engaged in strikes or slowdowns to "be immediately discharged" for at least a year, declared his intent "to replace as many of them as possible with white men."[1]

Given the racial overtones of the Birmingham strike, one might expect it to have forged an alliance between civil rights and labor activists similar to that which emerged to support the strike by African American sanitation workers less than a decade later in Memphis, Tennessee. Indeed, such a coalition was in many respects more likely in Birmingham, where civil rights and labor movements were both stronger and more closely interconnected than in Memphis. Martin Luther King Jr., who would be assassinated while supporting the Memphis strike, gave what the local African American newspaper called "a major" speech in Birmingham a few weeks before the 1960 strike began, and soon afterward ten Black students launched the first of many sit-ins against discrimination in downtown businesses. Later that summer, as the strike continued, King's Southern Christian Leadership Conference (SCLC) designated Birmingham "the most critical city in the South because of the hard-core resistance to any form of desegregation."[2]

Yet, while white labor leaders rallied behind the strikers, neither local nor national Black civil rights leaders connected the plight of the sanitation workers to their struggles for voting rights and integration. "Can They Vote?" asked an editorial in the *Birmingham World*, a Black-owned newspaper edited by pro-labor civil rights activist Emory O. Jackson. Taking no position on the legitimacy of the strike or the sanitation workers' demands, Jackson asserted that the strike raised only "three important questions" about organized labor: Had unions done enough to support the workers' right to vote? Did they involve "rank and file" workers in the decision to strike? And would they explain the issues involved to middle-class African Americans who had "political power and immense purchasing power"? Rejecting white union leaders' complaint that Waggoner had injected the "race issue" into the conflict by replacing strikers with white workers, Jackson argued that this was a problem only because unions had not fought to open other municipal jobs to Black workers. "The race issue has long been a job issue," he remarked. "How else can one explain the absence of Negro persons from so many of the jobs provided by the City of Birmingham?" Not until September of 1960, five months after the strike began, did the Alabama Council on Human Relations, the local affiliate of King's SCLC, protest Waggoner's "high-minded and undemocratic" dismissal of the sanitation workers "without a fair opportunity for an airing of their case."[3]

Jackson and other Black leaders hesitated to support the Birmingham strike not because they opposed unions but because their familiarity with organized labor made them acutely aware of the poor record that unions had in addressing the concerns of Black workers, bringing them into the leadership of unions, fighting racial discrimination in employment, and supporting voting rights in the South and elsewhere. Sanitation workers in both Memphis and Birmingham were represented by the American Federation of State, County, and Municipal Employees (AFSCME), which emerged in the 1960s as one of the most racially diverse and egalitarian unions in the United States. Three decades earlier, however, when AFSCME first entered the South, union leaders actively avoided African Americans and depicted its members and goals in racially exclusive terms. That position changed as sanitation workers launched strikes without support from unions during and after the Second World War, and AFSCME began supporting the organization of Black workers across the South. Lingering distrust and a political backlash against both unions and civil rights organizations limited their cooperation. Not until the late 1960s were labor and civil rights activists able to join forces as AFSCME and the SCLC did in Memphis.

This prehistory of the Memphis strike is significant given the central role that public employment acquired in the economic and political lives of African Americans in the decades following 1968. In their influential study of racial inequality, Michael B. Katz, Mark J. Stern, and Jamie J. Fader called government jobs "the principal source of black mobility, especially for women, and one of the most important mechanisms reducing black poverty," in the late twentieth-century United States. In fact, government had been an important source of employment for African Americans since the late nineteenth century. Yet, because public officials restricted Black workers to the lowest-paid, least-empowered positions, the sector served to reinforce rather than challenge broader patterns of racial inequality. In contrast, with the expansion of public sector unionism in the 1960s and 1970s, public employment was transformed into a significant vehicle for political empowerment and economic mobility for African Americans. This chapter seeks to explain how that transformation occurred and the role that Southern sanitation workers played in uniting unions and civil rights organizations around the concerns of Black public employees.[4]

AFSCME Goes South

Leaders of AFSCME signaled their intention to expand into the South by holding their second national convention in Atlanta, Georgia, in 1938, two years after the American Federation of Labor (AFL) authorized the union to organize employees of state and local governments across the United States. AFSCME leaders made it clear, however, that they were not interested in garbage collectors, janitors, and other mostly African American workers who formed the majority of the public workforce in Atlanta, Birmingham, and other Southern cities. Convention organizers sought to entice AFSCME members to travel from other regions with descriptions of local attractions, such as the Confederate Memorial Carving at Stone Mountain and the "cyclorama" painting of the Battle of Atlanta, that would not have been so appealing to Black members. The "Convention Forecast" printed in AFSCME's monthly magazine featured pictures of finely dressed white men and women dancing, eating, and listening to speeches, yet the only reference to an African American was a racist caricature of a Black man in overalls eating a large slice of watermelon.[5]

It was not only racism that prevented AFSCME from organizing Black workers but also a conception of public employees rooted in the union's founding by white-collar professionals in Wisconsin. Formed to defend and strengthen civil service regulations that governments had adopted to depoliticize and standardize public employment in the Progressive Era, the union encouraged new members to improve their wages and working conditions by appealing to elected officials and the broader public on the basis of their skill and dedication to the public good rather than confrontation. "An organization of public employees must be practical if it expects to accomplish results and justify its existence," AFSCME president Arnold Zander wrote in 1937. "Strikes in public service are impractical and therefore are not used."

That strategy worked well for formally credentialed professionals like Zander, who was the only president of an AFL union with a PhD, but it did little for manual laborers, like the Birmingham sanitation workers, who were excluded from most civil service systems. One of AFSCME's first locals outside Wisconsin was established by ten thousand employees of the Emergency Relief Bureau in New York City, which was created to provide jobs in public service for unemployed workers during the Great Depression. Workers organized when the city transferred their jobs to the New York State Department of Welfare and required them to pass a civil service exam in competition with fifty thousand recent college graduates. Local union leaders explained that Black workers were "especially affected," as they had "worked their way into the positions" and lacked the formal education and "poise, speech, personality" traits that were prioritized by the tests. AFSCME supported the workers, along with a coalition of Black ministers and labor leaders in New York, but expelled them after they went on strike to defend their jobs. The relief workers gained a charter from the Congress of Industrial Organizations (CIO), which broke away from the AFL to support strikes in private industry and, with relief workers in Philadelphia, Chicago, and Los Angeles, formed the State, County, and Municipal Workers of America (SCMWA). Dismissing the CIO as dangerously radical and subversive, Arnold Zander boasted that the "Perfect Purge" had rid the AFL of workers who "do not wish to be affiliated with such regular, ordinary, average American public employees" as those who remained in AFSCME.[6]

While Zander continued to oppose strikes by public employees, the rapid expansion of the CIO in the late 1930s and early 1940s led him to rethink AFSCME's focus on white-collar workers. In October 1938, soon after the

Atlanta convention, AFSCME issued a charter to an independent union of mostly African American garbage collectors and street sweepers in Philadelphia, Pennsylvania. While the AFL Teamsters Union represented white garbage truck drivers, unions showed little interest in the laborers until they launched a successful strike for better wages and working conditions in 1937. Rebuffing an offer to affiliate with SCMWA, the union remained independent through an even larger strike that the city settled by signing the first contract in the nation with a union of public employees. Recognizing the significance of that victory, white truck drivers offered to unite with the laborers in a new AFSCME local. Hopeful that the arrangement signaled a "new tradition of complete fairness and equality for Negroes with the AF of L," Philadelphia's Black newspaper urged the union to "admit—then encourage—Negroes to full and complete participation in ALL union affairs."[7]

Black Workers on Their Own

Impressed by the Black workers in Philadelphia, Zander encouraged AFSCME Southern regional director W. A. Florence to reach out to "colored employees" in Atlanta. Florence responded that the workers "were disgruntle[d] and a strike was brewing, which could hurt our organization rather than benefit it," but both men reconsidered after nearly two hundred "Negro laborers . . . virtually paralyzed" the city by walking off their jobs at the Department of Sanitation. As in Philadelphia, the Atlanta garbage collectors organized the strike with no assistance from a union. Sanitation Director H. J. Cates noted that the action "had all the earmarks of a well-organized and planned walk-out," but when city officials asked to speak with union representatives, workers responded, "We are all leaders." Inspired by the militancy of the collectors, white truck drivers switched their affiliation from AFSCME to the Teamsters and threatened a strike of their own. "This has been true elsewhere," Zander responded after both groups of workers won significant wage increases, "and I am about at the point where I feel that we cannot be permanently placed in the position of sacrificing the best interests of our people to a policy of avoiding strikes at almost any cost."[8]

Elected officials also noted the effectiveness of the Atlanta strike. Cates reported that only five of Atlanta's fifty-two garbage trucks left the garage the first day of the walkout, and three returned before noon. He contended that "those who wanted to work" were "accosted" and "actually threatened" by strikers who ordered them "to get off the job and abandon their equipment." The *Atlanta Constitution* compared the Black workers to German troops who were then pushing into Eastern Europe. "Not a wheel turned," read the caption for a photo of idled garbage trucks, "as the 'strike-krieg' stalled action on the garbage collection fronts all over town." The *Constitution* reported that strikers were headed toward a "showdown" with elected officials who were preparing to hire replacements and place armed guards on trucks to protect workers. "I don't think the people of Atlanta should be called upon to make additional sacrifices to raise salaries at this time," Cates told reporters, noting that the laborers made fifteen dollars a week with sick leave and had received a twenty-five-cent raise after threatening to strike the previous year. Emphasizing their obligations as public servants, Cates stated, "I do not believe the public will appreciate the fact that these men have stopped a vital service which if arrested too long will endanger the health of every citizen of this city."[9]

By the end of the week, city officials were forced to concede. White union leaders objected to a proposal to replace strikers with prisoners from the city jail, and federal authorities rejected the city's request for 175 "Negro workmen" from the Works Progress Administration. Florence reported to Zander that the white truck drivers waited until the laborers had "'clinched' the strike" and launched their own strike "after sanitary conditions in Atlanta had become almost unbearable." Facing a health crisis, Cates granted a fifty-cent raise for garbage collectors and a seventy-five-cent increase for truck drivers. "I'm doing so only because a vital health service on behalf of the citizens of Atlanta is threatened," he told reporters. "In fact, only because they have a gun in my ribs." Noting that white men gained more than Black ones, Florence added, "In my opinion, the drivers did not win the strike but rode the 'coat tails' on the negro laborers in their department to victory."[10]

Having won the strike without assistance from AFSCME, the Atlanta sanitation workers formed an unaffiliated union at a local Masonic Temple. That fall, the Sanitary Helpers Union marched alongside thirteen other "Negro locals" in the forty-first annual Labor Day parade. Meanwhile, W. A. Florence was "optimistic" about AFSCME's expansion among white-collar civil servants in the South. Just before the strike ended, locals from four cities gathered to form the Georgia State Council of the union. Two others were invited, and one promised to join the council "as soon as they get sufficiently organized." Florence reported that the Savannah local did not respond, as that city government is "purely a spoils system and is controlled by cliques." State employees were also resistant, as the governor "frankly states that he will not recognize a union of Government employees," and the president of the Georgia Federation of Labor believed it was "practically impossible" to organize them. Florence urged Zander to fund a regional organizing campaign, as local unions were "too busy with their own problems" to expand without assistance from an organizer prepared to work in the South. Nevertheless, he boasted soon afterward that the union had expanded to include police officers in Montgomery, Alabama, and won support from the Birmingham-based Alabama State Federation of Labor.[11]

While AFSCME continued to focus on white-collar civil servants, it was the militancy of African American laborers that drove the discussion about public employee unionism in the South. Early in 1942, the Atlanta City Council excluded the Department of Sanitation from a 10 percent bonus granted to other city workers on the grounds that laborers and truck drivers had already received an increase due to the 1941 strike. Sanitation Director H. J. Cates granted the raise to white truck drivers when they threatened to strike but held out when three hundred garbage collectors and street sweepers walked off their jobs. Admitting it would be hard to replace the workers due to a wartime labor shortage, he told reporters, "It is mighty hard work and it is almost impossible for men to stand up under it unless they are used to it." Cates restored service to downtown businesses by ordering convicts from the city jail to collect garbage with armed guards on trucks to protect the collectors and drivers. "We are out to whip this thing and are not compromising one single thing," Cates told reporters. The Atlanta Federation of Trades protested the use of prison labor to break a strike, but by that point Cates had recruited enough workers to restore normal service. He offered to rehire rank-and-file strikers, but leaders were told to seek work in other states.[12]

Southern Cities Fight Back

As garbage strikes became an annual rite of summer, officials in Atlanta and other Southern cities sought to expand their power to keep workers on the job. In 1943, truck drivers struck first, seeking a $1.00 raise to $6.50 a day. When the strike spread to white mechanics and engineers in the city garage and sewage plants, and to "Negro laborers" in construction, officials stemmed the tide by granting a wage increase to over two hundred workers, "mostly Negroes," in the Department of Sanitation. Warning that strikes by public employees undermined "the sovereignty of local government and the health and safety of the community," Mayor William B. Hartsfield threatened to lease garbage collection to private contractors as had been done in Cincinnati and several other cities. Suggesting his threat was taken seriously, local union leaders helped persuade workers to end the strike with "no promises" of a wage increase. The following winter, Hartsfield urged leaders of the U.S. Conference of Mayors to "take a firm and bold stand" on "the question of strikes against government."[13]

136   ORGANIZING PUBLIC WORKERS

While public officials in the United States had frequently taken the position that public employees could not strike, not until after the Second World War did they take legal action to prevent them. In an act that he would later credit for allowing him to win the presidency, then-governor Calvin Coolidge helped to crush a 1919 strike by police in Boston on the ground that "there is no right to strike against the public safety, anywhere, anytime." President Franklin D. Roosevelt agreed that strikes by public employees were "unthinkable and intolerable" but opposed a federal law to prevent them. Hartsfield shared Roosevelt's sympathy for unions and claimed that "of course, all progressive officials are willing to recognize and deal" with unions, "which we also do here in Atlanta." However, since "cities all over the nation have been subjected to a flood of strikes, many of them among garbage collections," it had become necessary to limit those "manifestations of power over the affairs of government" and to prevent unions from coming "between the people and their government." Citing the statements from Coolidge and Roosevelt, he urged fellow mayors to "consider this matter and take a firm stand on the subject which I am sure will meet with the approval of the American people."[14]

Hartsfield's call to action grew more pressing in 1946 as public employees joined an even larger strike wave than 1937 and as both AFL and CIO unions set out to consolidate the public sector unions they had established in the previous decade. In May 1946 the *New York Times* reported that CIO unions were launching "two major organizing drives" aimed at the nation's largest remaining groups of nonunion workers. One was "Operation Dixie," a million-dollar effort to organize industrial unions in the South. The other sought to organize nearly four million public employees under the banner of the United Public Workers of America (UPWA), which was created from a merger of SCMWA and the CIO's United Federal Workers of America. AFSCME launched a similar campaign at its 1946 convention in Chicago, with a focus on policemen, whose organization had been controversial since the Boston strike thirty years earlier. AFSCME leaders addressed concerns about similar conflicts by pointing out that all of their members were prohibited from striking but announced that they were taking legal action against Chicago, Los Angeles, and other cities that prohibited police from joining unions. The United Public Workers adopted a resolution that strikes would be used only as a last resort, although nearly a third of the delegates to the founding convention voted against it. Despite these disagreements over strikes, *Business Week* magazine reported, leaders of the UPWA and AFSCME agreed "that public employees should be given the same organization and bargaining rights now assured by law for other workers."[15]

Following Hartsfield's advice, elected officials responded by limiting rather than expanding public employees' rights to form unions and bargain collectively. "After World War II," writes legal historian Joseph Slater, "cities and states finally began to pass laws which explicitly covered public sector unions, but these laws were designed chiefly to provide draconian penalties for government workers who struck." Inspired by constraints imposed on industrial unions by the Taft-Hartley Amendment to the National Labor Relations Act, states ranging from Texas and Virginia to New York and Washington adopted laws banning strikes by public employees. Many cities followed with their own versions of those laws. In 1946 the Supreme Court of Florida ruled that cities had "no authority to enter into negotiations with a labor union" over hours, wages, or working conditions or to "make such negotiations the basis for fiscal appropriations." Echoing Mayor Hartsfield's warning that public sector strikes threatened democracy, the court added, "It would seem that a strike against the city would amount, in effect, to a strike against government itself—a situation difficult to reconcile with all notions of government."[16]

Those laws did not prevent government workers from organizing or going on strike, but they significantly slowed the expansion of public sector unions in the late 1940s. The return of veterans to civilian labor markets made it easier for administrators to hire replacement workers, and the ability of unions to improve wages and working conditions in manufacturing created a high rate of turnover that made it harder to organize workers in government, as well as agriculture, where no laws protected their right to organize or bargain collectively. AFSCME and the UPWA grew steadily in places, but neither expanded far beyond the seventy-five thousand members they each claimed in 1946. AFSCME had the most success among white-collar state employees, many of whom were already organized into independent associations, and among police, firefighters, and prison guards. The UPWA remained strongest in New York but made important gains among nonprofessional hospital, school, and sanitation workers in California and Alabama and among federal employees in Hawaii and the Panama Canal Zone. Organizing stalled, however, as both unions became embroiled in bitter disputes over charges of Communist infiltration of unions during the Cold War. That dispute culminated with the expulsion of ten unions, including the UPWA, from the CIO in 1950.[17]

AFSCME Gets a Second Chance

Yet that was not the end of the story. On August 20, 1951, three hundred garbage collectors walked off their jobs in Birmingham, Alabama. City Commissioner J. W. Morgan persuaded them to return to work by promising to take their demand for a wage increase from eighty cents to one dollar an hour to the city council, but they walked off again after the council rejected the request the following day. Workers distributed flyers to local residents apologizing for the inconvenience caused by lack of garbage collection and explaining that "the very high cost of living" meant a small wage increase was needed "to provide at least the necessities of life for ourselves and our families." Reprinting a newspaper report that state legislators had recently approved "handsome increases" in salary for county and city officials, including Morgan, Mayor Cooper Green, and Public Safety Commissioner "Bull" Connor, the flyer encouraged residents to contact Morgan and "urge him to do all in his power to help us secure a living wage so we can return to work and provide you with the services you deserve as a tax payer."[18]

In contrast to the strike ten years earlier in Atlanta, both elected officials and labor leaders recognized immediately that the Birmingham conflict could have widespread implications for public sector labor relations across the South. Commissioner Morgan agreed to study how wages in other cities compared to those in his department but threatened to fire any worker who joined the strike. "Well, you stop them," he ordered when strike leaders informed him that workers had voted to walk off their jobs. "Don't let some harum-scarum lead you into trouble because those garbage trucks are going if we have to put policemen on every one of them." A week later Morgan conceded that his threat failed to prevent the strike, but he insisted that state law prevented him from negotiating with Carey Haigler, a CIO organizer who claimed to represent a majority of the garbage collectors. "Confidentially, I am going to refuse to recognize the CIO," Morgan wrote to his counterpart in Montgomery, Alabama. "As I see it, if Birmingham allows the CIO to organize this department it could be a forerunner of other cities over the state, which might not be good." In 1952 the city council passed an ordinance prohibiting strikes or picketing "against the City of Birmingham."[19]

While public officials sought legal barriers to unionization and strikes by public employees, union leaders saw the Birmingham strike as an opportunity to establish stable unions and win collective bargaining rights in the public sector. Haigler was the Alabama director of the Government and Civic Employees Organizing Committee (GCEOC), which CIO leaders established to reorganize public sector locals after they expelled the UPWA. That effort was particularly effective in places where the UPWA had organized African American workers in sanitation, health care, and education, including Georgia, Alabama, Florida, and the Panama Canal Zone. The AFL's Building Service Employees International Union (BSEIU) also built on the UPWA, most notably in Los Angeles, where a union of mostly African American sanitation workers, janitors, and hospital workers became one of BSEIU's largest locals in the nation. Frustrated by AFSCME's lack of growth, Arnold Zander hired a cohort of young radicals and former CIO activists to organize hospital and sanitation workers in larger cities. He considered switching AFSCME's affiliation to the CIO but changed course when leaders of the two federations proposed a merger. Under the terms of the merger, which was completed in 1955, since the CIO had not yet chartered the GCEOC as a union, AFSCME gained jurisdiction over all of its locals.

The AFL-CIO merger gave AFSCME a second chance to act on the lesson that Zander had learned from the Atlanta garbage collectors' strike in 1941. In contrast to both federations' acceptance of prohibitions on strikes by public employees in the 1930s and 1940s, CIO leaders responded forcefully to Birmingham's 1952 prohibition on strikes and picketing by public employees. "We feel that this drastic law was hastily drawn during a time of hysteria," read a resolution adopted by the Birmingham Industrial Union Council, declaring it "a totalitarian approach to employer-employee relations." Placing the debate over public employee strikes in the context of the "great ideological struggle" during the Cold War between "those who believe in the dignity of man and those who would reduce him to slavery and servitude," union leaders called prohibitions on the right to strike "a step in the direction of slavery."[20]

In addition to supporting strikes by Black sanitation workers in the South, AFSCME leaders also changed their approach to the racial inequalities that were deeply intertwined in those conflicts. In 1950 Arnold Zander authored a resolution calling on the AFL to establish a civil rights department with at least three staff members. "We feel that the CIO is stealing a march in this field of discrimination not because they have actually accomplished more than the American Federation of Labor, but because they have a special committee activity for this purpose," the AFSCME president wrote to AFL leader George Meany. In 1956 AFSCME education director John Caldwell reported to Zander on a two-day institute to develop a "program of equal pay for all employees and integration of Negro members with white members in several of the locals." Acknowledging that the union would "face a possible withdrawal of some of our white members," Caldwell reported that local leaders of AFSCME and the Central Labor Union were committed to integrating unions and ending racial discrimination within the local labor movement. That same year, AFSCME leaders joined representatives from seventy-five churches, unions, and fraternal organizations to create "In Friendship," a fund-raising network to support "victims of race terror and economic reprisals in the South."[21]

140   ORGANIZING PUBLIC WORKERS

Despite its changing approach, AFSCME remained vulnerable to the charge of having ignored the concerns of African American workers in the past. In the spring of 1957, over two hundred Black and white workers packed the sanitation garage in Charlotte, North Carolina, to protest their exclusion from a wage increase that city officials had recently granted to police and firefighters. "We're giving them a chance to do something about it today. But tomorrow there might not be any garbage collection," said Ernest McCoy, a white truck driver. The men returned to work after managers threatened to fire them, but AFSCME sought to build on the protest by organizing "all rank-and-file" city employees into a single local union. However, while AFSCME emphasized the shared interests of Black and white workers, it faced competition from the United Southern Employees Association (USEA), an independent union that pledged to organize Black and white workers into segregated locals. "Look at that slave labor camp," USEA organizer W. A. Somersett told a Black laborer who signed a membership card. "Why didn't the AFL-CIO do something about this before?"[22]

AFSCME succeeded in building an interracial union in Charlotte but faced continued hostility from local officials. In 1958, city officials "urgently requested" assistance from the attorney general of North Carolina after the International Brotherhood of Teamsters supported an effort to organize the city's police officers. The state official assured local authorities that they had no need to negotiate with public employees, and a few weeks later, the state legislature passed a law prohibiting police officers and firefighters from joining a union and declaring any "agreement, or contract" between a union and a government agency to be "illegal, unlawful, void and of no effect." Nevertheless, city officials in Charlotte agreed to negotiate with garbage collectors and truck drivers who staged a one day "sit-down" strike in the fall of 1959. Although the mayor refused to discuss their demand for a wage increase until they resumed work, he and the superintendent of sanitation assured the workers that "there would be no repercussions against any" strikers and that "the city manager and council are acting in good faith" to meet their demands. "I told him we were concerned with getting the trucks moving and that nobody would be fired without just cause," the superintendent told reporters about his negotiations with the striker leader.[23]

AFSCME made similar gains in Miami, Florida, after four hundred African American sanitation workers walked off their jobs without authorization from the union. Rather than sanctioning the workers, Zander dispatched AFSCME's national director of publicity and "Shorty" Rowe, who had succeeded W. A. Florence as Southern regional organizer, to support them. After speaking with strikers and leaders of the Miami Central Labor Union,

Figure 6.1. Two decades after the American Federation of State, County, and Municipal Employees declined to organize Black Southern workers on the grounds that they were "disgruntle[d]" and prone to strikes, the union newspaper boasted of the success of its "concerted membership drive" among Black workers in Atlanta and other Southern cities. The article featured this photo of Atlanta Local 846 officers: (seated, l to r) Alton Leeds, Florence Capers, Luther Hayes, Ray Cainon, and John Harris, treasurer; (standing, l to r) Local 846 chaplain John Bell, Georgia State AFL-CIO president W. H. Montague, AFSCME organizer W. A. ("Shorty") Rowe, Atlanta City Employees Local 4 president E. H. Stewart, and AFSCME international vice president Leon G. Hay. (Courtesy of AFSCME.)

Rowe concluded that the walkout "had not only been inevitable, but was long overdue." Praising local labor leaders for "publicizing the walkout," pledging to oppose the mayor and other unsupportive elected officials in the next election, and winning support from the Miami Negro Ministerial Alliance, Rowe boasted that "considering the number of persons involved, this might be termed one of the best publicized work stoppages in U.S. labor history." He also noted that when the city attempted to break the strike with convict labor, twenty-three prisoners "staged their own 'walk-out'" and escaped during their first day on the job. Facing pressure from the publicity, the mayor backed down and agreed to rehire the strikers with a wage increase and vacation pay and no penalty for going on strike.[24]

Garbage In, Garbage Out

Despite those recent gains, AFSCME's longer history of avoiding Black workers hung over the union as it prepared for another sanitation strike in

Birmingham. In February 1960, leaders of the Birmingham Labor Council alerted AFSCME's national office that the city council was considering an ordinance prohibiting union membership by city employees. Asserting that such a prohibition would violate Alabama's "Right to Work" law, which prohibited discrimination based on membership, or lack of membership, in a union, AFSCME leaders assured local activists that they would continue to support the organization of workers in the Department of Sanitation. Soon afterward, leaders of the United Steelworkers of America, Birmingham's most powerful union, voted unanimously to go "on record as being strongly opposed" to Commissioner J. T. Waggoner's decision to reduce the salaries of laborers in the Department of Sanitation. Though the steelworkers were interracial, similar letters came from exclusively white unions. "Having members throughout the City who are entitled to the services of this department which are essential to the health and welfare of all citizens of the community," wrote leaders of the carpenters' union, "it was the opinion of this Local Union that the people in this department should not have their take home pay reduced approximately $3.00 per man per week after being put on a forty hour week, while similar employees take home pay was not reduced after going to a forty hour week."[25]

Efforts to support the sanitation workers were complicated by city leaders' staunch defense of segregation. The day after the carpenters sent their letter to city hall, the *New York Times* published the first of two articles detailing Birmingham's response to protests against discrimination in downtown businesses. "It is not accidental that the Negro sit-in movement protesting lunch-counter segregation has only lightly touched brooding Birmingham," wrote journalist Harrison E. Salisbury. "But even those light touches have sent convulsive tremors through the delicately balanced power structure of the community." Furious about Salisbury's reporting on collaboration between local authorities and the Ku Klux Klan, commissioners Waggoner and Connor and Mayor James Morgan sued the *Times* for libel. The following week, four hundred members of AFSCME Local 1184 voted to strike over the wage cut and the dismissal of workers without due cause.[26]

In the face of those tensions and the shadow of history, labor and civil rights leaders failed to unite behind the sanitation workers in Birmingham. Leaders of the Labor Council pleaded with Waggoner not to fire the strikers, but he insisted that his hands were tied by the 1952 ordinance and that white truck drivers had "requested that they be given white helpers." AFSCME organizer Robert Rogers reported to the national office that strikers were "getting good support from all union members in Birmingham, who are pressuring the commissioners to settle." Despite efforts to force them back to work, he claimed workers were "fighting for their lives" and "holding out one hundred percent."

Sanitation Workers and Postwar Public Employee Unionism

Yet, workers' resilience and support from labor leaders was not enough to win without civil rights leaders, who viewed the strike as a distraction from the struggle for integration and the right to vote. "In the long run the issue between City Hall and the garbage workers will have to be decided at the ballot box," read an editorial in the *Birmingham News*, advising that "organized labor will have to come to the public with a clear issue and with clear hands," and demonstrate that African American workers had opportunities for leadership in the union movement. Not until the following September did the Alabama Council on Human Relations write to Waggoner requesting that he rehire three hundred sanitation workers who remained out of work six months after joining the strike. Sanitation workers sustained the AFSCME local in Birmingham but failed to force city leaders back to the negotiation table.[27]

That task would fall to sanitation workers in Memphis and the alliance they forged between the civil rights and labor movements in 1968. A few weeks after the strike began in Birmingham, a committee of sanitation workers began to organize with support from the Teamsters Union in Memphis. They voted to strike after Sanitation Commissioner William Farris refused to recognize the union but backed down when the Teamsters withdrew support. Workers formed an independent union in 1963 and affiliated with AFSCME the following year. The March on Washington for Jobs and Freedom, which strengthened cooperation between civil rights and labor organizations at the national level, set the stage for an alliance between AFSCME and the SCLC in Memphis. Cooperation faltered after a failed sanitation strike in 1966, which civil rights leaders feared would undermine a mayor who they hoped would support their demands for integration. When workers launched a second strike in 1968, the two movements were prepared to unite behind them. The result was a transformation of the civil rights and labor movements as well as the role of public employment in African American life.[28]

* * *

As we face continued opposition to public employee unions, and to the expansion of public spending on services such as sanitation, health care, and transportation, it is critical to recall that public employment remains one of the most important sources of economic security for African Americans in the twenty-first-century United States. Those opportunities stemmed not simply from the concentration of Black workers in public sector jobs, nor even from the expansion of unions into the public sector, but, rather, from the militancy and organization of Black workers themselves. The sanitation strikes of the 1940s and 1950s forced both elected officials and labor leaders to recognize the power and importance of Black public workers in Atlanta and other Southern cities while forging alliances between labor and civil rights organizations that would appear in Memphis and other cities after 1968. The forgotten history of Black public employee unionism in the postwar South is thus a critical component in the broader history of Black public employment in the twentieth-century United States.

Further Reading

Berger, Jane. *A New Working Class: The Legacies of Public-Sector Employment in the Civil Rights Movement*. Philadelphia: University of Pennsylvania Press, 2021.

Eskew, Glenn T. *But for Birmingham: The Local and National Movements in the Civil Rights Struggle*. Chapel Hill: University of North Carolina Press, 1997.

Honey, Michael K. *Going Down Jericho Road: The Memphis Strike, Martin Luther King's Last Campaign*. New York: W. W. Norton, 2007.

Huntley, Horace, and David Montgomery, eds. *Black Workers' Struggle for Equality in Birmingham*. Champaign: University of Illinois Press, 2004.

Jones, William P. *The March on Washington: Jobs, Freedom, and the Forgotten History of Civil Rights*. New York: W. W. Norton, 2013.

Ryan, Francis. *AFSCME's Philadelphia Story: Municipal Workers and Urban Power in the Twentieth Century*. Philadelphia: Temple University Press, 2011.

Notes

Thanks to the Jerry Wurf Memorial Fund for supporting the research and writing of this chapter.

1. "White Replacements," *Birmingham (AL) World*, April 23, 1960; M. H. Nelson to James Morgan, J. T. Waggoner, and Eugene Conner, April 11, 1960, James Morgan Papers, Birmingham Public Library, Birmingham, AL.

2. On the Memphis strike, see Michael K. Honey, *Going Down Jericho Road: The Memphis Strike, Martin Luther King's Last Campaign* (New York: W. W. Norton, 2007). On Birmingham's civil rights movement, see Glenn T. Eskew, *But for Birmingham: The Local and National Movements in the Civil Rights Struggle* (Chapel Hill: University of North Carolina Press, 1997); Horace Huntley and David Montgomery, eds., *Black Workers' Struggle for Equality in Birmingham* (Champaign: University of Illinois Press, 2004); and Max Krochmal, "An Unmistakably Working-Class Vision: Birmingham's Foot Soldiers and Their Civil Rights Movement," *Journal of Southern History* 76, no. 4 (2010): 923–60; "City Laborers Vote to Strike," *Birmingham Post Herald*, April 20, 1960; "Dr. King to Speak at New Pilgrim Baptist, March 6th," *Birmingham World*, March 5, 1960; "10 Students Arrested by Birmingham Police," *Birmingham World*, April 2, 1960; "SCLC Nonviolent Institute Moves to Birmingham," *Birmingham World*, August 17, 1960.

3. "Can They Vote?" *Birmingham World*, April 30, 1960.

4. Michael B. Katz, Mark J. Stern, and Jamie J. Fader, "The New African American Inequality," *Journal of American History* 92, no. 1 (2005): 77. On older patterns of exclusion, see Philip F. Rubio, *There's Always Work at the Post Office: African American Postal Workers and the Fight for Jobs, Justice, and Equality* (Chapel Hill: University of North Carolina Press, 2010); David Goldberg, *Black Firefighters and the FDNY: The Struggle for Jobs, Justice, and Equality in New York City* (Chapel Hill: University of North Carolina Press, 2020); Eric S. Yellin, *Racism in the Nation's Service: Government Workers and the Color Line in Woodrow Wilson's America* (Chapel Hill: University of North Carolina Press, 2016).

5. "Atlanta Attractions," *Journal of State and Local Government Employees* 2, no. 7 (1938): 14; "Convention Forecast," *Journal of State and Local Government Employees* 2, nos. 8–9 (1938): 19.

6. "Relief Workers Vote 6 to 1 for Strike," *New York Amsterdam News*, November 14, 1936; Adam Clayton Powell Jr., "Soap Box: Civil Service Only Secure," *New York Amsterdam News*, December 5, 1936; Arnold Zander, "The Perfect Purge," *Journal of State and Local Government Employees* 1, no. 1 (1937): 9.

7. Francis Ryan, *AFSCME's Philadelphia Story: Municipal Workers and Urban Power in the Twentieth Century* (Philadelphia: Temple University Press, 2011), 63.

8. W. A. Florence to Arnold Zander, July 24, 1941, and Zander to Florence, July 30, 1941; both in folder 2, box 42, AFSCME President Zander Papers, Walter Reuther Library, Wayne State University, Detroit, MI (hereafter, AFSCME President's Office Collection); "Garbagemen Back on Job as Wage Demand Is Met," *Atlanta Daily World*, July 27, 1941; "City's Garbage Piles Up as 175 Here Walk Out," *Atlanta Constitution*, July 23, 1941.

9. "Garbagemen Back on Job as Wage Demand Is Met," *Atlanta Daily World*, July 27, 1941; "City's Garbage Piles Up as 175 Here Walk Out," *Atlanta Constitution*, July 23, 1941; "Strike of Garbage Men Spreads: Incinerator Forced to Close," *Atlanta Daily World*, July 24, 1941.

10. "Garbagemen Back on Job as Wage Demand Is Met," *Atlanta Daily World*, July 27, 1941; W. A. Florence to Arnold Zander, September 17, 1941, box 42, folder 1, AFSCME President's Office Collection.

11. "Garbagemen Back on Job as Wage Demand Is Met," *Atlanta Daily World*, July 27, 1941; "Observance of Labor Day to Be Varied," *Atlanta Daily World*, September 1, 1941; W. A. Florence to Arnold Zander, September 17, 1941, box 42, folder 1, AFSCME President's Office Collection; W. A. Florence, "AFSCME Organizing in Alabama," to Arnold Zander, December 12, 1941, box 41, folder 2, AFSCME President's Office Collection.

12. "Garbage Piles High as 300 Workers Strike," *Atlanta Daily World*, July 22, 1942; "City Acts to Whip Strikers," *Atlanta Daily World*, July 23, 1942; "Garbage Strike May End This Weekend, *Atlanta Daily World*, July 24, 1942; "Prisoners Doing Work of Strikers," *Atlanta Daily World*, July 25, 1942; "Garbage Strike Ends," *Atlanta Daily World*, July 26, 1942.

13. "Garbage Piles Up as Workers Seek Wage Hike," *Atlanta Daily World*, July 16, 1943; "Citizens Aiding Officials during Garbage Strike," *Atlanta Daily World*, July 20, 1943; "No New Turn in Garbage Strike," *Atlanta Daily World*, July 21, 1943; "Garbage Strike Ends, Mayor Says," *Atlanta Daily World*, July 23, 1943; William B. Hartsfield to H. R. Betters, January 13, 1944, Collection #368.13.9, Cooper Green Papers, Department of Archives and Manuscripts, Birmingham Public Library, Birmingham, AL.

14. Joseph Slater, *Public Workers: Government Employee Unions, the Law, and the State* (Ithaca, NY: IRL Press, 2004); Hartsfield to Betters, January 13, 1944.

15. "CIO Unions to Open Organizing Drives," *New York Times*, April 22, 1946; "New Union Urges Wider Labor Law," *New York Times*, April 26, 1946; "Double Campaign," *Business Week*, May 4, 1946.

16. Slater, *Public Workers*, 94.

17. William P. Jones, "The Other Operation Dixie: Public Employees and the Resilience of Urban Liberalism," in *Capitalism Contested: The New Deal and Its Legacies*, ed. Romain Huret, Nelson Lichtenstein, and Jean-Christian Vinel, 224–39 (Philadelphia: University of Pennsylvania Press, 2020).

18. "Garbage, Trash Men Ask Pay Hike after Brief Stoppage," *Birmingham Post-Herald*, August 20, 1951; Garbage and Brush Collectors and Street Cleaners of the City of Birmingham, "A Message to the People of Birmingham," file 20.22, James W. Morgan Papers, Department of Archives and Manuscripts, Birmingham Public Library, Birmingham, AL (hereafter, James W. Morgan Papers).

19. "Garbage Collectors May Strike Here," *Birmingham Post-Herald*, August 21, 1951; Carey E. Haigler to J. W. Morgan, August 30, 1951, and J. W. Morgan to Mr. Ed Reid, August 31, 1951, both in file 20.20, James W. Morgan Papers.

20. Birmingham Industrial Union Council, CIO, "Resolution on Anti-Strike Ordinance," folder 2, box 12, AFSCME Secretary Treasurer's Office, GCEOC Records, Walter Reuther Archive, Wayne State University, Detroit, MI.

21. Arnold Zander, "AFSCME Resolution for AFL Civil Rights Department," letter to George Meany, August 30, 1950, box 8, folder 131; and John P. Caldwell to Arnold Zander, June 14, 1956, box 51, folder 2; AFSCME President's Office Collection; William P. Jones, *The March on Washington: Jobs, Freedom, and the Forgotten History of Civil Rights* (New York: W. W. Norton, 2013), 109.

22. Murray Kempton, "The Garbage Collectors," unidentified newspaper clipping in folder 11, box 2775, AFL-CIO Region 5/8 Papers, Special Collections, Georgia State University, Atlanta, GA.

23. Michael G. Okun, "Public Employee Bargaining in North Carolina: From Paternalism to Confusion," *North Carolina Law Review* 59 (1980): 218–20; Dick Young, "Garbage Strike Is Over, Trucks Roll," *Charlotte News*, September 2, 1959.

24. "Miami, Fla, City Manager Attempts to Break Strike of City's Laborers with Convict Scabs, Fails Miserably," *Public Employee*, September 1959, 12–13.

25. Henry Wilson, "Birmingham, Alabama, City Employees," memo, folder 3, box 84, AFSCME President's Office Collection, Arnold Zander Collection, Walter Reuther

Library; M. H. Nelson to James Morgan, J. T. Waggoner, and Eugene Connor, April 11, 1960, folder 15, box 13, James W. Morgan Papers.

26. Harrison Salisbury, "Fear and Hatred Grip Birmingham," *New York Times*, April 12, 1960; Salisbury, "Race Issue Shakes Alabama Structure," *New York Times*, April 13, 1960; "3 in Birmingham Sue the Times," *New York Times*, April 16, 1960; "City Laborers Vote to Strike," *Birmingham Post*, April 20, 1960.

27. "Can They Vote?" editorial, *Birmingham World*, April 30, 1960; C. Herbert Oliver and J. W. Ellwanger to J. T. Waggoner, folder 7, box 5, Waggoner Papers, Birmingham Public Library, Birmingham, AL.

28. Honey, *Going Down Jericho Road*; Jones, *March on Washington*.

CHAPTER 7

"They Won't Work for a Cop of Any Kind"

The 1970 Sanitation Slowdown and the Struggle for Black Independent Politics in Philadelphia

FRANCIS RYAN

At daybreak on February 26, 1970, three hundred Philadelphia sanitation workers gathered at the Domino Lane and Umbria Street truck yard before starting out on their routes. Despite the ten-degree temperature, the men were in an upbeat mood, celebrating the end of a twenty-three-day trash slowdown that had successfully pressured city officials to reconsider the controversial appointment of a police inspector as head of the Streets Department. Meeting the men inside the district service building was the sanitation union's business agent, Earl Stout, a blunt spokesman who had threatened to continue to disrupt trash services in the city for as long as it took to achieve their goal. An African American worker in blue overalls put his arm around the leader, saying, "You did it Earl, goddam." Addressing the men as they broke into cheers, Stout shouted back, "It was not Earl Stout that done this, it was you."[1]

In the first three months of 1970, job actions by government employees surged across the United States as twenty-four cities "ranging from hamlets to metros" witnessed similar walkouts, besides shutdowns of twenty-eight public school districts and a nationwide wildcat strike of postal workers that halted mail delivery for two weeks.[2] Philadelphia's monthlong protest stood out in this period of upheaval, with national media coverage emphasizing not just its duration but the reason it was called: the refusal of the predominantly African American sanitation force to accept the appointment of a white police officer with no prior background in municipal public works as their boss as streets commissioner. While defending the integrity of professional standards and upward mobility in the civil service were critical factors in the struggle, the protest went beyond economics and united African Americans across the city to curb what many felt was an overextension of police power in municipal government. In a few weeks' time, an alliance of Black business leaders, clergy, civil organizations, and ordinary citizens came together to back the sanitation workers, manifesting the kind of labor–civil rights coalition that Martin Luther King Jr. had called for the previous decade.

Government employee engagement within urban liberal regimes remains an understudied aspect of the public workers movements of this era.[3] With worksite power relations determined by the policy decisions of a range of elected officials and their appointees, unionized public workers, from the federal level down to county governments, were bound within a highly politicized context, one that necessitated a struggle not only over service delivery but also over how priorities that impacted these workers were ultimately determined at the ballot box. Efforts to build support with voters with shared social interest characterize such campaigns. While efforts to secure alliances with the publics they served were not always a given in the history of the varied public worker organizations in the United States, moments when such initiatives coalesce merit attention. Philadelphia's trash slowdown of 1970 provides a case study of how workplace-community concerns briefly aligned in a major city and how, in the weeks it played out, it showed how the struggle encapsulated not just on-the-job issues but the position of the broader African American electorate in the urban power structure. This chapter outlines the contexts and prospects for this labor–civil rights coalition in February 1970 and the months that followed and accounts for the varied reasons for its eclipse over a sixteen-year period.[4]

"My People Don't Want to Work for a Policeman"

The twenty-three-day standoff began on January 30, 1970, when city managing director Fred T. Corleto announced the appointment of Joseph F. Halferty, a veteran police inspector and director of the police department's Traffic Division as streets commissioner. Halferty's selection, which quickly followed the resignation of David Smallwood, a civil engineer who had served in the post since 1956, drew immediate fire. With no prior experience in municipal public works—his main qualifications being his knowledge of city geography and the fact that he had coordinated parades and traffic at sporting events—

Halferty was deemed below standard by both the Pennsylvania Society of Professional Engineers and the American Society of Civil Engineers, which sent Mayor James H. J. Tate letters denouncing the choice and offering assistance in the selection of a qualified expert. Good government advocates also scored the appointment, as political factors had clearly factored in. Hours after the announcement, Corleto confirmed rumors that he had consulted with Police Commissioner Frank L. Rizzo before making the call, revealing how internal political priorities had sidestepped normal protocol.[5]

Commissioner Rizzo's nod to Halferty underscored his increasing influence in the Tate administration by early 1970. Since joining the police force as a motorcycle patrolman in 1943, Rizzo had moved up the department ranks, gaining notoriety as "the toughest cop in America" for his hard, no-nonsense tactics and uncompromising defense of police practice. Appointed commissioner in 1967, Rizzo's relations with the African American community were particularly strained. While interactions between the police and the Black community had been difficult for decades, Rizzo's handling of the department in an era of increased protest, including the beating of public high school students demanding curriculum changes, made it even worse. Boisterous media pronouncements rejecting calls for police reform and retraining, and repeated demands for the disbanding of the Police Review Board, the city government police watchdog agency, set a tone for mistrust. Rizzo's support base, in contrast, came from a sizable section of the city's white working class, many of whom respected his hardline attitude toward what was perceived as a new array of threatening social forces. By 1970 such support gave the commissioner a viable platform for political power.[6]

Like many big-city urban machines of this era, the social turmoil of the 1960s had fractured Philadelphia's New Deal coalition of row home working-class voters. Seeking to maintain the dominance of the Democratic Party, Mayor Tate and other party chiefs turned to the controversial police chief as a potential unifying figure. While Rizzo claimed to have no interest in running for public office, it was obvious that he did. One week prior to Halferty's appointment, Rizzo had secured Police Inspector Robert R. Taylor as deputy commissioner of the city's License and Inspection Division, passing over more qualified civil servants with long careers in the bureau.[7] Such promotions fortified Rizzo's control of the police department and secured him loyalists in critical municipal posts on the eve of a mayoral bid. To many, such power moves marked a disturbing return to the kind of blatant nepotism that characterized the city's rule before the advent of postwar reform measures. In an editorial a few days after Halferty's appointment, the *Philadelphia Evening Bulletin* editorialized on Rizzo's increasing influence, noting, "The

The Struggle for Black Independent Politics in Philadelphia   151

aggregation of so much power into any single focus is a dangerous signal that cannot be ignored."[8]

Of all the opposition to Chief Inspector Halferty's appointment, none was as vehement or as consequential as that of Philadelphia's three thousand unionized sanitation workers. By 1970 the union representing these men—AFSCME Local 427—was one of the most militant in the city, regularly calling service disruptions to address a range of issues, especially during tense collective bargaining sessions. Founded in 1938 during a violent six-day strike, the union's early history was marked by bold actions that resulted in job security and pay boosts; such militant traditions were sidelined in the 1950s when white union leaders tied organizational gains to bureaucratic adjustments sponsored by the reform administrations of mayors Joseph S. Clark and Richardson Dilworth. Impatient with the glacial pace of pay raises, a group of Black insurgents took over the leadership of Local 427 in 1965 promising better wage deals in future contract negotiations. Combining direct action at the point of service and coordinated political mobilization, modest improvements were gained. In these standoffs, the sanitation local and its parent body, the eighteen-thousand-member AFSCME District Council (DC) 33, representing the bulk of the blue-collar labor force in the city's streets, water, public property, airport and health departments, placed pay equity with the mostly white uniformed police and fire departments as a major focus, an objective that continued into the new decade.[9]

More than just pay differences marked this discontent among Streets Department employees. In some basic ways, Philadelphia's trash collection service resembled that of Southern cities like Memphis, Tennessee, and Birmingham, Alabama: over 90 percent of the men driving trucks or lifting trash cans were Black, supervised by managers who were almost entirely white. Such stark disparity continued despite the promise that civil service regulations established in the reform era of the 1950s would facilitate upward advancement. Contemporary surveys of civil service systems, however, revealed that across the nation, racial disparities persisted, with African Americans concentrated at the lowest rung of the government service. Commissioner Rizzo's boosting of a police official into the top job in the trash service, and his public boast that he had done so, underscored how corrupt the system was.[10]

On January 30, 1970, AFSCME DC 33's executive board called an emergency meeting authorizing Local 427's business agent Earl Stout to meet with Mayor Tate to demand Halferty's withdrawal. The most outspoken of the union's new Black leadership, the forty-seven-year-old Stout worked as a trash truck mechanic for twenty years before defeating union founder Bill

152   ORGANIZING PUBLIC WORKERS

McEntee for the sanitation post in 1965. Hearing that Mayor Tate refused to meet with him, Stout called a press conference and addressed the racial undertones of Smallwood's replacement. "When white men controlled this union, they were consulted about appointments," he declared. "Now there are black men here and the mayor doesn't. If I were a white man, the mayor would have talked to me." Stout was clear, however, that union opposition did not pivot on race alone but was a response to the new commissioner's lack of experience. Other, more qualified men with long tenure in the Streets Department, such as Deputy Commissioner Robert Doyle—a white man who started in the division as a laborer in 1928 and who, over time, advanced to an engineer post—should have been tapped. "My people don't want to work for a policeman," Stout reiterated. "They won't work for a policeman of any kind."[11] If Mayor Tate did not rescind Halferty's promotion, trash service disruptions would commence within a day.

Anyone who lived in Philadelphia in these years knew this was not an idle threat; by 1970, trash slowdowns, often called during contentious collective bargaining sessions, had become part of the cycles of the year. While illegal strikes marked the first years of the union's history, sanitation crews now used informal leverage that arose out of the daily routines that marked the workday. By mid-decade, budget cutbacks and equipment shortages required men to work at least two hours overtime to complete assigned routes; by 1968 the city paid over six hundred thousand dollars in overtime due to such conditions. Although some citizens believed sanitation crews deliberately bilked the system, extra hours on the streets resulted, in large part, from perennial shortcomings of the bureau's truck fleet. Most of the city's 511 sanitation trucks were over five years old, considered "over-age," and in need of constant repair. Although the city contracted for new trucks from the Ford Motor Company, delivery of the ordered compactors stalled a year behind schedule, as production orders for military vehicles for the war in Vietnam took priority. Add to this the fact that a Streets Department hiring freeze enacted the previous summer exacerbated an already existing manpower shortage. No wonder trash collection lagged behind.[12]

News coverage of the developing trash crisis showed congested streets across the city, at points hampering movement of traffic and bus routes. In South Philadelphia, residents put trash cans and bags out in roadways as others burned piles in empty lots and playgrounds. While this public health breakdown was a primary concern, a serious political crisis raged for Mayor Tate and the city's Democratic Party establishment. In poor health and vacationing in Florida at the time of Halferty's appointment, Tate returned to a fractious situation as a number of high-ranking Democratic Party officials,

The Struggle for Black Independent Politics in Philadelphia   153

including city council president Paul D'Ortona, publicly criticized the decision to name a police inspector to the job as a predictable and avoidable dilemma. During a televised press conference on February 5, Mayor Tate, known for his short temper, rebuked members of his administration for their handling of the service disruption and humiliated city managing director Fred T. Corleto by stripping him of his duties. In this tirade, Tate made clear his determination to stand by Halferty, no matter what actions sanitation crews took.[13]

Mayor Tate's press conference underscored the problems now confronting the Quaker City's already fragmented Democratic Party. Divided by opposing views on the Vietnam War, law and order, civil rights, and internal reform measures, the trash impasse exposed Mayor Tate's loss of administrative control in a year when a range of local council offices and the Pennsylvania governor's seat were in play. Having secured reelection in 1967 by less than eleven thousand votes—and doing so without the support of the city's Democratic Party chair—Tate's battle with the sanitation men brought out into the open his deteriorating relations not only with a critical union that he had previously counted on but also with the wider African American community. This crumbling of the political masonry was compounded by the immensity of the trash crisis. Alarm over mounting fire hazards and reports of rats roaming the streets led the city's health department to declare a city-wide emergency on February 10. Two days later common pleas court judge Vincent A. Carroll issued a preliminary injunction requiring sanitation crews to work overtime to relieve the backlog as city engineers determined that 4,324 truckloads of curbside trash had accumulated.[14]

AFSCME Local 427 instructed members to adhere to the ruling but issued a statement that the protest would continue by other means. Critical staff at city incinerators called in sick as trucks lined up outside district garages for repairs, drivers citing a range of deficiencies such as broken turn signals, missing headlight bulbs and fire extinguishers, balding tires, and defective windshield wipers. By the start of the slowdown's second week, merchants and business associations contracted with independent trash haulers to remove accumulating tons of rubbish. For private homeowners, the city made available almost a million dollars' worth of plastic trash bags, encouraging citizens to transfer rubbish to incinerators on their own. A steady stream of cars transported trash to relay points, the residents' comments underscoring a sense of frustration. Dropping off some bags at an incinerator in the city's Roxborough section, Ed McMahon, a retired railroad employee commented, "Who are they to tell the city who they want to work for? If I'd done that when I was working, I would have gotten fired."[15]

154   ORGANIZING PUBLIC WORKERS

Building Community Alliances

Nothing united Philadelphia's African American community at the start of the 1970s more than the issue of police brutality. Since the early twentieth century, police mistreatment of Black citizens had been a perennial concern voiced to city administrators and a rally point for political action.[16] During the reform period of the 1950s, in response to calls for better police oversight, Mayor Richardson Dilworth authorized the creation of a Police Advisory Board, establishing a formal process by which claims of misconduct could be investigated. Even after this, police-community relations in Black neighborhoods remained tense. In the summer of 1964, rumors that a pregnant African American woman had died in police custody sparked three days of rioting that resulted in 2 deaths, 339 injuries, and millions of dollars in damaged property. Reports of aggressive arrests, beatings of suspects in custody, random stop-and-frisk practices, verbal harassment, phone tapping, surveillance, and reprisals against those critical of police practices were common, drawing the criticism of Philadelphia's chapter of the National Association for the Advancement of Colored People (NAACP) and liberal groups such as the American Civil Liberties Union and Americans for Democratic Action.[17]

Through the summer of 1969, incidents of hyperpolicing featured prominently in the city's most prominent Black newspaper, the *Philadelphia Tribune*. In early September, following a deadly police shooting of a fifteen-year-old mentally disabled youth, outraged citizens met with district police chiefs, but no effective means of curbing such actions was ever promised. Reflecting the frustration many in the community felt, Jack Levine, president of Philadelphians for Equal Justice said, "I'm afraid that there's just no effective vehicle for disciplinary action against policemen who act in a brutal or racist fashion." In turn, Commissioner Rizzo turned up his defense of aggressive policing, calling for the hiring of one thousand more officers and the purchase of armored personnel carriers for the department's arsenal. By the end of the year, Rizzo, along with the city's lodge of the Fraternal Order of Police, swayed Mayor Tate to abolish the Police Advisory Board. Incidents continued to spike in the first weeks of 1970. Three days before the trash slowdown started, police shot and killed seventeen-year-old Harold Brown and injured a companion as the two youths fled on foot following a stolen car chase. Besides two gunshot wounds, Brown had abrasions across his upper body and several of his teeth were knocked out. Some who witnessed the arrests signed affidavits claiming two officers beat the suspects after both were wounded and in custody.[18]

In response to police violence, a range of neighborhood-based organizations such as the Council of Organizations on Philadelphia Police Accountability and Responsibility (COPPAR), Philadelphians for Equal Justice, and the Kensington Council for Black Affairs had formed in the 1960s to publicize incidents of abuse and to provide legal assistance for victims.[19] At the start of the trash slowdown, Earl Stout appealed to such groups for support. On February 13, 1970, thirty-eight Black leaders of the North City Congress (NCC), an umbrella group of neighborhood associations, which included the Opportunities Industrialization Center, the Congress of Racial Equality, the Black Economic Development Conference, and the Black Ministers Conference of Philadelphia, among others, issued a statement backing Local 427's demand.[20] In an unprecedented move, the NCC also announced a petition campaign in North Philadelphia to remove Mayor Tate from office. Encouraged by the example of Black militants who launched a similar offense to oust Newark mayor Hugh J. Addonizio three years earlier, NCC's efforts drew on a section of Philadelphia's 1951 city charter that outlined an executive removal process. If 10 percent of registered voters who cast ballots in the previous municipal election signed a petition demanding a recall, a plebiscite would be held. Based on turnout from the 1967 election, 175,000 signatures were needed to initiate this process—a number that advocates believed was attainable. The following day, Local 427 joined the campaign, aiding NCC volunteers in canvassing neighborhoods to bring in signatures despite Mayor Tate's threats that they would be fired.[21]

With 200,000 registered voters in North Philadelphia wards, the recall campaign posed a serious challenge to Mayor Tate and the Democratic Party. Public opinion in the area solidly backed the trash crews. "When the sanitation men come to our doors with their petitions, it is our responsibility to see that we sign our names and be counted, for the day is near when the Black man will be completely garroted and castrated by total police rule and garrison troops," one woman implored.[22] Black radio stations also publicized the effort, with Georgie Woods, a popular radio disc jockey and civil rights activist, coming out in favor of the trashmen, urging listeners to get involved. Things turned even hotter when Philadelphia's Republican Party Policy Committee announced it would consider joining the recall push. With chaos engulfing the city, and a mayor unable to provide necessary leadership, Republican city chairman William J. Devlin expressed confidence that his ward leaders could quickly gather enough signatures from the city's 373,889 registered GOP voters to secure the recall provision in November.[23]

The emerging community-union coalition marked a serious blow to a Democratic Party bloc that maintained its power by a razor-thin margin.

Mayor Tate would not have won reelection without overwhelming support from the city's predominantly Black precincts. While Black churches and the NAACP exercised some influence in voter outreach, Election Day turnout in these wards was often uncoordinated and lacking in financial resources.[24] Thousands of eligible African American voters remained unregistered; while they were just under half of the city's overall population, only one-fourth of Blacks showed up at the polls. In this vacuum, the city's municipal workers union was an important power broker. AFSCME DC 33's predominantly Black rank-and-file members in the Streets Department proved a bastion of votes, thanks in part to voter registration drives implemented at municipal worksites. With all of its membership included across ten locals, the union, when bulking immediate family of members in the fold, claimed to control as many as fifty thousand votes.[25] While such a figure was speculation, the union's mobilization force in Black neighborhoods in North and West Philadelphia, and in Germantown, Mount Airy, and Point Breeze was undeniable. Union leaders and members knew this. "We worked to elect Tate," stated Howard McCall, president of DC 33's AFSCME Local 403, which represented a thousand mostly Black street maintenance employees. "We put him in office, he didn't elect us."[26]

AFSCME DC 33's role as a political mobilization force was not lost on the city's African American political activists. Impatient with the lack of responsiveness of the city's political regime to the growing demands of Black citizens, a new wave of independent Black Democrats had emerged in the previous decade to secure greater control of the party's machinery. Among the groups backing Local 427's slowdown and the community-based campaign to recall Tate was the Black Political Forum (BPF), the most prominent African American political organization in the city. Founded in the basement of a West Philadelphia row house in 1968 by John F. White Sr., Hardy Williams, and W. Wilson Goode, the forum focused on expanding Black political engagement. To the BPF, Tate's refusal to compromise on the Halferty appointment epitomized the white party leadership's disdain for the Black electorate and the need for a separate organization within the machine that would support self-determination. "The Forum calls upon the black community to express its dissatisfaction with the outrageous way that Mayor Tate forfeited the qualifications of men already experienced in the field of sanitation," John F. White Sr. stated on February 12.[27]

The Black Political Forum was critical of most of the city's Black Democratic Party leaders, which in 1970 included sixteen ward leaders in West and North Philadelphia. While providing a range of basic services to voters, these leaders, like all ward heads in the city, were bound within the dictates of the Democratic Party Executive Committee, controlled by Mayor Tate. According to John F. White Sr., these politicos acted as lackeys to white city bosses at city hall. The city's three Black councilmen—West Philadelphia's Edgar C. Campbell Sr., North Philadelphia's Thomas McIntosh, and civil rights attorney Charles H. Durham, who represented West Philadelphia's 3rd Council District—were no different, and their response to the sanitation crisis left no doubt. While all believed Tate had erred in naming a policeman to head the Streets Department, only McIntosh put his name on a resolution drafted by Councilman David Cohen, a white liberal, demanding Halferty's immediate release. McIntosh's break with Tate was soon patched over, as a few days later he joined the majority of Democratic council members in a unity meeting in a show of support for the mayor. The limits of Black political independence under the current leadership seemed clear. "The three of them are walking worms," wrote Edna Thomas, president of Philadelphia Women for Community Action to the *Philadelphia Tribune*. "It infuriates me to think that we could elect such low-quality people for public office."[28]

Other important African American leaders within the Democratic Party establishment joined in defense of the sanitation men and implored the Tate administration to rethink its position. Addressing the political fallout of the policy gaffe, Austin Norris, one of the city's Black political patriarchs since the 1930s, who now served as legal counsel for Local 427, said, "The mayor is wrong if he takes the position that one man is more important than 700,000 Negroes in Philadelphia." The consequences of Halferty's appointment reverberated well beyond the Streets Department. "This is a ridiculous situation that could destroy the Democratic Party. He will ensure the defeat of the party in the next state election," Norris observed, indicating that many Black residents were preparing to vote Republican later that year.[29] As the wife of a trash truck driver noted in a letter to the *Philadelphia Tribune*, Halferty's recent promotion was leading ordinary voters to rethink their political allegiances. "I and my husband voted for Mayor Tate along with sanitation men and until now we thought Mayor Tate to be fair and above board. But the appointment of Mr. Halferty gives us much cause to wonder about our vote, cause also to wonder about the Democratic Party."[30] As sanitation men and their community partners redoubled the recall drive, pressure mounted. Even after the city's Republican Party announced that it would not join in the movement, the ongoing campaign—signature by signature—hit hard.

As the crisis entered its third week, the sanitation men's determination to limit the city's trash collection stayed strong. In his public statements, Mayor Tate remained firmly behind Halferty, but behind the scenes a movement toward compromise was building.[31] On February 24, Tate met union officials

158   ORGANIZING PUBLIC WORKERS

Figure 7.1. Philadelphia mayor James H. J. Tate with African American Democratic Party leaders at a press conference following the end of a twenty-three-day trash slowdown, February 1970. AFSCME Local 427 business agent Earl Stout stands with his arm on the lectern. (Courtesy of Special Collections Research Center, Temple University Libraries, Philadelphia, PA.)

face-to-face for the first time and proposed a revision to the city charter that would remove the Sanitation Division from the Streets Department and create a new trash service unit, which, the mayor promised, would be overseen by an African American commissioner. In this split, the Streets Department's Highway Division, which employed just over one thousand mostly Black workers in road repair and traffic engineering, would remain under direction of Joseph F. Halferty. Stout dismissed the proposal as a sellout of the highway workers and abruptly left the meeting.[32] That same day, the union's protest spread as the Highway Division workers, represented by DC 33's AFSCME Local 403, announced a curtailing of basic street maintenance and traffic light oversight. Faced with further operational breakdown, Halferty resigned on February 25.[33]

As word spread, sanitation men and their supporters celebrated an important victory. Making clear that he did not want a say in who would now be appointed, Earl Stout confirmed that his members would work full-on to clean up the city. "As long as they take someone from our ranks, or an engineer or something like that, we'll do a job for him," he said. On March 3, Fred T. Corleto announced that Leo Goldstein, a deputy commissioner from the city's Department of Licenses and Inspections, had agreed to serve as streets commissioner. Appointed along with Goldstein as deputy commissioner was Stuart W. Adams, a city waste collection superintendent who had started with the division thirteen years earlier as a clerk, becoming the first African American to hold the number two position in the department.[34]

More Than Cash?

The day after Halferty's resignation, *Philadelphia Inquirer* reporter Al Haas interviewed Earl Stout outside the Domino Lane Streets Department service building. Sitting with Haas in his idling 1970 Oldsmobile, Stout recapped the previous weeks' events, stressing its political origins. African American citizens were the reason Tate had been reelected, and the mayor's refusal to consider Black demands in municipal policy had resulted in a breakdown in urban order. The majority-Black sanitation crews had the solid backing of the wider African American community, and Stout, who some now urged to run for political office himself, promised to strengthen this political alliance in the new decade.[35]

While service disruptions marked the union's early history and were common through the 1960s, the community and political coalition building that characterized the February 1970 job action was something new. For progressive labor activists, the successes of Black-led unions like AFSCME Local 427 marked a hopeful start to a new phase of the labor movement, one that would fulfill the broader promise of social democracy begun in the 1930s. Ultimately, the transformation in policy and government focus on human needs would improve conditions for white working people as well. In unions across the nation, minority-led caucuses among auto, transit, and health care pivoted workplace struggles in alignment with community concerns. Militant Black leadership was fundamental in this change. Writing in the magazine *Dissent*, journalist Thomas R. Brooks observed these developments and noted that "greater black participation in the unions will reinvigorate social unionism." More so than most of their white coworkers, Black men and women looked to more vigorous government activism in boosting living standards and, especially in the public sector, had a capacity to bring these solutions to the fore. "Local union leadership is a power base, and if that base can be utilized for action to solve community problems black labor leaders are going to act," Brooks continued. "It'll be worth watching."[36]

Since the momentous 1968 Memphis sanitation strike, AFSCME had been associated more than any other national union with the empowerment of African American workers. The iconic Black male sanitation worker had become part of the public imagination, linked to the impatience of Black communities with the status quo of political and economic second-class citizenship. Across the nation, Black Power groups formed new working-class organizations like the League for Revolutionary Black Workers to secure African American demands of control both on the job and where they lived. For some, the endgame was the overthrow of what they termed "white capitalism."[37] Though a small percentage of its members may have advocated such positions, AFSCME stood apart from these more radical aims, seeking not the destruction of urban liberal regimes but more say within them. By the end of 1972, AFSCME's secretary treasurer William Lucy helped launch the Coalition of Black Trade Unionists (CBTU), a national organization of Black trade union officers committed to advancing African American leadership within unions as a step toward realizing the political aims of Black working people in both national and local arenas.[38] Even with such emphasis, Lucy and other Black AFSCME leaders knew that pragmatic, interracial alliances were critical. Securing this kind of political coalition was at the top of the union's agenda in the early 1970s.

Organizing an average of one thousand members a week before the end of the 1960s, AFSCME had become a political powerhouse under the leadership of Jerry Wurf, who gained the union's national presidency in 1964. Calling for the continuation of Great Society–type programs, Wurf outlined a federal Freedom Budget based on Martin Luther King Jr.'s original platform to supplement local tax bases, a key step in securing living wages for city workers across the nation. Urban service expansion, free school lunch programs, an immediate end to the war in Vietnam, and a guaranteed annual living wage for all were pillars of the union's bold platform.[39] Legislative power was tantamount to attaining this, and Wurf prioritized a mobilization of the union's membership to forge a working-class, interracial political coalition. By 1972 the union had established a political action committee, the Public Employees Organized for Political Empowerment (PEOPLE), to strengthen the organization's legislative arm.

With polls showing growing public support for government sector unions, Jerry Wurf believed a historic moment for labor-community alliances was at hand. Addressing the surge in militant tactics, Wurf argued that civic concerns just as much as wage adjustments were at their root. "If you think the dynamic of unionization among city employees is cash and the desire for more of it, you are dead wrong," he said in May 1971. While economic betterment was no doubt part of this trend, "the voice that is provided the city worker through unionization and collective bargaining mechanisms helps him find his way out of the frustrating powerlessness of his situation." A quest for a more democratic lifestyle, for a say in all aspects of urban life, undergirded the public sector union movement and aligned these workers to the needs of their neighbors in the communities they served. "It is that same feeling of powerlessness that permeates our cities today, and, as surely as I know the city worker must have a voice through collective bargaining, I know, too, that the citizen of the community must share more of the power in decisions governing his and her life," Wurf argued.[40]

In the months after the trash slowdown, Earl Stout remained a highly visible public figure, considered by many to be the most powerful Black man in Philadelphia. Speaking at community forums and on radio programs, Stout called for Black political engagement and was more vocal in his opposition to the Vietnam War.[41] He remained an outspoken opponent of Frank Rizzo, who by now had launched a mayoral campaign. "I will not buy having a policeman as boss over my sanitation workers," Stout made clear in November 1970.[42] Such vehemence was common across the African American community, and the commissioner's mayoral bid sharpened efforts to increase voter registration. Black independents in the BPF looked to Hardy Williams, an African American state legislator from West Philadelphia, as their choice for mayor instead of Rizzo.[43] Many knew what chances Hardy had depended upon the candidate gaining the support of the groups that had backed the sanitation workers the previous year and thus hoped for the formal endorsement of their union. Earl Stout did not give it. His actions in these weeks pointed to a different path, one in which Black working-class leaders would stake an independent position from middle-class professionals.

In early 1971, Stout helped found a new organization, the United Black Labor Political Committee (UBLPC). Claiming to represent between thirty and forty thousand workers across the city, UBLPC was headed by United Steelworkers representative James Jones, the president of the city's Negro Trade Union Leadership Council, which eight years earlier had led a campaign to desegregate the city's building trades. The committee organized an independent political organization, the Save Our City Party, slating Joseph G. Feldman, a white lawyer and former school board member for mayor.[44] Quickly, the new party raised three hundred thousand dollars and moved forward with additional nominations, including Howard McCall, the Af-

162   ORGANIZING PUBLIC WORKERS

rican American president of AFSCME Local 403, for sheriff and, for a city council seat, Ray Turchi, a white man who had long served as president of Philadelphia's Joint Council of Hotel and Restaurant Employees.[45] Hardly political neophytes, the men of this slate were seasoned Democrats—and their break with the Tate wing of the party made clear the persistent divide in the party establishment and a lack of consensus over Rizzo's candidacy in these weeks. By splitting the party between Black communities across the city and whites who were uneasy about Rizzo, the Save Our City Party aimed to win a narrow primary win and provide the core for a new Democratic organization in the fall.

The Democratic Party City Committee took this challenge seriously and worked to block the UBLPC's independent party. Weeks later the board of city commissioners, which proctored city election regulations, barred it from the November ballot, claiming a shortage of prerequisite signatures of supporters.[46] The Tate-controlled Democratic Party Policy Committee in turn endorsed Rizzo, who also received the backing of the city's building trades and trucking unions. Charting an independent route, AFSCME DC 33 backed Congressman William J. Green III, citing his experience in Congress that would make him a champion in securing more federal funding. "I think this means that approximately 50,000 votes should go into the Green camp, and we will work for more," DC 33 president Charles Dade said.[47] Earl Stout joined the candidate on a door-to-door campaign in West and South Philadelphia and defended the candidate against claims from Hardy Williams that he ran a racist campaign.[48] On primary day, Frank Rizzo took the nomination with white working-class support, defeating Green by forty-six thousand votes, Hardy Williams trailing in third.

In predominantly Black divisions in North and West Philadelphia, Congressman Green outpolled Hardy Williams, a fact seasoned observers attributed to DC 33's mobilization efforts. Now, with Frank Rizzo as the 1971 Democratic Party candidate, the union was a key base for the opposition. Republican W. Thacher Longstreth, the Princeton-educated president of the city's chamber of commerce, who had no prior record of union support, became the unlikely candidate around which the city's African American and white liberals coalesced. Black membership strongholds of AFSCME Streets Department Locals 427 and 403 endorsed Longstreth, although DC 33, which had many sections of blue-collar whites working in public property, correctional facilities, and the airport pushing for Rizzo, remained officially uncommitted.[49] Politics again shaped this. Through primary season, union leadership took part in tense negotiations with the outgoing Tate administration. That June, seven thousand AFSCME members gathered in West

The Struggle for Black Independent Politics in Philadelphia   163

Philadelphia in a boisterous show of strength, approving a strike resolution if the city did not give in to demands by July 1. In an unusual move, Mayor Tate then took over contract negotiations himself and eventually offered a sizable one-year $650 across-the-board raise for all union members. Political observers saw this for the raw power move it was: in turn for this pay deal, DC 33 would sit out the November election.[50]

With the city's AFL-CIO support and the backing of a majority of the white blue-collar voters in South Philadelphia, Kensington, and Northeast sections of the city, Frank Rizzo won in November by fifty thousand votes. While claiming a "great victory," Rizzo knew that, by Philadelphia standards, his win was a close one. Philadelphia's electoral map showed a stark racial split. Rizzo won only one predominantly Black ward, in contrast to Jim Tate, who had won all of them just four years earlier. Close analysis revealed the untapped potential of the Black electorate: although Rizzo lost North Philadelphia's predominantly Black 28th Ward by a 5–1 margin, only four thousand of eighty-seven hundred registered voters showed up at the polls. In other North Philadelphia wards, more than half of eligible voters stayed home, a trend seen in West Philadelphia as well.[51] Looking to future power, Black political advocacy groups like the BPF doubled down on efforts to increase voter outreach and education. The city's unionized public sector organizations were now, more than ever, a needed partner in building a Black independent organization with an interracial, cross-class liberal coalition.

The Limits of Social Justice Unionism

While the prospect for broad coalition building between municipal workers and community groups seemed a given at the start of the decade, this hope soon faded. Even as more African American city officials attained office, the Black electorate—never a monolith—fractured along class lines. As voter registration drives in predominantly Black wards succeeded, and subsequent turnout on Election Day boosted, AFSCME DC 33's role as the city's primary Black political mobilization force waned. Traditions of independent action long ingrained in the history of Philadelphia's unionized blue-collar city workers, compounded by broader shifts in the nation's political culture, also influenced this turn.

As mayor, Frank L. Rizzo proved as polarizing a figure as he had as commissioner, his administration tainted by charges of corruption and poor services in Black communities. Police misconduct remained an underlying aspect of this criticism. Rizzo's governing style alienated key Democratic chieftains, and as in 1967, bitter internal fracture was apparent on the eve of the 1975 mayoral election. In the lead-up to this campaign season, John S. White Sr. noted that although Rizzo had previously maligned the Black community, in his need to manage party turmoil he now sought alliances, promising Black ward leaders greater influence at city hall. Such détente, White made clear, was not acceptable if Blacks wanted an independent political voice. "We consider any black that willfully joins an administration that is demonstrably anti-black an enemy," he said in April 1974.[52]

Forging alliances with white liberals with a shared dislike for Mayor Rizzo, and who might support a Black mayoral candidate in 1975, remained a primary goal for the Black Political Forum. Organized labor's progressive wing, which had some influential Black leaders at the helm, was a key bloc on which such a citywide interracial coalition could be built. Foremost among these was the National Union of Hospital and Health Workers Local 1199c, which over a five-year period had organized more than ten thousand mostly Black hospital service workers. Highly politicized, 1199c was led by Henry Nicholas, the son of Mississippi sharecroppers and a veteran civil rights activist who was one of Rizzo's most fervent critics. Wendell W. Young III, a white man who led the city's eleven-thousand-member Retail Clerks Union, which represented hundreds of African American liquor store clerks across the city, joined Nicholas in alliance against Rizzo. Following a bitter, monthlong strike in 1973, the city's seventeen-thousand-member Philadelphia Federation of Teachers also promised political resistance to another Rizzo term, as did AFSCME District Council 47, a small but militant section of municipal white-collar employees and social workers, many of whom came out of the student protest, antiwar, feminist, and gay rights movements. While not as numerous as the conservative building trades and Teamster unions that remained Rizzo's staunchest base, this labor-liberal section was an important hinge of the anti-Rizzo movement.[53]

Despite its fierce opposition to Frank Rizzo during the 1970 trash slowdown, AFSCME's three-thousand-member Sanitation Local 427 stood on the fringes of this emergent coalition. Practical priorities account for this. In 1974 Earl Stout succeeded Charles Dade as DC 33 president and, as he went into collective bargaining sessions with the city, promised real gains.[54] Aware of the kinds of political leverage that led to pay boosts under Mayor Tate, Stout built a pragmatic relationship with his former nemesis, a move that Rizzo seconded in his need to gain votes in a contested Democratic primary. Brokering a settlement just before the May election, the mayor signed off on a 13 percent pay boost—which granted each city employee a $1,100 raise— the largest ever recorded for blue-collar municipal workers in Philadelphia history, at a cost of $26.2 million. With this payoff, Stout mobilized union voters in African American wards across the city, gaining the mayor vital support. Black independents like John S. White Sr. were dismayed by this compromise, and even more so when AFSCME endorsed Rizzo over the BPF-endorsed candidate, Charles Bowser, who ran as an independent on the Philadelphia Party ticket. With white ethnic voters and labor support, Rizzo scored a resounding win. Still, the final ballot tally revealed a seismic shift in the city's political terrain as Bowser outpolled Republican Thomas Foglietta. Securing second place underscored the possibilities for Black political power, and leaders looked to 1979 as a time when their emerging political coalition might come through.[55]

With the 1975 deal, Earl Stout advanced his members' pay scales and reinforced his status as one of the city's most powerful union heads; simultaneously, however, it left him an isolated figure in the movement to secure an independent Black political organization. Assessing the city's power brokers in 1975, *Philadelphia Inquirer* reporter Lenora Berson acknowledged the significance Black labor leaders held in securing greater representation for African American citizens, identifying Henry Nicholas as the movement's most consequential figure. Stout seemed a more likely figure to play this role, she observed, but now that he was identified with Rizzo, his position had diminished. "It is hard for a black man to be a Rizzo man and still lay claim to leadership in his own community," Berson noted.[56] Earl Stout's reasoning was plain. Boasting that he had the power to shut down any city department with one phone call, he could act alone. He dismissed building community coalitions as a union aim and no longer saw the city's African American citizenry as a bulwark of support. Taxpayers, regardless of racial background, were not allies in the struggles faced by unionized city workers. "They've never been with us. No matter what we do to try and improve our image, they'll always be against us," Stout said in 1976.[57] While Jerry Wurf's earlier claim that more than just pay matters shaped AFSCME's programs in big cities, Stout's pronouncements suggest otherwise.

By the start of the 1980s, Stout's role as a lone power broker gained only limited payoffs for Philadelphia's blue-collar city workers. With the election of Ronald Reagan to the White House, drastic cuts in urban aid followed, and Philadelphia, like other big cities across the country, saw both service curtailments and public sector layoffs. In early 1983, Earl Stout positioned DC 33 behind the mayoral campaign of W. Wilson Goode, an African American liberal and a cofounder of the Black Political Forum, who had recently served as Mayor William J. Green III's managing director. Like other key representatives of the city's Black labor leadership and middle class, Stout believed the election of an African American mayor would be a historic achievement,

166   ORGANIZING PUBLIC WORKERS

opening better consideration for city workers. Following Goode's election later that year, the new mayor faced an unprecedented set of urban problems compounded by homelessness, the AIDS epidemic, further industrial decline, and suburban flight. City revenues dwindled and, compounded by the loss of federal aid, little money was available for wage boosts.[58]

In the face of Mayor Goode's demands for union givebacks, Stout led a three-week strike in the summer of 1986. This time the confrontation was a stark contrast to the one sixteen years earlier, as the sanitation, highway, and other city workers garnered little support, even from within the city's Black community. When reporters questioned whether he would imprison striking sanitation men who ignored an injunction to return to work, Goode responded, "Tell them to try me."[59] Having managed a difficult first few years in office, many saw the mayor's strong handling of this strike, which soon ended with the union's capitulation, as the reason he secured a second term.[60]

The events that transpired in 1986 resembled other public sector strikes in this period. In strategizing a response to the walkout, Mayor Goode consulted with former Atlanta mayor Maynard Jackson, that city's first Black executive, who had successfully resisted a 1977 strike by a majority–African American municipal workforce. Both the Atlanta and Philadelphia strikes revealed the transformed position of unionized Black municipal workers and their relation to ascendant Black political leaders. Reflecting on the impact of these changes in both public attitude and among African American elites, labor historian Robert Zeiger noted that, while seen as important icons of Black political rights after 1968, by the 1980s these "impoverished and victimized black workers had become greedy saboteurs of economic progress."[61] Sifting public views characterized by a national anti-tax movement and the corresponding rise of political conservatism severely limited the continued advancement of public sector unionists.[62] Such shifts marked the end of the line for the civil rights and Black working-class alliance. By this time, the hopes of the early 1970s, with militant Black sanitation workers at the lead, had been, for the most part, abandoned.

While inflation, a resurgent conservative movement, deindustrialization, and the corresponding decline of the labor movement were key factors in the curtailment of nascent public worker power in Philadelphia in the 1970s, other causes must also be factored in. By the 1980s, as W. Wilson Goode, Joseph Coleman, Lucian Blackwell, and other Black leaders gained more control over the powerful Democratic City Committee, overseeing financial resources that had previously been unavailable to them, AFSCME DC 33's influence in the local political order waned. Black voter registration surged, diminishing the union's former role as the primary voter-mobilizing force of a fragmented Black electorate. The union's limited economic program, based on its control of municipal service, and its rejection of coalition building with the communities they served, left it with little to offset this new dynamic. As twenty-first-century municipal workers and their union leaders struggle to redefine effective strategies in a new period of upheavals, an awareness of this earlier brief moment represented in the Philadelphia trash slowdown of 1970 may once again inspire broader, pragmatic, class-based urban alliances.[63]

Further Reading

Berger, Jane. *A New Working Class: The Legacies of Public Sector Employment in the Civil Rights Movement.* Philadelphia: University of Pennsylvania Press, 2021.

Honey, Michael K. *Going Down Jericho Road: The Memphis Strike, Martin Luther King's Last Campaign.* New York: W. W. Norton, 2007.

Johnston, Paul. *Success While Others Fail: Social Movement Unionism and the Public Workplace.* Ithaca, NY: ILR Press, 1994.

McCartin, Joseph A. "'Fire the Hell out of Them': Sanitation Workers' Struggles and the Normalization of the Striker Replacement Strategy in the 1970s." *Labor: Studies in Working-Class History* 2, no. 3 (2005): 67–92.

———. "'A Wagner Act for Public Employees': Labor's Deferred Dream and the Rise of Conservatism, 1970–1976." *Journal of American History* (June 2008): 123–48.

Ryan, Francis. *AFSCME's Philadelphia Story: Municipal Workers and Urban Power in the Twentieth Century.* Philadelphia: Temple University, 2011.

Saso, Carmen D. *Coping with Public Employee Strikes.* Chicago: Public Personnel Association, 1970.

Spero, Sterling D., and John Capozzola. *The Urban Community and Its Unionized Bureaucracies: Pressure Politics in Local Government Labor Relations.* New York: Dunellen, 1973.

Notes

1. Al Haas, "Brother Stout: A Job to Be Done," *Philadelphia Inquirer,* February 27, 1970.

2. Carmen D. Saso, *Coping with Public Employee Strikes* (Chicago: Public Personnel Association, 1970), iii; Aaron Brenner, "Striking against the State: The Postal Wildcat of 1970," *Labor's Heritage* 7, no. 4 (1996): 4–27; Stephen C. Shannon, "Work Stoppage in Government: The Postal Strike of 1970," *Monthly Labor Review* 101, no. 7 (1978): 14–22; "Trash Piles Growing in Job Dispute," *Asbury Park (NJ) Press,* February 18, 1970; "Trash Plagues Big City," *Palm Beach Post,* February 12, 1970; "Trash Crisis Hits City of Brotherly Love," *Bridgeport (PA) Telegram,* February 12, 1970; "In Philadelphia: 'A' for Effort at Cleanup," *Boston Evening Globe,* February 25, 1970; "Garbage Piles Up," *New York Daily News,* February 13, 1970; "Trash Is Accumulating in Philadelphia Dispute," *Chicago Tribune,* February 7, 1970.

3. Paul Johnston, *Success While Others Fail: Social Movement Unionism and the Public Workplace* (Ithaca, NY: ILR Press, 1994), 15–16.

4. For additional treatment of this topic in the 1970s, see Joseph A. McCartin, "Turnabout Years: Public Sector Unionism and the Fiscal Crisis," in *Rightward Bound: Making America Conservative in the 1970s*, ed. Bruce J. Schulman and Julian E. Zelizer (Cambridge, MA: Harvard University Press, 2008), 211.

5. "New Equipment for Street Cleaners," *Philadelphia Evening Bulletin*, September 27, 1969; H. James Laverty, "Smallwood Resigns as City Streets Chief; Halferty Gets Job," *Philadelphia Evening Bulletin*, January 30, 1970); Daniel J. McKenna, "Smallwood Cites Delay, Frustration for Quitting," *Philadelphia Evening Bulletin*, February 2, 1970; Wendell W. Young III, *The Memoirs of Wendell W. Young III: A Life in Philadelphia Labor and Politics*, ed. Francis Ryan (Philadelphia: Temple University, 2019), 150–51.

6. Charles Gilbert, "Police Are Human, Rizzo Says; Rejects Charges of Brutality," *Philadelphia Inquirer*, August 17, 1967; Ed Cunningham, dir., *Rizzo*, television documentary (Philadelphia: WHYY, 1999); Timothy J. Lombardo, *Blue-Collar Conservatism: Frank Rizzo's Philadelphia and Populist Politics* (Philadelphia: University of Pennsylvania, 2019), 52–60, 68–76, 140–41; Matthew J. Countryman, *Up South: Civil Rights and Black Power in Philadelphia* (Philadelphia: University of Pennsylvania, 2006), 230–57.

7. Michael von Moschzisker, "Police Venture into Politics," *Philadelphia Evening Bulletin*, February 12, 1970.

8. "Dropping the Engineer," *Philadelphia Evening Bulletin*, February 5, 1970.

9. Francis Ryan, *AFSCME's Philadelphia Story: Municipal Workers and Urban Power in the Twentieth Century* (Philadelphia: Temple University, 2011).

10. Michael K. Honey, *Going Down Jericho Road: The Memphis Strike, Martin Luther King's Last Campaign* (New York: W. W. Norton, 2007), 56–57. For a contemporary survey of civil service and race, see Ewart Guinier, "Impact of Unionization on Blacks," Unionization of Municipal Employees, *Proceedings of the American Academy of Political Science* 30, no. 2 (1970): 173–81; Martin J. Herman, "Trashmen Insist Tate Appoint from Ranks," *Philadelphia Evening Bulletin*, February 12, 1970.

11. Robert Rafsky, "Streets Workers Protest Appointment of Halferty," *Philadelphia Evening Bulletin*, January 31, 1970.

12. Joseph H. Trachtman, "Truck Shortage Boosts Costs of Trash Pick Up," *Philadelphia Inquirer*, February 15, 1968; Bill Fidati, "Workers in Clear on Street Grime, Union Aide Says," *Philadelphia Daily News*, August 20, 1969.

13. Bill Fidati, "Mayor Blisters Aides, Assumes Corleto's Job," *Philadelphia Daily News*, February 6, 1970.

14. "Trashmen Begin Removing Piles of 'Overtime' Rubbish," *Philadelphia Inquirer*, February 14, 1970.

15. Daniel J. McKenna and Brian C. Feldman, "City Trashmen Obey Order, Work Overtime," *Philadelphia Evening Bulletin*, February 13, 1970; "500 Leave Jobs to Picket Talks on Trash Dispute," *Philadelphia Daily News*, February 17, 1970; Alan L. Phillips, "Merchants Turn Trashmen," *Philadelphia Inquirer*, February 15, 1970; Robert Fowler, "Citizens Haul Trash, Look to Better Days," *Philadelphia Inquirer*, February 20, 1970.

16. Vincent P. Franklin, "The Philadelphia Race Riot of 1918," *Pennsylvania Magazine of History and Biography* 99, no. 3 (1975): 336–50.

17. Countryman, *Up South*, 154–71; Lombardo, *Blue-Collar Conservatism*, 49–51; "ACLU Assails Police Board," *Philadelphia Inquirer*, October 30, 1969; "Blacks Contest Police Story in Frankford Fight," *Philadelphia Inquirer*, April 3, 1969.

18. "Police, Politicians Turn Up at Funeral of Boy Shot by Cop," *Philadelphia Tribune*, September 6, 1969. For Levine quote, see *Philadelphia Tribune*, August 19, 1969; Frank Donner, *Protectors of Privilege: Red Squads and Police Repression in Urban America* (Berkeley: University of California Press, 1990), 197–229; "ADA Calls for Ghetto Action," *Philadelphia Inquirer*, March 17, 1968; Saul Kohler, "'Repeaters' Mock Law, Rizzo Says," *Philadelphia Inquirer*, September 22, 1967; Dennis Kirkland, "Slain Youth Attacked Officer, Report Says," *Philadelphia Inquirer*, February 2, 1970; "Rizzo Will Release Report, Shooting Probe Continues," *Philadelphia Inquirer*, March 6, 1970.

19. Donner, *Protectors of Privilege*, 226–27; Countryman, *Up South*, 290–93.

20. "38 Black Leaders Ask Tate to Recall Halferty," *Philadelphia Evening Bulletin*, February 14, 1970; "Hearing Today May End Hectic Trash Dispute," *Philadelphia Tribune*, February 21, 1970; Rev. J. J. Cooper to *Philadelphia Tribune*, February 24, 1970. See also "Ministers Too," Rev. T. C. Kilebrew, *Philadelphia Tribune*, February 24, 1970.

21. "Sanit Men Weigh Recall Move on Mayor," *Philadelphia Daily News*, February 17, 1970; "Tate Recall Petitions Taboo for City Aides," *Philadelphia Tribune*, February 24, 1970; Komozi Woodward, "It's Nation Time in NewArk: Amiri Baraka and the Black Power Experiment in Newark, New Jersey," in *Freedom North: Black Freedom Struggles Outside the South, 1940–1980*, ed. Jeanne F. Theoharis and Komozi Woodward (New York: Palgrave Macmillan, 2003), 287–311, esp. 298.

22. Doris E. Ballon, "Police State," *Philadelphia Tribune*, February 24, 1970.

23. Robert Fowler, "Trashmen Join Campaign to Remove Tate," *Philadelphia Inquirer*, February 17, 1970; Joseph Miller, "Tate Ouster May Be Sought," *Philadelphia Inquirer*, February 12, 1970; "GOP Looks Ahead, Scraps Tate Recall Effort," *Philadelphia Daily News*, February 27, 1970; Joseph H. Miller, "11th Hour Drives Begun by Parties to Get Out Heavy Vote Tuesday," *Philadelphia Inquirer*, November 2, 1969.

24. Joseph H. Miller, "Democrats Get Labor Funds for Aid in Negro Areas," *Philadelphia Inquirer*, November 5, 1968.

25. In 1956 Mayor Richardson Dilworth initiated a voter registration drive among Streets Department employees, securing over 90 percent participation. See David Smallwood to Mayor Dilworth, October 5, 1956, Mayor Richardson Dilworth Papers, folder: Streets, box A 491, Philadelphia City Archives. For union claims to control fifty thousand votes, see Desmond Ryan, "City Union Supports Green," *Philadelphia Inquirer*, April 22, 1971.

26. Pamala Haynes, "Street Cleaners Strongly Oppose Police Inspector as Commissioner," *Philadelphia Tribune*, February 7, 1970.

27. "Piled Up Refuse Called 'Menace' to Public Health, *Philadelphia Tribune*, February 14, 1970; Countryman, *Up South*, 308–313.

28. Len Lear, "No Man Can Serve 2 Masters Same Time," *Philadelphia Tribune*, March 3, 1970; Edna Thomas, "Walking Worms," *Philadelphia Tribune*, March 3, 1970.

29. Pamala Hayes, "Mayor Tate's Response Rejected by Trashman, Their Attorney Says, Halferty's Dismissal Is All They'll Accept[,] Norris Tells Tribune," *Philadelphia Tribune*, February 24, 1970. For a detailed overview of African American politics in Philadelphia in the twentieth century, see Clemmie L. Harris Jr., "Race, Leadership, and the Local Machine: The Origins of the Struggle for Political Recognition and the Politics of Community Control in Black Philadelphia, 1915–1968" (PhD diss., University of Pennsylvania, 2013).

30. Mrs. Henry C. Bailey Jr., "A Truck Driver's Wife," *Philadelphia Tribune*, March 3, 1970.

31. Daniel J. McKenna, "Tate Says He Can't Yield to Union on Halferty," *Philadelphia Evening Bulletin*, February 23, 1970.

32. Bill Fidati, "Sanit Men, Tate to Air Protest," *Philadelphia Daily News*, February 24, 1970.

33. "City Trashmen Back on Job, Cheer Victory," *Philadelphia Evening Bulletin*, February 26, 1970.

34. Francis M. Lordan and Leonard J. McAdams, "L.&I. Aide Gets Streets Post, New Deputy Also Appointed," *Philadelphia Inquirer*, March 4, 1970; Tom Fox, "Black Power Puts a Man with Class in City Hall," *Philadelphia Daily News*, March 4, 1970.

35. Al Haas, "Brother Stout: A Job to Be Done," *Philadelphia Inquirer*, February 27, 1970. For commentary on the possibilities of this new political alliance, see James Smith, "A Man Concerned: Support the Trashmen at the Ballot Box," *Philadelphia Tribune*, February 28, 1970.

36. Thomas R. Brooks, "Black Upsurge in the Unions," *Dissent* (March-April 1970): 124–34.

37. For a fuller treatment of the intersection of the Black Power movement and labor, see Dan Georgakas and Marvin Surkin, *Detroit: I Do Mind Dying: A Study in Urban Revolution* (Cambridge, MA: South End Press, 1998); David Goldberg and Trevor Griffey, eds., *Black Power at Work: Community Control, Affirmative Action, and the Construction Industry* (Ithaca, NY: Cornell University Press, 2010); Erik S. Gellman, "In the Driver's Seat: Chicago's Bus Drivers and Labor Insurgency in the Era of Black Power," *Labor: Studies in Working-Class History of the Americas* 11, no. 3 (2014): 49–76; Cedric Johnson, *Revolutionaries to Race Leaders: Black Power and the Making of African American Politics* (Minneapolis: University of Minnesota, 2007), 67–68. Earl Stout was a member of the A. Philip Randolph Institute, an organization formed by Randolph and Bayard Rustin in 1963 to foster labor–civil rights coalitions, advancing a program that understood black working-class advancement to the realization of a powerful national alliance with white workers, bound together through the AFL-CIO. For further overview of Black leadership challenges within the AFSCME international and the U.S. labor movement of this era, see Philip S.

Foner, "Organized Labor and the Black Workers in the 1970s," *Insurgent Sociologist*, 8 nos. 2–3 (1978): 87–95.

38. Manning Marable, *Race, Reform, and Rebellion: The Second Reconstruction and Beyond in Black America, 1945–2006*, 3rd ed. (Jackson: University of Mississippi Press, 2007), 115.

39. "Statement of the American Federation of State, County, and Municipal Employees, AFL-CIO to the Black Political Convention, March 11, 1972," AFSCME Secretary Treasurer Office: Chapman/Ames Records, box 11, folder 5, Archives of Labor and Urban Affairs, Wayne State University, Detroit, MI.

40. "Wurf: Conference on Cities, Indianapolis, Indiana, May 1971," AFSCME Secretary Treasurer Office: Ames/Chapman Records, box 9, folder 44, Archives of Labor and Urban Affairs, Wayne State University, Detroit, MI.

41. "Leaders of Antiwar Groups Meet, Issue Joint Statement," *Philadelphia Evening Bulletin*, December 30, 1971; "Delegates to Draft List of Blacks for City Posts," *Philadelphia Inquirer*, January 20, 1971.

42. "Stout Hints Sanitation Men Would Oppose Bid by Rizzo," *Philadelphia Evening Bulletin*, November 22, 1970.

43. Charles Thomas, "Policemen 'Enjoyed' Breaking Up Protest, Union Aide Testifies," *Philadelphia Inquirer*, January 3, 1968; Dennis Kirkland, "300 Delegates Draw Platform at Convention," *Philadelphia Inquirer*, February 14, 1971; Acel Moore, "Slate of Black Candidates Headed by Williams Endorsed by Blacks," *Philadelphia Inquirer*, February 15, 1971; Dennis Kirkland, "Leroi Jones Urges Blacks to Use 'Ballots, Not Bullets,'" *Philadelphia Inquirer*, February 13, 1971.

44. Acel Moore, "Rizzo Must Be Stopped in Bid for Mayor, SCLC Aid Says," *Philadelphia Inquirer*, March 22, 1971; Dan Lynch, "3rd Party Is Formed by Black Unionists to Help Beat Rizzo," *Philadelphia Inquirer*, March 13, 1971.

45. Orrin Evans, "New Political Party Formed by Negro Labor Leaders," *Philadelphia Evening Bulletin*, March 12, 1971; Dan Lynch, "3d Party Is Formed by Black Unionists to Help Beat Rizzo," *Philadelphia Inquirer*, March 13, 1971; "Feldman Vows Strong Effort in Mayor Race," *Philadelphia Evening Bulletin*, March 13, 1971; "An Independent Files for Mayor before Deadline," *Philadelphia Inquirer*, April 1, 1971; "Feldman Loses Right to Place on City Ballot," *Philadelphia Evening Bulletin*, April 9, 1971; Harmon Y. Gordo, "Save Our City Faction Loses Ballot Fight," *Philadelphia Evening Bulletin*, July 7, 1971.

46. Orrin Evans, "New Political Party Formed by Negro Labor Leaders," *Philadelphia Evening Bulletin*, March 12, 1971; Dan Lynch, "3d Party Is Formed by Black Unionists to Help Beat Rizzo," *Philadelphia Inquirer*, March 13, 1971; "Feldman Vows Strong Effort in Mayor Race," *Philadelphia Evening Bulletin*, March 13, 1971; "An Independent Files for Mayor before Deadline," *Philadelphia Inquirer*, April 1, 1971; "Feldman Loses Right to Place on City Ballot" *Philadelphia Evening Bulletin*, April 9, 1971; Harmon Y. Gordo, "Save Our City Faction Loses Ballot Fight," *Philadelphia Evening Bulletin*, July 7, 1971.

47. Desmond Ryan, "City Union Supports Green," *Philadelphia Inquirer*, April 22, 1971.

48. Cliff Linedecker, "Shapp Joins Green's Motorcade, Predicts His Victory," *Philadelphia Inquirer*, May 16, 1971; "Green Not 'Racist' Earl Stout Declares, *Philadelphia Inquirer*, April 15, 1971.

49. Tom Fox, "The Press Conference," *Philadelphia Daily News*, October 13, 1971.

50. "Blackmail to Us," *Philadelphia Daily News*, June 11, 1971; Fred Smigelski, "City Workers Vote for Strike if Pact Isn't Signed by July 1," *Philadelphia Inquirer*, June 17, 1971; Don McDonough, "Employees Union Frequently Plays Politics Despite Prohibition in Home Rule Charter," *Philadelphia Inquirer*, June 20, 1971; "Get Ready, Jim Tate," *Philadelphia Daily News*, June 18, 1971; Jeremy Heymsfeld and Thomas Madden, "Did the Mayor Play Politics on Employees' Wage Raise?," *Philadelphia Inquirer*, June 28, 1971; Harold J. Wiegand, "No Politics: Jim Is Just Big-Hearted," *Philadelphia Inquirer*, July 2, 1971.

51. Dan Lynch, "White Working Class Elects Rizzo Despite Blacks, Liberals, Youth," *Philadelphia Inquirer*, November 3, 1971.

52. "Black Political Forum Has List of Its 'Enemies,'" *Philadelphia Evening Bulletin*, April 29, 1974; Laura Murray, "Blacks Must Dump Rizzo, Bowser Says," *Philadelphia Evening Bulletin*, June 10, 1974.

53. Young, *Memoirs of Wendell W. Young III*, 134–98.

54. John T. Gillespie, "$2500 Wage Rise to Be Sought by Our City Employees," *Philadelphia Evening Bulletin*, November 27, 1974.

55. Young, *Memoirs of Wendell W. Young III*, 188–89; Ryan, *AFSCME's Philadelphia Story*, 193.

56. Lenora Berson, "The Power Game," *Today: Philadelphia Inquirer*, March 23, 1975, 24–28, esp. 28.

57. "Unresolved Contracts Delay Layoff of Philadelphia Workers," *Philadelphia Inquirer*, July 9, 1976.

58. Ryan, *AFSCME's Philadelphia Story*, 201–204.

59. Vernon Loeb and Robin Clark, "As the Trash Goes, the Strike Weakens," *Philadelphia Inquirer*, July 20, 1986.

60. Young, *Memoirs of Wendell W. Young III*, 235–36; Ryan, *AFSCME's Philadelphia Story*, 204–209.

61. Robert H. Zieger, *For Jobs and Freedom: Race and Labor in America since 1865* (Lexington: University Press of Kentucky, 2007), 206; Ronald H. Bayor, "African-American Mayors and Governance in Atlanta," in David R. Colburn and Jeffrey S. Adler, *African-American Mayors: Race, Politics, and the American City* (Urbana: University of Illinois, 2001), 178–99, esp. 180–86; Joseph A. McCartin, "'Fire the Hell Out of Them': Sanitation Workers' Struggles and the Normalization of the Striker Replacement Strategy in the 1970s," *Labor: Studies in Working Class History* 2, no. 3 (2005): 67–92; Nelson Lichtenstein, *State of the Union: A Century of American Labor* (Princeton, NJ: Princeton University Press, 2002), 232. See also Bruce J. Schulman,

The Seventies: The Great Shift in American Culture, Society, and Politics (Cambridge, MA: Da Capo Press, 2002), 193–217.

62. Joseph A. McCartin, 'A Wagner Act for Public Employees': Labor's Deferred Dream and the Rise of Conservatism, 1970–1976," *Journal of American History* (June 2008): 123–48; Joseph A. McCartin, "Turnabout Years: Public Sector Unionism and the Fiscal Crisis," in *Rightward Bound: Making America Conservative in the 1970s*, ed. Bruce J. Schulman and Julian E. Zelizer, 210–226 (Cambridge, MA: Harvard University Press, 2008).

63. For an overview of the ecology of urban power in the early twenty-first century, see Michael B. Katz, "Why Aren't U.S. Cities Burning?" *Dissent* (Summer 2007): 23–29.

PART IV

Public Workers in the Neoliberal Age

This pairing of chapters by Amy Zanoni and Jon Shelton allows us to pause and reflect upon just how invisible public sector workers can be; even key, nationally significant positions can be overlooked with popular mainstream interest, hyperfocused on high-profile entertainers or capitalists. Yet, two groups of laborers who silently report for duty, all to our collective relief, are hospital workers and teachers. One shudders to think just how different and difficult life would be if these individuals abandoned their responsibilities all at once. Most likely, the public would become enraged, upset that these workers violated an implicit social contract of sorts—in other words, their work is so important, the public virtually requires that these laborers dutifully report for work out of a sense of moral obligation.

If society implicitly understands the importance of these contributions, what remains curious is why these groups of workers continue to struggle in less than ideal working conditions with less than ideal pay. Ironically, the government's paternalistic assumptions about the caretaking value of these workers prompted both groups to organize, using the union model as a means to defend collective interests for undervalued and overworked employees who have little room to negotiate.

Both chapters raise resonant questions concerning economic security and how it directly affects economic citizenship and the contributions demanded of public workers. Namely, when those who work directly for the common good recognize their common interest to personally profit from their efforts, sacrifices, and labors, does it then become problematic for society? In publicly run institutions such as hospitals and schools, the quality of work and care are often interconnected. Zanoni and Shelton force us to wrestle with the larger epistemological question of whether an economic premium should be assigned and assessed for such labor or whether the work—insofar as it serves the greater good—is sufficient reward unto itself.

CHAPTER 8

Sick-Ins, Feed-Ins, Heal-Ins, and Strikes

Labor Organizing at Chicago's Public Hospital in the 1960s and Its Legacy for the 1970s

AMY ZANONI

"In my job," Lillie Jones told an interviewer in the early 1990s, "you had to have compassion for the patient—you put yourself in that patient's place." Although an experienced food service worker at Cook County Hospital (CCH, or County) since 1963, Jones herself had been a patient at CCH a few years before starting in her position. In the 1960s, Jones remembered, CCH "was not so clean. They had roaches and rats crawling over your feet." The atmosphere was depressing, with the hospital lobby painted a dour color Jones described as "battleship gray." Labor conditions for the almost entirely Black female food service or dietary staff were poor as well. For these workers tasked with preparing food and delivering it to patients, according to Jones, "the pay was lousy" and employees were overworked.[1] Other food service workers described an unsafe environment and hospital management's "complete lack of respect" for staff.[2] Supervisors used threatening and degrading language when giving directives to employees. Rather than "asking you to do something, it was, 'You better or you're going to get fired,'" Jones remembered.[3]

Like other public hospitals in the twentieth-century United States, CCH was a vital safety net for uninsured and other marginalized Chicagoans in need of health care as well as a major employer for the city's working-class residents and medical professionals. But as Jones's memories suggest, patients and workers alike faced grim circumstances at CCH in the 1960s. In response, hospital employees, including Jones, organized. This chapter analyzes how public hospital employees turned to collective action to improve labor and patient conditions in this period. Their collective struggles for accountability and dignified work and care at the public institution led to tangible changes in leadership and hospital conditions and formed the foundation for resistance against threats to this crucial institution in the years that followed.[4]

For marginalized Chicagoans in need of healing in the 1960s, CCH was in certain ways a citadel from discrimination and the private medical care system. At the time, it was Chicago's only public hospital and the largest public hospital in the United States.[5] In the mid-1960s, the public hospital cared for upward of 750,000 Chicagoans each year, the vast majority of whom were African American and medically indigent or unable to afford medical care. At excess capacity, the hospital had twenty-eight hundred beds.[6] Private hospitals sometimes refused care for Black patients, sending them instead to County. It was not only that the growing numbers of Black Chicagoans were uninsured and unable to pay for medical care; some private hospitals denied care to Black Chicagoans even when they carried insurance. This common practice of private hospitals sending patients they deemed undesirable to the public hospital, which treated all who came through its doors, was known as patient "dumping."[7] CCH counted over four thousand people on its staff to care for patients and maintain the building.[8]

Serving as the city's health care safety net without adequate resources and under the leadership of public officials known for working in undemocratic ways meant that CCH conditions suffered, sometimes severely. Throughout the 1960s, CCH was "an institution in trouble," one *Chicago Daily Defender* reporter wrote in 1964. The hospital was crammed with patients and understaffed across all echelons of labor; patient care was suffering and so were the hospital employees who were providing it. In 1964 crowding at CCH was so severe that patients were "placed on cots in the corridor" because wards were at maximum capacity. Two infants died after CCH staff sent them home from the hospital's packed emergency room.[9] Later in the decade, crowding persisted, and overworked personnel were frustrated by their inability to provide the care they thought necessary. "We have to steal equipment from each other," one nurse told the *Defender*. It was difficult to keep up with the workload, which sometimes meant patients were left to sit in soiled linens.[10] To free up beds, physicians had to discharge patients before they were medically ready. The predominantly white union leadership who represented support staff and the public officials who ran the hospital engaged in backdoor political dealings, undermining accountability on the hospital floor.

In the face of these circumstances, CCH workers organized for labor rights, social justice, and decent treatment for patients and workers in the public sector. With expectations for labor and health care conditions rising in the context of the Black freedom movement, hospital employees joined together to demand improvements at the hospital and accountability from public officials, hospital management, and union leaders. CCH workers fought for control over their labor through unionization and opposition to patronage politics; they threatened and used strikes and other job actions to achieve just wages and safe working and patient conditions. The nature of their demands suggests that these worker struggles must be seen as an integral part of Black freedom and other social justice movements of this era and central to efforts to defend the public sector.

Public hospitals were not the only organizing hot spots in the late 1960s. Private hospital workers were also organizing, and in their struggles they often centered on demands for racial justice.[11] As the organized labor power of mostly white male industrial workers plateaued, many white women, as well as Black and Latinx men and women, working in the public and service sectors across the country formed new unions to assert their rights. Historians of these struggles have drawn attention to the alternative organizing models of nonindustrial workers, who often enlisted the support of their clients and patients when they demanded the professionalization and state protection of their labor in the 1960s and after.[12] Scholars of public sector unionism have documented how those struggles were central to the Black freedom movement in the 1960s.[13] And historians of Chicago's Black freedom movement have traced the intersections between labor, Black liberalism, and Black Power, shedding light on mostly failed attempts to dislodge the prejudice built into Chicago's labor system, particularly in the construction trades.[14] By looking to organizing in the public hospital, an underexplored site in which caring labors and the public sector intersected, I suggest that these workers waged struggles for racial justice but also pioneered movements for public accountability and the public good.[15]

In this period of growing social movement activity, public hospital employees—from dietary staff, to registered nurses, to physicians—participated in efforts to better conditions at the public hospital. I argue that a series of public labor actions at Cook County Hospital in the late 1960s and early 1970 helped launch a tradition of organizing that shaped the hospital's history for years to come. Women workers—including women of color in low-wage positions—carried out the first large-scale job actions at CCH, using tactics that would come to be almost commonplace in the next decade. Nurses criticized the effect that Democratic machine control of CCH had on patient care and demanded labor rights to improve conditions for themselves and patients. Hospital support staff, predominantly Black and working class like their patients, brought a new level of militancy to CCH when they fought for union recognition, dignity, and accountability in their workplace. The activism of physicians followed, focusing on patient care more explicitly. Together, these struggles were part of a larger movement to rein in Chicago's Democratic machine and to make the public institution more accountable to its employees and patients. The organizing tradition these public workers launched in the 1960s formed a solid foundation on which struggles over the survival of CCH were fought in the following decades, when, in the context of inflation, revenue shortfalls, and mounting deficits, many public officials and their allies in the private sector called for CCH's closure.

Exposing Labor and Patient Conditions

One hundred years after county officials established Cook County Hospital to care for the medically indigent in 1866, conditions were dire. Due to the ongoing problem of patient dumping, the hospital was crowded. There were scarcities in staff and funding, leaving physical hospital conditions deteriorated and triggering a crisis in 1963. That year, the Joint Commission on the Accreditation of Hospitals (JCAH), the body charged with granting accreditation to hospitals, called CCH "grossly and dangerously overcrowded," particularly in obstetrics-gynecology, and "below minimal requirements for registered nurses for all services."[16] The hospital, like the rest of the nation, faced a nursing shortage.[17] The 1965 passage of the first national public health insurance programs, Medicaid and Medicare, did mean fewer patients coming through CCH's doors, since some formerly uninsured, including the elderly and those who qualified for the means-tested Medicaid program, could now turn to private providers for their care. But crowding continued in the years immediately after these Great Society programs were instituted, since private providers were still turning away patients and the lack of effective public education meant that not all who qualified knew about Medicaid.[18]

The 1967 death of Lena Fulwiley epitomized the severity of another aspect of the crisis: grave problems with the quality of health care being delivered. The fifteen-year-old African American girl arrived at County suffering from severe abdominal pains and holding a doctor's note indicating that she might have appendicitis. Instead, the CCH interns staffing the emergency room diagnosed her with venereal disease. Fulwiley died the next day of a ruptured appendix.[19] With the dilapidated state of hospital conditions, Fulwiley's death prompted *Chicago Daily Defender* associate editor Betty Washington and photographer Bob Black to investigate CCH in late 1967 and early 1968 and to publish a series of articles exposing County conditions. After she and Black spent a Saturday night at the hospital, Washington reported, "A walk through the wards at Cook County Hospital is an enlightening and depressing experience, particularly if you are familiar with facilities at other hospitals." She described a pool of blood on the floor, already hardened when they arrived and "not yet mopped up" when they left two hours later. They found "double rows of beds down the center of the large wards in the men's building," and privacy limited to a "single drape across the entrance to the ward." The journalists recounted flaking paint falling into a crib where a child was sleeping and included a photograph to let readers see the conditions for themselves.[20]

In her investigative reporting, Washington elevated the voices of employees, especially nurses. Most registered nurses (RNs) at County were white in the mid-1960s. Just over one-fourth of CCH RNs were women of color. A much greater percentage of licensed practical nurses (LPNs) and other support staff were Black.[21] The nurses criticized the patronage system of appointing hospital employees. There was a long tradition of hospital hiring going through precinct captains and aldermen, who demanded Democratic Party work in exchange for jobs. The Cook County Board of Commissioners, which oversaw CCH's budget and operations, was usually in the grip of Chicago's Democratic machine.[22] The nursing staff, employed by the Cook County School of Nursing rather than directly by the hospital, had escaped patronage but criticized patronage hiring of their CCH coworkers.

Nurses opposed patronage on the basis that it undermined professionalism and patient care. Five hundred of seven hundred nurses, nurses' aides, and orderlies signed a petition against a 1964 proposal to bring the nursing school under the direct administration of the hospital. In the *Daily Defender*, nurses complained that patronage employees disappeared from their hospital posts on Election Day; the mostly housekeeping, laundry, and dietary department staff, nurses said, were instead away helping party officials secure votes. This arrangement threatened care, the nurses argued. RN Hortense Thomas told the *Defender*, "We are concerned about the bedside care of the patients. We must be on the alert for their care and available for their service 24 hours of every day. Holidays and election days are unthinkable when human lives are in the balance."[23] Cook County Board president Richard Ogilvie—a Republican reformer—implemented a civil service system in 1966, the year he was elected.[24] Civil service meant that elected officials would no longer appoint hospital staff. Instead, employees would be hired according to merit, determined by civil service exams. Some workers, including food service worker Lillie Jones, had left their appointed positions and returned to County through the Civil Service Commission.[25] But still, in November 1967, nurses complained that the practice persisted and that patronage workers were not pulling their weight.[26]

After Fulwiley's death, nurses spoke out against broader trends compromising the quality of care at CCH. The School of Nursing filed a report with the Cook County Board in December 1967, in which they detailed a lack of equipment so severe that patients were required to share aspirators, and extreme overcrowding, with bassinets stacked practically on top of each other. They decried poor lighting, lack of refrigeration and ice, corroded equipment, and overall filthy conditions.[27] Individual nurses told the *Defender* that understaffing and overcrowding made it difficult for them to do their work well.[28] Employees described diarrhea epidemics among children, and one confessed, "I would not want my baby to go there." Washington claimed that "in the midst of this the nurses still managed to be Florence Nightingales." One nurse told the reporter that they were doing "the best we can."[29]

Nurses and support staff pushed for improvements for patients on a daily basis. Lillie Jones reminisced about this legacy of agitating for better, more dignified treatment for patients in a 1993 oral history interview. The job was difficult, she remembered: "I served food all over the hospital. There were so many patients to be served. A hundred and forty on some wards, 175 on others. It was hard work." Still, she took on the additional task of advocating for patients: "The food was awful when I started [in 1963]. Garbage." But "in the years later, the food improved, I think because we raised Cain," Jones said, highlighting the impact of her rabble-rousing.[30] Nurses also took credit for improvements: "When new curtains go up in this place it is because the nurses have made the curtains or purchased them." They bought TVs with their own money, to "take way some of the gloom on the wards."[31]

Building an Organizing Momentum

Many CCH employees saw bettering their own working conditions through collective action as a way to improve hospital care. Yet, there were substantial barriers to organizing for public hospital workers in the 1960s. In Illinois there was no labor legislation guaranteeing collective bargaining for public workers. The National Labor Relations Act of 1935 did not extend to those employed in the public sector, and the State of Illinois did not formally grant public employees collective bargaining rights until 1983, despite repeated attempts starting in 1945. The lack of legal protections, however, did not mean a lack of organizing. Industrial relations scholar Milton Derber estimates that in 1967 a third of nonfederal public employees in Illinois were part of unions or other collective bargaining organizations, with professional workers including teachers, social workers, and nurses making the most substantive gains.[32] Still, organized public workers, including CCH staff, had murky legal standing.

In the 1960s, the Illinois Nurses Association (INA), originally founded in 1901 as a professional organization, deployed bolder pressure tactics to secure labor rights and higher wages. In 1966, CCH nurses promised mass resignations if they were not granted collective bargaining rights. They succeeded in getting a contract.[33] Soon after, and on the heels of a successful public hospital nurses' strike in San Francisco, CCH RNs pushed for a wage increase they said would ameliorate the hospital's nursing shortage. To shed light on what the shortage meant for patient care, RNs organized what they called a "feed-in." One day in September, off-duty nurses volunteered their labor during lunchtime, helping feed pediatric and disabled patients. By stuffing the wards with extra hands, they hoped to address—and probably to expose—the dire implications of understaffing, which included those who needed assistance going unfed. Days later when they again threatened mass resignations, nurses received their raise.[34]

As nurse militancy escalated, the INA continued to draw connections between the quality of patient care and labor rights.[35] Nurses threatened another strike in 1967, this time for salary increases, and vowed to bring licensed practical nurses out with them.[36] As nurses prepared for their job action, they promised to help the hospital develop a contingency plan to ensure care for the hospitals' approximately two thousand patients. The plan included the provision of emergency care and helping transfer patients to other hospitals. Quality patient care and workers' rights, they showed, were not at odds. One county commissioner drew on common tropes about women's work in caring sectors to criticize the nurses' demands for the right to higher compensation. "They seem to have forgotten their obligations to suffering humanity and appear to be thinking only of their own selfish interest and pay checks," he wrote in a *Chicago Tribune* opinion piece.[37] But county officials gave in to nurses' demands at the final hour, preventing the strike from taking place.[38] Later that year, nurses threatened to strike over pay, arguing that wages at County should be higher than those at private hospitals; otherwise, they would not be able to attract workers to care for the city's sickest patients.[39] They also demanded improvements to hospital equipment, supplies, working conditions, and the building itself, linking labor demands to the quality of public sector services and infrastructure.[40]

Amid growing militancy and nationwide movements tying public and service sector work to civil rights and feminist struggles, CCH's LPNs, clerical staff, and dietary workers—all predominantly women of color—also organized. In many instances, these were the members of CCH staff who interacted most closely with hospital patients and thus were most attuned to their challenging experiences. Many CCH employees also came from the same class and race backgrounds as patients. Some employees were patients or had been previously, as with food service worker Lillie Jones.[41] The memoir of a white nurse who trained at County in the early 1970s described a Black CCH clerk who had delivered children and received cardiac care at County and who recommended the hospital to family and friends who encountered discrimination elsewhere. She also remembered a classmate who had been inspired to pursue a nursing career after being treated for a gunshot wound at County.[42] These connections often spurred hospital staff to push for improvements in County conditions, both for themselves and for the patients for whom they helped care.

These workers frequently highlighted the relationship between employment conditions, including racial discrimination, and the quality of patient care. In 1964 an anonymous letter to the *Defender* charged that Black nursing attendants were given the "largest and heaviest assignments," tasked at times with caring for fifty to one hundred patients on their own. Another reported "deplorable . . . treatment of some of their employees of darker skin from the islands and the U.S.A." Both letters connected employment discrimination to the care provided at CCH, suggesting that understaffed wards compromised the quality of care. "Patients are suffering because of this prejudice," one wrote.[43]

Many of the support staff's early organized labor actions prioritized higher wages. Motivated by RNs who had threatened mass resignations, LPNs sought raises at CCH using similar tactics. In October 1967 all but three LPNs, an estimated 350 in total, called in sick for two days in October, forcing the hospital to stop admitting patients except for in emergency cases. This work disruption yielded results. The nurses received a 12–15% wage increase the next day.[44]

Perhaps inspired by the spirit of organizing traveling through County's aging corridors, clerks and attendants also organized but focused on transforming the existing system of labor organization that failed to protect low-wage workers of color. Service Employees International Union (SEIU) Local 46, a service worker union, nominally represented many CCH and other Chicago service workers.[45] During negotiations between Local 46 and administration in early 1969, a militant majority of ward clerks and attendants organized a "wildcat sick call" to add pressure to their demands for a wage increase, paid health insurance, more vacation time, increased pay for night shifts, and reimbursement for their uniforms. The wildcat group, made up of workers who did not feel adequately represented by their union, included eight hundred of eleven hundred clerks and attendants.[46] Dissatisfaction with the current labor arrangement was widespread. In response, a white union official representing another SEIU local wrote to SEIU president David Sullivan, who was also white, that the public worker union American Federation of State, County, and Municipal Employees (AFSCME) had "stepped in" to organize clerks at County two years earlier. The extent of AFSCME's involvement in the wildcat action is unclear. The representative's comment might have referred to an explicit AFSCME campaign to organize the clerks, or perhaps to the union's efforts in recent years to organize Chicago public sector workers. AFSCME District Council 19 had lent its support to racial justice causes and sharply criticized political control of unions.[47] In response, SEIU seemed to view AFSCME and Black freedom groups similarly bent on undermining the city's political machine as a threat. "We do not want this to happen again nor do we want such an 'Operation Bread Basket' to replace the union," the SEIU representative said. He was referring to the Chicago chapter of the Southern Christian Leadership Conference's racial and economic organization, led by Jesse Jackson. In recent years, Operation Breadbasket had organized job training programs, boycotts to pressure Chicago businesses to hire Black workers, and a statewide campaign against hunger. SEIU seemed to fear that with Operation Breadbasket's backing, AFSCME could usurp SEIU's control.[48]

The "First Strike"

Food service workers were also dissatisfied with SEIU Local 46 and directly embraced AFSCME as a path to collective bargaining and a better work environment. SEIU Local 46 claimed to have represented food service workers—along with housekeeping, laundry, and janitorial staff—since the 1940s, but many did not consider themselves to be part of the local, or at least did not find the union to be a reliable or effective advocate.[49] Local 46 "was like a company union," Jones remembered. A reporter sympathetic to the workers called Local 46 president John Masse a "political hack." Instead of negotiating contracts, the union leaders made backroom deals with hospital supervisors and county officials.[50] Workers still saw unionization as integral to their struggle against persistent workplace grievances. In 1969 they rejected SEIU and opted to join AFSCME District Council 19 to address working conditions that one employee described as "a slave system."[51] "When you think of what happens to us in our everyday work life, you get angry!" members of the organizing committee wrote. "And when you get angry enough, you decide to do something about it." Like the better-documented campaigns of groups such as the Coalition for United Community Action, who during the summer of 1969 were fighting for workplace justice for Black men in the construction industry, members of AFSCME Council 19 were attempting to reform Chicago's labor system, which organizers saw as corrupt and racist. Food service workers said of their decision to join AFSCME, "WE KNOW THERE IS NO OTHER WAY."[52]

With no public sector legislation in place, public hospital dietary staff pointed to precedent when insisting on their right to bargain with county officials. In July 1969, Council 19 staff representative Neal A. Bratcher, an outspoken racial justice advocate, wrote to Cook County Board president George Dunne to ask for a meeting, telling him that the majority of County's food service employees had signed union cards indicating they wanted AFSCME to represent them.[53] Dunne, who replaced Republican Richard Ogilvie when he was elected governor in January 1969, was part of the Democratic machine. He refused to meet with workers on the basis that the state legislature had failed to pass public sector labor legislation. AFSCME Council 19's director Carmen Mendoza wrote to Dunne that the union was "shocked" at his "basically anti-union attitude." Mendoza, a Chicago native of Mexican descent, had joined AFSCME's staff in 1964, after working with the Cardinal's Committee for the Spanish Speaking, a Catholic organization that formed in the 1950s to assist new immigrants adjusting to life in Chicago. (The organization had advocated for translation services at CCH and protested the termination of such services in the early 1960s.)[54] Though she chided the state legislature for failing to enact bargaining legislation, Mendoza insisted that because of a Chicago teachers' union precedent, Dunne had the option to recognize the public employees' union on behalf of the Cook County Board of Commissioners.[55] Mendoza charged that Dunne's antiunionism echoed "employer attitudes of the 1930s as well as the more recent attitudes of the Southern Mayors towards public employee unions." She warned, "We do not want a repetition of Charleston," referring to the 113-day hospital worker strike that lasted from March through June in Charleston, South Carolina.[56]

The mostly Black female hospital workers at two Charleston hospitals rallied the support of national civil rights leaders as well as the Charleston community, which waged a boycott in support of striking workers. In the end, the administrations gave in to some worker demands, such as new grievance procedure, but meaningful gains, including union recognition, remained at bay in the right-to-work state.[57]

Other unionists saw Council 19's organizing efforts as a viable threat to the established order of labor relations wherein white union leaders engaged in backdoor negotiations with white management and political officials and failed to represent all workers. In mid-September, the leadership of SEIU Local 46 called AFSCME's unionization struggle a "raid" and declared their intentions to file a charge against AFSCME for violating Article XX of the AFL-CIO constitution, which prohibited unions from attempting to organize already organized workers.[58] SEIU officials anticipated difficulty, especially from AFSCME's alliance with Chicago Black freedom organizations. One official wrote that he saw AFSCME's organizing drive as "a very serious problem" that could threaten Local 46's stronghold in sectors made up of predominantly Black workers: "I feel certain that if successful, State County will launch a major organizing campaign. I believe also that a breakthrough into Local 46 could result in some of the militant civil rights organizations becoming involved due to the large percentage of Negro employees involved."[59]

Local 46's suspicions may have derived, at least in part, from the convergence of Black freedom and labor activism in Chicago in recent months. Historians have chronicled how the Coalition for United Community Action (CUCA), a Black Power coalition group that included Operation Breadbasket, other civil rights and community groups, and members of Chicago youth gangs, supported efforts to increase the number of Black workers in the building trades in this period. To force the construction industry and unions to hire Black men, who were disproportionately unemployed in the context of ongoing discrimination and deindustrialization, CUCA shut down federal construction sites in the summer of 1969—part of what historian Erik Gellman has called CUCA's "formidable challenge to deep-seated institutional racism" in Chicago.[60] Like the Black trade worker organizing campaign, the efforts of this mostly Black female segment of public workers to have AFSCME represent them challenged existing labor relations.

Food service workers and their AFSCME representatives were building momentum around their campaign for recognition, wages, and dignity. On September 9, 1969, dietary workers took their unionization struggle to the next level by waging a "sick-in." Union representatives estimated that 83 percent of workers participated, protesting the hospital administration's and the County board's refusal to recognize their union, along with grievances including wages that fell below the federal poverty level ($393/month starting salary).[61] The workers warned that a more drastic action was in store if the county government continued to not recognize their union. Nine days later, workers decided unanimously to picket the County Building in an attempt to "express themselves directly to the County Board members." They handed out flyers that detailed their reasons for picketing—low wages and poor working conditions—as well as their demands, including "the dignity of being treated like men and women, not like children!" The workers were dedicated to collective bargaining through a union and blamed their protest on their employer's refusal to recognize them as such.[62] Workers had been appealing to the County board for union recognition since July and were running out of patience.[63] On September 26 the union took a strike vote but vowed to give the board "every opportunity to respond to justice and equality."[64] The board agreed to offer the union dues check-off and a grievance procedure but no contract. The workers were not satisfied.[65] Cook County Board president Dunne asked for ten days to consult legal experts about how to proceed. State's Attorney Edward Hanrahan took weeks to respond and cited Illinois statutes when he advised on October 30, "The Cook County Board does not have the power to enter into a collective bargaining agreement."[66]

In this sector dominated by Black women, food service workers focused their struggle on "dignity and respect," which included more control over their labor and racial justice. In early October, Mendoza listed member grievances. She criticized the "arbitrary way" workers' schedules were made up. Understaffing led to "excessive" workloads for employees. The scheduling system made it so "we can't get sick on weekends." Work injuries were ignored. Employees' wages lagged in comparison with the cost of living. They were also vulnerable to the whims of their supervisors, despite since 1967 being part of a civil service rather than patronage system. They criticized demeaning treatment by a white female supervisor who was verbally abusive.[67] And there were many uncompensated expectations attached to their work, such as training new employees and highly skilled labor, such as "being as familiar with nutrition, reading charts, and nutritious food combinations as anyone trained in school."[68] They asserted themselves as skilled workers who deserved decent compensation as well as respect for the vital work they did to make the city's public hospital run. They rejected paternalism and demanded professionalism.[69]

Workers viewed their militant pursuit of union recognition, a contract, and "real FIRST CLASS CITIZENSHIP!" as matters of democracy and racial justice.[70] On October 29, with the support of some of the city's influential Black community groups, including Operation Breadbasket, the strike began. The strikers, almost all of them Black women over the age of thirty, were determined in their struggle for unionization and the larger racial and economic justice it represented. "We will stay here 'til hell freezes over, if necessary!" declared Ida Harris, the chairperson of the union strike committee. "We know we are right and we are going to win this fight no matter what it takes! We have had enough of working under a slave system!" The strikers picketed from 4 a.m., when the final food service worker shift began, until 4:30 p.m.

"They are showing remarkable determination as a group, almost superhuman individual integrity and bravery," wrote a reporter for the *West Side Torch*, the weekly paper of the West Side Organization, a Black Power community group. Their "commitment to stick the matter out is plainly evident in the firm, steady motion of their bodies and feet and the strong resonance of their voices raised in freedom and labor songs, that fill the frosty morning air." Reporter Sig Wimberli also noted that many on strike had over twenty years of service and therefore "the most to lose."[71]

The dietary workers' vigorous job action gained the support of fellow workers. On the first day, only twenty-six of a total of three hundred food service employees reported to work. "Picketing is good with 50 to 55 on duty," one union official reported back to AFSCME president Jerry Wurf. Though union representatives had predicted that hospital administration would "try to operate the hospital by trucking in food from other hospitals via Teamsters and by some volunteer help on a shoe-string basis," the strike effectively thwarted food delivery, at least for a time. About sixty laundry and sixty housekeeping staff expressed interest in joining the union.[72] On the fifth of November, a strike settlement was expected, the *Chicago Daily Defender* reported on its front page.[73] When such settlement did not come to fruition and workers stayed out, the hospital fired six to eight striking workers and threatened to dismiss others. Workers responded by picketing the County Building.[74] By November 7 the county reported that only fifty were on strike, but the union claimed two hundred.[75]

Support for the strike was not unanimous, however, and often cleaved along gender lines. Notably, all but one of the strikers were women, while many of the strikebreakers were men. Some workers never joined, and many had returned to work by the second week of November. "These scabs are sneaking into the hospital through tunnels, rear entrances, and side doors" with the aid of hospital administration as well as Chicago police, Wimberli reported. The strikers remained militant, on one occasion violently so, beating up one worker who attempted to cross the picket line. Jones remembered the striking women as unsparing in their criticism of the men who had the power to strengthen the strike by withholding their kitchen labor—food service was divided along gender lines, with men mostly staffing the kitchen and women delivering food on wards. Instead, the men snuck into the hospital before strikers arrived. Bratcher suggested that the men "had been bought," according to strike reporting in *Muhammad Speaks*, the Nation of Islam newspaper.[76] Jones supposed the men were "scared to death."[77] Another worker agreed: "These bastards are the poorest excuse for a man I ever did see." She added, "And they got the nerve to always be tryin' to hit on somebody." Striking workers condemned the men who would not support their labor action but continued to harass the women. "If they can't help us out here . . . where we need them, then they can't do nothin' for me!" Women led the action and were keenly aware of the strength this leadership required.[78]

As strike numbers diminished, workers and AFSCME organizers looked for additional outside support, especially from Black freedom groups. They already claimed the support of several unions, including the United Auto Workers, the Independent Union of Public Aid Employees, the local representing the city's cab drivers, and other AFSCME locals, who sent them donations and letters of support to Cook County Board president Dunne.[79] Wimberli reported in the strike's second week that the workers had received "encouragement" from noted Black leaders, including Rev. C. T. Vivian, who headed the Coalition for United Community Action, and Bob Williams of the Lawndale People's Planning Action Committee, both of which had participated in CUCA's campaigns for construction jobs for Black men that summer.[80] In internal correspondence, AFSCME representatives regularly reported on the status of the support they were receiving from members of Operation Breadbasket and CUCA, both of which expressed support for the food service workers at press conferences. In late November an AFSCME representative described an upcoming strike rally whose participants included Operation Breadbasket's Rev. Calvin Morris and Al Raby, as well as state senator Richard Newhouse, as "extremely important." AFSCME saw community support as vital in the uphill battle they were fighting.[81] Workers circulated a flyer calling on the community to "join us as the other workers and citizens did in Memphis and Charleston," referring to the 1968 sanitation worker strike and the 1969 hospital worker strike, both of which had garnered much more extensive community support and the backing of the SCLC.[82]

But despite the attempts of workers and their allies to draw greater attention to the public workers' cause, support for the mostly Black women on strike paled in comparison to other recent labor actions and struggles. Reporter Sig Wimberli had attempted to use his platform—a Black Power community organization newspaper—to boost the strike. "The sisters eagerly welcome the help of the black youth nations, wearing their berets on the picket lines," he reported. He invited members of the city's more militant Black Power groups and politicized gangs to come out in support, "so that the scabs and [County Board president] Dunne and [State's Attorney] Hanrahan can know that the black sisters are being supported by the brothers in the community."[83] *Muhammad Speaks* condemned the failure of civil rights groups and Black politicians to support the workers. "The 100 middle-aged Black women expressed disappointment because no Civil Rights organization came to their aid," a photo caption read.[84] The city's Black freedom organizations may have been preoccupied with the December 1969 murder of Illinois Black Panther Party chairman Fred Hampton.[85] Whatever the explanation, the lack of solidarity with striking workers likely undermined their struggle.

Workers also tried to build support within the hospital itself. "Together we can win decency for ALL County workers," they wrote on one flyer calling for worker solidarity within the massive public institution. "We are weak divided, but think what we can do if we all stand up and be counted! We all need basic dignity and better working conditions on the job. What we would win through our common struggle would be for all employees at County!" They encouraged their colleagues, saying, "Join your sisters and help them and help yourself!"[86] But here too there is little evidence of widespread support.

In the face of declining power, AFSCME pursued legal action. In September SEIU Local 46 had filed a complaint against AFSCME with the AFL-CIO, charging that the union was attempting a "raid." SEIU then withdrew its complaint in late November, when representatives concluded that they were "over the initial crisis" and thought the raid case might hurt Local 46's reputation at CCH by drawing attention to the union's lack of formal collective bargaining power.[87] A few days later, Local 46 reported to its members that it had secured a number of crucial gains for County workers, including wage increases, full family hospital benefits, and responsibility for keeping uniforms "furnished, laundered, and maintained."[88] Tensions again flared.[89] On December 10, AFSCME District 19 filed a federal suit against SEIU Local 46. Workers charged that CCH supervisors had forced food service workers to join Local 46 and intimidated those who had signed AFSCME cards. They alleged that Dunne had "unlawfully used his position as President of the County Board to recognize Local 46" by engaging in backdoor negotiations with union leadership.[90] When Council 19 members tried to "deal with their employer in a constructive, democratic way," as AFSCME's attorney put it, Dunne had forced them out into the street on the basis that the county had no authority to bargain with their members, they claimed. At the same time, he suggested, the county was maintaining a "fraudulent sweetheart arrangement" with Local 46. Claiming violations of the Fourteenth Amendment and the Civil Rights Act, AFSCME asked for an injunction to stop the county from negotiating with Local 46.[91] With only somewhere between thirty and one hundred members still out on strike, AFSCME looked to the courts to make their case that workers' civil right to collectively bargain was being violated.[92] On December 15 food service workers Willa Mae Jackson, Lenta Whaley, Ruby Levi, and Ann Stanek testified that Local 46 forced new hires to pay union dues even though the local did not bargain on their behalf; if

Organizing at Chicago's Public Hospital and Its Legacy   191 they didn't pay those dues, they were "viced," or discharged. Levi added, "I had other grievances and I felt like can stand up for my rights."[93] SEIU Local 46 reinstated their raid charges on December 18, the same day that the district court denied AFSCME Council 19's injunction.[94]

* * *

Though some employees, including Lillie Jones, stayed on strike for four months, AFSCME Council 19 did not win union recognition for the food service workers. The strike lasted until March 1970, when an arbiter ruled that AFSCME had indeed violated the AFL-CIO's constitution in trying to organize dietary workers. The strike was "quietly settled," the fired workers reinstated, and SEIU Local 46 designated the representative of the food service workers.[95] But the struggle for the rights of public hospital workers and for holding the public health care institution accountable was under way. The AFSCME's efforts seemed to improve the responsiveness of Local 46 leadership, who, still feeling pressure from the public sector union's organizational push for racial justice and accountability, vowed to "do everything possible" to bolster its own organizing efforts.[96] Perhaps most saliently, the action empowered hospital workers. Jones boasted that the food service workers' job action was the first strike at CCH. Reminiscing, she said, "They gave us hell. But we were rebels and we held out."[97] The workers' rebellious spirit would not soon leave the public hospital.

The "Heal-In"

The food service workers' militant and sustained protest seemed to rouse other Cook County Hospital workers to action. In mid-December, eleven hundred RNs and LPNs were again threatening to strike over their 1970 contract, which they won in January.[98] And in April, x-ray technicians conducted a "sick-in" over wages.[99] Physicians also organized, focusing primarily on issues of crowding and accountability, including restructuring CCH leadership. Before food service staff had even returned to work, the hospital's Residents and Interns Association (RIA) waged what they called a "heal-in" in February 1970.[100] Perhaps because their voices reverberated more loudly in the halls of governance than did those of low-wage, predominantly female staff of color, physician activists more successfully disrupted the status quo of hospital governance.

Residents and interns, known as the "house staff," provided the bulk of medical care at CCH. In the late 1960s and early 1970s, many physicians came to train at County out of commitment to social justice. Some of these mostly white activist physicians were part of a national health care justice movement that often focused its energies on public hospitals. There were also many foreign-born physicians, most of whom were nonwhite, who had attended medical school abroad.[101] Because of Illinois's discriminatory medical licensing system, there were few Black physicians in the state or at County.[102] The RIA worked to align members of the house staff across backgrounds, for example, by advocating for the rights of noncitizen physicians.[103] United, physicians mobilized to improve patient care at CCH. Surgeon and then–hospital director Robert Freeark suspected that the house staff's motives were selfish—or at least "mixed." They were really after higher wages and more comfortable working conditions, but "they were smart enough to cloak their demands in what's best for the patient," he told an oral historian over two decades later. Freeark correctly identified the rebellious doctors' facility with sympathetic language, but he underestimated their earnest desire for change. He conceded that when they mobilized for accountability and higher-quality care at CCH, they "quite literally blew the whistle on what was then an obsolete system."[104]

Residents and interns organized the "heal-in" during February 1970. In the heart of a Chicago winter, when many vulnerable city residents were sick with the flu and frostbite, the hospital's organized house staff decided that they "were no longer willing to compromise the welfare of their patients" by discharging them to free up hospital beds.[105] Participating physicians vowed to admit all sick patients and wait to discharge patients until they were "medically ready." The "heal-in," as they called it, lasted ten days. Their action meant to shed light on how overcrowding and understaffing at CCH was seriously undermining hospital staff's ability to deliver quality or even adequate care, as well as the hospital's role as a safety net. Whether or not they knew it, the "heal-in" resembled the "feed-in" that nurses had carried out in 1966, when off-duty nurses reported to work to help feed patients and for once get everyone fed. Over the course of the heal-in, admissions reached 2,150 when hospital capacity was just 1,850.[106] Administrators declared a crisis at CCH and the hospital director closed admissions—the first time in the hospital's history.[107] Community groups demanded the hospital reopen, the leader of the Woodlawn Organization telling the press, "The black community will not accept the closing of the only hospital we have immediate access to, when we are living in the second richest city in the world."[108] Members of Operation Breadbasket called on the federal government to set up field hospitals in the predominantly Black areas most affected by the crisis at CCH.[109]

Like the nurses who spoke out against patronage as a way to ensure patient care, and like food service workers who demanded responsive union representation to advocate for their dignity as workers, the physicians fought to make the hospital more accountable to the people who worked and received medical care there. Specifically, the RIA demanded a change in leadership and, especially, the end to political control of the hospital. In theory the independent Health and Hospitals Governing Commission had been running the hospital since the beginning of 1970. But the Cook County Board had retained control of the hospital's budget. By controlling the purse strings, the board still held power. A consensus eventually emerged among hospital employees and the wider community over the need to give the independent governing commission more meaningful control of CCH. Medical personnel threatened mass resignations in order to achieve the change in leadership they thought necessary to fully meet the needs of patients. When politicians met crisis conditions with threats to close all but CCH's trauma unit, physician, nurses, and support staff wore black armbands to signify that they were mourning the death of CCH.[110] Facing mounting pressure from hospital employees and community members who picketed Dunne's office, the Cook County Board agreed to cede control of the hospital's finances to an independent governing commission in May.[111] A few months later, the commission appointed Black obstetrician James G. Haughton its executive director.[112] Governor Ogilvie expressed his satisfaction with the apparent resolution, saying, "The recurring problems of this great hospital, the crisis in service, and the battle for control should now end."[113] Ogilvie could not know then that those problems, that crisis, and struggles for control were just beginning.

A Democratic Organizing Tradition for the 1970s

As the 1970s wore on, the newly created governing commission improved some aspects of hospital care, though new difficulties soon emerged. The commission clashed with hospital employees, conflicts that grew more heated as inflation and diminishing revenues led to budgetary shortfalls. But the late 1960s surge of employee activism persisted, and over the next several years, community members and CCH staff continued to fight for accountable, representative leadership; adequate wages and benefits for workers; adequate conditions for patients; and dignity for all. New alliances also formed among hospital staff. In 1972, LPNs joined RNs on a four-day strike.[114] When the governing commission announced a thousand layoffs, mostly of low-wage workers, in late 1972, one hundred employees, including nurses and physicians, signed petitions opposing the layoffs.[115]

By the mid-1970s, politicians, government watchdog groups, and private sector interests were arguing for the closure of CCH. When this push came, the hospital staff was organized and played a pivotal role in defending Chicago's public hospital. The resident and intern union went out on an eighteen-day strike in 1975, demanding more substantial investment in the public hospital and the right to bargain over patient conditions. They claimed the support of nurses and support staff who "leant out of the window and cheered the house Staff marches, reflecting a conscious concern about patient care at the institution and about the validity of job actions."[116] Employees as well as a number of religious and community groups formed a coalition called the Committee to Save Cook County Hospital in 1976. After a budgetary crisis at CCH became so acute that hospital employees were sent home without paychecks in 1979, CCH staff turned out hundreds of people at demonstrations.

This stream of vigorous protest during the 1970s, vital in saving CCH from closure, built on an organizing tradition developed a decade earlier. In the late 1960s, the women working at CCH, many women of color in low-wage jobs, pioneered organizing traditions that carefully centered on patients, emphasized accountability, and pointed to the tied fates of the public sector and public workers. Through the day-to-day care they provided and their organized labor actions, these CCH employees helped build an organizing momentum and a movement focused on accountability and care.

Hospital employee activism sheds light on Cook County Hospital's troubled late twentieth-century history. CCH was consistently underfunded and, increasingly in the 1970s, subject to vituperative critique, disinvestment, and near closure. The continuous struggles of hospital employees could be read as their failure to meaningfully improve hospital conditions for patients and workers. But the fact that County was a public institution meant it was accountable to the people who relied on CCH for care and who worked there—or that it ought to be. We might see the sustained activism at CCH, then, as democracy at work. After all, it was with a triumphant air that Lillie Jones remembered the food service workers' job action that started in 1969. The strike was "the first strike in the history of County," Jones told the interviewer, "and ever since that time *everybody's* been protesting."[117]

Further Reading

Fernández, Johanna. *The Young Lords: A Radical History*. Chapel Hill: University of North Carolina Press, 2020.

Fink, Leon, and Brian Greenberg. *Upheaval in the Quiet Zone: 1199 SEIU and the Politics of Health Care Unionism*. 2nd ed. Urbana: University of Illinois Press, 2009.

Johnston, Paul. *Success While Others Fail: Social Movement Unionism and the Public Workplace*. Ithaca, NY: ILR Press, 1994.

Opdycke, Sandra. *No One Was Turned Away: The Role of Public Hospitals in New York City since 1900*. Oxford: Oxford University Press, 1999.

Sacks, Karen Brodkin. *Caring by the Hour: Women, Work, and Organizing at Duke Medical Center*. Urbana: University of Illinois Press, 1988.

Notes

1. Interview with Lillie Jones, in Sydney Lewis, *Hospital: An Oral History of Cook County Hospital* (New York: Berkley Books, 1994), 278, 279.

2. Letter, Carmen Mendoza to George Dunne, October 6, 1969, folder 15-21, box 15, American Federation of State, County, and Municipal Employees Central Files Department, Walter P. Reuther Library, Archives of Labor and Urban Affairs, Detroit, MI (hereafter, AFSCME Central Files).

3. Interview with Jones, in Lewis, *Hospital*, 278.

4. Here I build on the insights of scholars who have highlighted the role public sector employees played in struggles in defense of a welfare state under attack. See, for example, Paul Johnston, *Success While Others Fail: Social Movement Unionism and the Public Workplace* (Ithaca, NY: ILR Press, 1994); Sandra Opdycke, *No One Was Turned Away: The Role of Public Hospitals in New York City since 1900* (Oxford: Oxford University Press, 1999), 125–29, 154–55, 166; Kim Phillips-Fein, *Fear City: New York's Fiscal Crisis and the Rise of Austerity Politics* (New York: Metropolitan Books, 2017). Work that touches on public hospital worker organizing includes, for example, Joshua B. Freeman, *Working-Class New York: Life and Labor since World War II* (New York: New Press, 2000), 207–214; Johanna Fernández, *The Young Lords: A Radical History* (Chapel Hill: University of North Carolina Press, 2020), 271–304. On the vulnerability of women of color to public sector retrenchment, see Jane Berger, "'There Is Tragedy on Both Sides of the Layoffs': Privatization and the Urban Crisis in Baltimore," *International Labor and Working-Class History*, no. 71 (Spring 2007): 29–42.

5. CCH was Chicago's only full-service public hospital until 1993, when Provident Hospital opened as the city's second public hospital. In 1955 the *Chicago Daily Tribune* called CCH "the world's largest medical charity institution." Quoted in Robert Wiedrich, "Why County Hospital Lacks Sterile Smell," *Chicago Daily Tribune*, March 7, 1955.

6. Statistics and quote from Lloyd General, "Cook County Hosp. in Crisis: County Hospital: A Time of Crisis," *Chicago Daily Defender*, May 25, 1964. A 1966 city report estimated 2,538 beds. Chicago Board of Health, *Preliminary Report on Patterns of Medical and Health Care in Poverty Areas of Chicago and Proposed Health Programs for the Medically Indigent* (Chicago: Chicago Board of Health, September 1966). In 1968 the Cook County Board president described a 2,500-bed facility (plus 200

bassinets) treating 724,354 patients per year. *Annual Message of Richard B. Ogilvie*, 1968, folder 21, box 15, AFSCME Central Files.

7. On the role public hospitals played as safety-net health care institutions that did not turn patients away, see, for example, Harry Filmore Dowling, *City Hospitals: The Undercare of the Underprivileged* (Cambridge, MA: Harvard University Press, 1982); Odycke, *No One Turned Away*; David Oshinsky, *Bellevue: Three Centuries of Medicine and Mayhem at America's Most Storied Hospital* (New York: Doubleday, 2016). On Black patients refused care regardless of income, see Dowling, *City Hospitals*, 161.

8. Reporter Lloyd General wrote that in 1964 "a great number" of the hospital's 4,384 employees were Black. General, "Cook County Hosp. in Crisis."

9. Lloyd General, "What Can Save County Hospital?," *Chicago Daily Defender*, May 28, 1964.

10. "Having a Baby Here Is a Crime," *Chicago Daily Defender*, December 18, 1967.

11. On the joint campaign of Teamsters Local 743 and Service Employees International Union (SEIU) Local 73 to organize Chicago private hospital workers under the banner of the Hospital Employees Labor Program (HELP) in 1959–1960 and again starting in 1966, see David Nicolai and Milton Derber, "Hospital Employees Labor Program," in Milton Derber, *Labor in Illinois: The Affluent Years 1945–1980* (Urbana: University of Illinois Press, 1989), 142–58. Illinois private hospital workers were granted the right to strike in November 1969. "Hospital Workers' Strike Right Upheld," *Chicago Sun Times*, November 26, 1969; Nicolai and Derber, "Hospital Employees Labor Program," 148. On private hospital workers organizing around the United States, see Karen Brodkin Sacks, *Caring by the Hour: Women, Work, and Organizing at Duke Medical Center* (Urbana: University of Illinois Press, 1988); Leon Fink and Brian Greenberg, *Upheaval in the Quiet Zone: 1199 SEIU and the Politics of Health Care Unionism*, 2nd ed. (Urbana: University of Illinois Press, 2009). On the Charleston hospital worker strike, which targeted both a public hospital and a private one, see, for example, Jewell Charmaine Debnam, "Black Women and the Charleston Hospital Workers' Strike of 1969" (PhD diss., Michigan State University, 2016); Jewell C. Debnam, "Mary Moultrie, Naomi White, and the Women of the Charleston Hospital Workers' Strike of 1969," *Souls* 18, no. 1 (2016): 59–79; Otha Jennifer Dixon-McKnight, "'We Shall Not Always Plant While Others Reap': Black Women Hospital Workers and the Charleston Hospital Strike, 1967–1970" (PhD diss., University of North Carolina at Chapel Hill, 2017).

12. On nonindustrial worker organizing, particularly in the caring and public sectors, see, for example, Deborah E. Bell, "Unionized Women in State and Local Government," in *Women, Work, and Protest: A Century of US Women's Labor History*, ed. Ruth Milkman (Boston: Routledge, 1985); Dorothy Sue Cobble, *Dishing It Out: Waitresses and Their Unions in the Twentieth Century* (Champaign: University of Illinois Press, 1992); Dorothy Sue Cobble, "'A Spontaneous Loss of Enthusiasm': Workplace Feminism and the Transformation of Women's Service Jobs in the 1970s," *International Labor and Working-Class History* 56 (1999): 23–44; Dorothy Sue Cobble,

"A 'Tiger by the Toenail': The 1970s Origins of the New Working-Class Majority," *Labor: Studies in Working-Class History of the Americas* 2, no. 3 (2005): 103–114; Dorothy Sue Cobble and Michael Merrill, "Promise of Service Worker Unionism," in *Service Work: Critical Perspectives*, ed. Marek Korczynski and Cameron Lynne Macdonald, 153–74 (New York: Routledge, 2009); Eileen Boris and Jennifer Klein, *Caring for America: Home Health Workers in the Shadow of the Welfare State* (Oxford: Oxford University Press, 2012); Premilla Nadasen, *Household Workers Unite: The Untold Story of African American Women Who Built a Movement* (Boston: Beacon Press, 2015).

13. On public sector organizing and civil rights, see, for example, Bell, "Unionized Women in State and Local Government"; Michael K. Honey, *Going Down Jericho Road: The Memphis Strike, Martin Luther King's Last Campaign* (New York: W. W. Norton, 2007); Thomas J. Sugrue, "'The Largest Civil Rights Organization Today': Title VII and the Transformation of the Public Sector," *Labor: Studies in Working-Class History of the Americas* 11, no. 3 (2014): 25–29.

14. Examples include Erik S. Gellman, "'The Stone Wall Behind': The Chicago Coalition for United Community Action and Labor's Overseers, 1968–1973," in *Black Power at Work: Community Control, Affirmative Action, and the Construction Industry*, ed. David A. Goldberg and Trevor Griffey (Ithaca, NY: Cornell University Press, 2010); Jeffrey Helgeson, *Crucibles of Black Empowerment: Chicago's Neighborhood Politics from the New Deal to Harold Washington* (Chicago: University of Chicago Press, 2014); Toussaint Losier, "The Rise and Fall of the 1969 Chicago Jobs Campaign: Street Gangs, Coalition Politics, and the Origins of Mass Incarceration," *University of Memphis Law Review* 49, nos. 1–4 (2018): 1–36.

15. Here I build on the work of sociologist Paul Johnston, who has theorized that the structure of public work lent itself to more expansive visions that foregrounded the public good rather than hewing to market terms like wages. Johnston, *Success While Others Fail.*

16. Quoted in Chesly Manly, "New Dilemma Faced by County Hospital," *Chicago Daily Tribune*, February 4, 1963, box 2, Seymour Simon Papers, Chicago History Museum, Chicago, IL (hereafter, Seymour Simon Papers).

17. The *Defender* reported that aides and volunteers were playing a more important role in the context of the shortage. "Cook County Nursing School Caps 18 Volunteer Nurse Aides," *Chicago Daily Defender*, June 26, 1962.

18. Lawrence S. Bloom, Peter R. Bonavich, and Daniel Sudran, "Medicaid in Cook County: Present Status and Future Prospects," *Inquiry* 5, no. 2 (1968): 12–23.

19. "Claim County Hospital Erred," *Chicago Daily Defender*, November 9, 1967; Betty Washington, "Medic Raps Hospital's Callousness," *Chicago Daily Defender*, November 14, 1967. In an oral history interview, former hospital superintendent Dr. Robert Freeark explained Fulwiley's death by pointing to the high volume of patients and to the fact that when Fulwiley entered the emergency room, she encountered "the greenest, least experienced person in the world." Interview with Dr. Robert Freeark, in Lewis, *Hospital*, 114.

20. Betty Washington, "The Truth about County Hospital," *Chicago Daily Defender*, December 19, 1967.

21. Ingeborg G. Mauksch, "How Did It Come to Pass?," *Nursing Forum* 10, no. 3 (1971): 265. The *Defender* reported that closer to 50 percent of nurses were African American in this period, a number that might have included nursing staff, not only registered nurses. See Betty Washington, "Too Many Patronage Jobs," *Chicago Daily Defender*, December 20, 1967. At the time, between a quarter and a third of Chicago's population was African American. In 1960 Chicago was approximately 22.9 percent African American and by 1970, 32.7 percent. Campbell Gibson and Kay Jung, "Historical Census Statistics on Population Totals by Race, 1970 to 1990, and by Hispanic Origin, 1970 to 1990, for Large Cities and Other Urban Places in the United States by Population Division, Working Paper No. 76," U.S. Census Bureau, Washington, DC (February 2005). On the history of the racial and gender stratification of health care labor, including the exclusion of women of color from professional nursing and the grading of nursing labor in the 1930s, see Evelyn Nakano Glenn, "From Servitude to Service Work: Historical Continuities in the Racial Division of Paid Reproductive Labor," *Signs: Journal of Women in Culture and Society* 18, no. 1 (1992): 19–22, 24–28. On the history of Black women in nursing, see Darlene Clark Hine, *Black Women in White: Racial Conflict and Cooperation in the Nursing Profession, 1890–1950* (Bloomington: Indiana University Press, 1989).

22. Management scholar David Lewin described the city's labor relationships as informal arrangements where labor leaders met with Mayor Richard J. Daley each autumn and through discussions decided on a prevailing rate. Public sector wages were often higher than private sector rates, what Lewin called the "'price' Daley willingly paid to keep formal collective bargaining out of city government and yet preserve the support of organized labor." Lewin said Daley encouraged more formalized bargaining at the county level, but that doesn't seem to have been the case at CCH, where negotiations between union officials and political leaders seemed to resemble those Lewin described. David Lewin, "Mayoral Power and Municipal Labor Relations: A Three-City Study," *Employee Relations Law Journal* 6, no. 4 (1981): 652–53. On complaints of politically appointed employees being paid more and being unaccountable, see Ronald Kotulak, "Political Aids Get Cream of Hospital Pay: Among Highest Paid in County," *Chicago Tribune*, April 6, 1964.

23. Lloyd General, "Nurses Still Fight County Takeover," *Chicago Daily Defender*, May 27, 1964; "Nurses at Cook County Hospital Protest Change," *Chicago Daily Defender*, March 30, 1964; quote from Ted Coleman, "County Nurses Protest," *Chicago Daily Defender*, March 31, 1964. See also Ronald Kotulak, "Nurse School Fears Merger with Hospital," *Chicago Tribune*, March 31, 1964; Ronald Kotulak, "Forget the Sick," *Chicago Tribune*, April 15, 1964.

24. On Ogilvie's reform efforts, see "Ogilvie Promises Reforms: Civil Service Overhaul to Get Priority," *Chicago Tribune*, December 6, 1966; Thomas Buck, "County Tells of Plan to Give Hospital Civil Service Tests," *Chicago Tribune*, January 24, 1967;

Thomas Buck, "Board Urged to Reorganize Cook Hospital," *Chicago Tribune*, September 26, 1968.

25. Interview with Jones, in Lewis, *Hospital*, 277.

26. Washington, "Too Many Patronage Jobs."

27. Betty Washington, "A Study in Misery," *Chicago Defender* (national edition), December 16, 1967.

28. Washington, "Too Many Patronage Jobs."

29. Washington, "Truth about County Hospital."

30. Interview with Jones, in Lewis, *Hospital*, 277.

31. Washington, "Truth about County Hospital."

32. Following the 1935 passage of the NLRA, states worked to devise their own legislation dictating the organizing rights of public sector workers. In 1945 public sector worker legislation passed the Illinois House and Senate; however, Governor Dwight Green vetoed it on the basis that it would conflict with civil service laws. The legality of collective bargaining remained ambiguous for decades, with a variety of informal arrangements occurring. Milton Derber acted as vice chairman of the commission that Governor Otto Kerner appointed to research and recommend policy on public sector legislation in 1966. In 1967 the commission recommended a public labor statute that allowed bargaining and prohibited strikes. The Illinois legislature could not agree on legislation, and after a series of bills and amendments were proposed, efforts ultimately failed in 1967. Governor's Advisory Commission on Labor-Management Policy for Public Employees, *Reports and Recommendations*, Springfield, State of Illinois, March 1967; Milton Derber, "Labor-Management Policy for Public Employees in Illinois: The Experience of the Governor's Commission, 1966–1967," *Industrial Labor Relations Review* 21, no. 4 (1968): 541–58; Milton Derber, "American Federation of State, County, and Municipal Employees," in *Labor in Illinois: The Affluent Years, 1945–1980* (Urbana: University of Illinois Press, 1989), 159–73. The state wouldn't enact its first comprehensive public sector labor legislation until 1983. Gregory M. Saltzman, "Public Sector Bargaining Laws Really Matter: Evidence from Ohio and Illinois," in *When Public Sector Workers Unionize*, ed. Richard B. Freeman and Casey Ichniowski, 41–79 (Chicago: University of Chicago Press, 1988); Richard R. Nelson, "State Labor Legislation Enacted in 1983," *Monthly Labor Review* (January 1984): 64–65. On the absence of federal public sector labor legislation and its implications for the labor movement, see Joseph A. McCartin, "'A Wagner Act for Public Employees': Labor's Deferred Dream and the Rise of Conservatism, 1970–1976," *Journal of American History* 95, no. 1 (2008): 123–48.

33. On the INA tactic of threatening strikes, see Derber, "Labor-Management Policy for Public Employees in Illinois." On bargaining rights, see "County Gives Nurses Rights of Bargaining: Open Meetings on Pay Raises," *Chicago Tribune*, August 31, 1966.

34. On the San Francisco nurses' strike, see "Nurse Strike Hits 3 Coast Hospitals," *Chicago Tribune*, August 31, 1966, folder 130, box 6, Zimmerman Papers, University of Illinois at Chicago Health Sciences Library, Chicago, IL (hereafter, Zimmerman

Papers). On the "feed-in" and the larger campaign, see Mauksch, "How Did It Come to Pass?" The *Chicago Daily News* described a "voluntary assistance program," which was likely the same action. See "34% County Hospital Rate Hike Likely," *Chicago Daily News*, September 7, 1966, folder 081.012, box 81, Civic Federation Papers, DePaul University Special Collections (hereafter, Civic Federation Papers). On threats to resign and the notices of resignation nurses handed in, see "Raise for Now—Simon," *Chicago Daily News*, September 8, 1966, folder 081.012, box 81, Civic Federation Papers; "364 Nurses Resign over Pay: Simon Urges County Act to Halt Walkout," *Chicago News American*, September 9, 1966, folder 134, box 6, Zimmerman Papers; Robert S. Kleckner, "Hold 1st Talks on County Nurse Pay," *Chicago Sun Times*, September 9, 1966, folder 132, box 6, Zimmerman Papers; Phillip J. O'Connor, "363 Nurses Resign at County Hospital: Submit Notice in Pay Fight," *Chicago Tribune*, folder 133, box 6, Zimmerman Papers; Illinois Nurses' Association, For Release, September 13, 1966, folder 135, box 6, Zimmerman Papers; Agreement, September 14, 1966, folder 139, box 6, Zimmerman Papers.

35. INA executive administrator Anne Zimmerman discussed this national rise in militancy in Louise Hutchinson, "Nurses New Militancy Is a Bitter Pill for Some," *Chicago Tribune*, November 5, 1967.

36. Sara Jane Goodyear, "May Avoid Nurse Strike: Agreement Is Reached after Talks," *Chicago Tribune*, February 19, 1967.

37. Commissioner Charles F. Chaplin criticized that while patient censuses had decreased, the numbers of nurses as well as their wages had increased. Charles F. Chaplin, "Voice of the People: Working Conditions at County Hospital," *Chicago Tribune*, February 18, 1967.

38. "Draft Plans in Event of Nurse Strike," *Chicago Tribune*, January 20, 1967; Thomas Buck, "County Faces Nurse Strike over Pay Hike," *Chicago Tribune*, February 11, 1967; Donna Gill, "County Girds for Strike at 2 Hospitals: Nurses Prepared to Walk Out," *Chicago Tribune*, February 14, 1967; Thomas Buck, "Kerner Vows to Help Keep County Open," *Chicago Tribune*, February 17, 1967; Arthur Siddon, "Crisis at County Hospital!: Admissions Cut in Strike Preparation," *Chicago Tribune*, February 23, 1967; Thomas Buck, "Vote to Call Off Strike Plans," *Chicago Tribune*, February 24, 1967.

39. "County Nurses Pay Hike Asked," *Chicago Tribune*, November 17, 1967; Thomas Buck, "500 County Nurses Threaten to Strike," *Chicago Tribune*, December 12, 1967.

40. Washington, "Study in Misery."

41. Interview with Jones, in Lewis, *Hospital*, 279.

42. Interview with Jones, in Lewis, *Hospital*; Carol Karels, *Cooked: An Inner-City Nursing Memoir* (Englewood Cliffs, NJ: Full Court Press, 2005), 39, 23–24.

43. A Reader, "Negroes, Whites Get Different Jobs," *Chicago Defender* (national edition), January 25, 1964; One Who Knows, "Color Decides Hospital Duties," *Chicago Defender* (national edition), January 25, 1964.

As early as the 1930s, African Americans protested discrimination toward CCH staff. For example, Black nursing trainees at Cook County School of Nursing who

Organizing at Chicago's Public Hospital and Its Legacy   201 provided care at CCH were barred from living in the nursing residence. See, for example, "Begin Fight on Discrimination at Co. Hospital," *Chicago Defender* (national edition), October 26, 1935; "To Force Action in Fight against Jim Crow Nurses Home," *Chicago Defender* (national edition), May 16, 1936; "Citizens Rap Color Bar at Nurses Home," *Chicago Defender* (national edition), July 4, 1936.

44. On the strike, see "Practical Nurses Walk Out," *Chicago Tribune*, October 18, 1966; Rob Warden, "Office Help May Join Walkout," *Chicago Daily News*, October 18, 1966, folder 15, box 9, Institute of Labor and Industrial Relations Library Labor Clippings File, University of Illinois, Urbana, IL (hereafter, ILIR Clippings); "Nurses Still Out; Welfare Strike in Air," *Chicago Daily Defender*, October 19, 1966; Thomas Buck, "All Expected to Return to Work Today," *Chicago Tribune*, October 19, 1966, folder 142, box 6, Zimmerman Papers; "Hospital, Nurses Back to Normal," *Chicago Daily News*, October 20, 1966, folder 81.012, box 81, Civic Federation Papers; "County Hospital Back to Normal as Strike Ends," *Chicago Daily Defender*, October 20, 1966.

45. SEIU was previously called Building Service Municipal Employees Union (BSMEU); both names are used in records. For simplicity I use only SEIU.

46. These clerical workers were technically employed by the School of Nursing, which meant that their negotiations involved nursing school administration. Larry Green, "County Threat: Hospital Aides Plan 'Sick Call' in Pay Dispute," *Chicago Daily News*, February 11, 1969, folder 9-4, box 9, SEIU Executive Office, David Sullivan Records, Walter P. Reuther Library, Archives of Labor and Urban Affairs, Detroit, MI (hereafter, Sullivan Records).

47. The leadership of Victor Gotbaum, a white reformer virulently critical of patronage, from 1959 to 1964 fueled AFSCME Council 19's opposition to the Democratic machine. Gotbaum left Council 19 to assume leadership of Illinois AFSCME in 1964 and vowed to wage an organizational drive focused on Chicago city workers. In a speech at a 1966 rally in support of the Independent Union of Public Aid Employees, Gotbaum criticized local labor leaders as "slobs who are still at the business of breaking strikes." William Kling, "Vow Longer Aid Strike: Union Chiefs Demand Right to Organize," *Chicago Tribune*, May 23, 1966; Edward Schreiber, "Civil Service a Farce, Says Union Leader: Raps Maneuvering of Politicians," *Chicago Tribune*, November 19, 1963; quote from "City Workers Name Gotbaum as State Chief," *Chicago Tribune*, June 9, 1964. Council 19 seems to have supported the Black freedom movement in a number of ways. For example, four days after Martin Luther King Jr. was assassinated in Memphis while supporting a public sanitation worker strike, Council 19 formed a "Memphis, U.S.A. Committee" to send aid and support to the workers. "Union to Aid Striking Group in Tennessee," *Chicago Tribune*, April 6, 1968.

48. Letter, John A. Coleman to David Sullivan, February 28, 1969, folder 9-4, box 9, Sullivan Records. On Operation Breadbasket campaigns, see, for example, Gordon K. Mantler, *Power to the Poor: Black-Brown Coalition and the Fight for Economic Justice, 1960–1974* (Chapel Hill: University of North Carolina Press, 2013), 224–26; Jakobi Williams, *From Bullet to Ballot: The Illinois Chapter of the Black Panther Party and Racial Coalition Politics in Chicago* (Chapel Hill: University of North Carolina

Press, 2013), 98; Helgeson, *Crucibles of Black Empowerment*, 89–190, 192–93; Martin L. Deppe, *Operation Breadbasket: An Untold Story of Civil Rights in Chicago, 1966–1971* (Athens: University of Georgia Press, 2017).

49. In a 1969 letter, Local 46 president John J. Masse claimed the union had represented food service works "for the past twenty years." A 1969 memo from Eugene P. Moats said "approximately 23 years." Letter, John J. Masse to David Sullivan, folder 9-5, box 9, Sullivan Records; Memo, Eugene P. Moats to David Sullivan, September 18, 1969, folder 9-5, box 9, Sullivan Records.

50. Interview with Jones, in Lewis, *Hospital*, 278; quote from Sig Wimberli, "Workers Strike for Union Contract," *West Side Torch*, November 7–14, 1969, folder 15-21, box 15, AFSCME Central Files.

51. Wimberli, "Workers Strike for Union Contract." On Black Chicagoans' long movement against machine politics, or what activist Timuel Black called "plantation politics," see Helgeson, *Crucibles of Black Empowerment*, 248–58.

52. Organizing Committee to Co-Worker, October 6, 1969, folder 15-21, box 15, AFSCME Central Files.

53. Letter, Neal A. Bratcher to George Dunne, July 24, 1969, folder 15-21, box 15, AFSCME Central Files. When Democratic Illinois secretary of state Paul Powell called Mayor Daley and the Chicago Police Department's violent response to protesters at the May 1968 Democratic National Convention "restrained," AFSCME's Neal A. Bratcher called Powell's comment racist, saying, "The tactics used by the Chicago police were the same that they have been using against the black community for 300 years." Bratcher threatened that if Democrats continued to defend such actions, Black voters would switch their political allegiance from the Democrats to the Republicans. James Strong, "Powell Lauds Daley, Kindles Racism Charge: Union Delegate Warns of Negro Vote Switch, *Chicago Tribune*, September 25, 1968.

54. On the Cardinal's Committee, see Rev. Leo T. Mahon to Robert Healy, December 20, 1962, box 2, Seymour Simon Papers; Lilia Fernandez, *Brown in the Windy City: Mexicans and Puerto Ricans in Postwar Chicago* (Chicago: University of Chicago, 2012), 76. On Mendoza, see Judy Nicol, "A Mother Nurtures the Stepchild of Unions," *Chicago Sun Times*, September 30, 1969, folder 29, box 11, ILIR Clippings; Carmen Mendoza Obituary, *Chicago Tribune*, November 23, 2000.

55. Letter, Carmen Mendoza to George Dunne, August 13, 1969, folder 15-21, box 15, AFSCME Central Files.

56. Letter, Carmen Mendoza to William A. Lee, August 18, 1969, folder 15-21, box 15, AFSCME Central Files.

57. On the centrality of Black women as leaders and participants in the Charleston hospital workers' strike of 1969, see Debnam, "Black Women and the Charleston Hospital Workers' Strike of 1969"; Debnam, "Mary Moultrie, Naomi White, and the Women of the Charleston Hospital Workers' Strike of 1969," 71; and Dixon-McKnight, "We Shall Not Always Plant While Others Reap." On its connection to the national movement of Local 1199, see Fink and Greenberg, *Upheaval in the Quiet Zone*, 129–58.

58. Letter, John J. Masse, to David Sullivan, September 9, 1969, folder 9-5, box 9, Sullivan Records.

59. The SEIU vowed to deploy other strategies to preserve their status as the exclusive representative of County food service workers, including "beef[ing] up our membership within the unit" and trying to get the Cook County Board to "clearly indicate that they have and continued to recognize Local 46 for the contested unit." Eugene P. Moats to General President Sullivan Re: Local 46 Re: AFSCME & Food Services Dept. Cook County Hospital, September 18, 1969, folder 9-5, box 9, Sullivan Records.

60. They achieved symbolic successes, but ultimately their efforts failed in the context of the violent crackdown on Black Power in Chicago. Gellman, "'Stone Wall Behind,'" 113. See also Derber, *Labor in Illinois*, 77–80; Helgeson, *Crucibles of Black Empowerment*, 196–97; Losier, "The Rise and Fall of the 1969 Chicago Jobs Campaign." On the gendered aspects of CUCA's campaign, see Gellman, "'Stone Wall Behind,'" 118–19.

61. For immediate release, September 10, 1969, folder 15-21, box 15, AFSCME Central Files; "Sick-In by County Hospital Food Workers Seeking Affiliation," *Chicago Sun Times*, folder 15-21, box 15, AFSCME Central Files. The hospital disputed the union's claims of participation, with *Chicago Today* reporting 25 percent workers calling in sick. "Hospital Staff Sick-In," *Chicago Today*, September 9, 1969, folder 15-21, box 15, AFSCME Central Files; "53 Hospital Food Aides on Sick-In," *Chicago Daily News*, September 9, 1969, folder 15-21, box 15, AFSCME Central Files; "Hospital Food Workers Hold Union 'Sick-In,'" *Chicago Tribune*, September 10, 1969.

62. For immediate release, September 9, 1969, folder 15-21, box 15, AFSCME Central Files. On the picket, see Letter, Carmen Mendoza to George Dunne, September 19, 1969, folder 15-21, box 15, AFSCME Central Files; "Why We Are Picketing," September 19, 1969, enclosed in Letter, John J. Masse to David Sullivan, September 23, 1969, folder 9-5, box 9, Sullivan Records.

63. Letter, Carmen Mendoza to George Dunne, September 19, 1969, folder 15-21, box 15, AFSCME Central Files.

64. Organizing Committee to Co-Worker, October 6, 1969, folder 15-21, box 15, AFSCME Central Files.

65. Charley Bussey to unknown, September 30, 1969, folder 15-21, box 15, AFSCME Central Files; Letter, Carmen Mendoza to George W. Dunne, October 1, 1969, folder 15-21, box 15, AFSCME Central Files.

66. Letter, Carmen Mendoza to George Dunne, September 19, 1969, folder 15-21, box 15, AFSCME Central Files. On response, see Letter, Edward Hanrahan (State's Atty) to Edward J. Barrett, October 30, 1969, enclosed in Letter, Les Keck to Winn Newman, November 4, 1969, folder 15-21, box 15, AFSCME Central Files. SEIU efforts to prosecute the raid were ongoing, but AFSCME representatives remained unfazed by SEIU's case against the union, since they thought only fifteen or twenty people considered themselves part of Local 46. Letter, Bob Bollard to Joe Ames Re: Cook County Hospital (Chicago) Strike Pending !!!, October 21, 1969, folder 15-21, box 15, AFSCME Central Files. "Local 46 is nosing around but has a bad reputation here and does not worry us too much," they reported in a memo from Robert D. Bollard to Joseph L. Ames, November 6, 1969, folder 15-21, box 15, AFSCME Central Files.

67. Letter, Carmen Mendoza to George Dunne, October 6, 1969, folder 15-21, box 15, AFSCME Central Files.

68. Quote from Wimberli, "Workers Strike for Union Contract." See also "300 Hospital Aides Strike," *Chicago Daily Defender*, October 30, 1969.

69. On paternalism that plagued pre-union hospital workers in voluntary hospitals in New York City, see Fink and Greenberg, *Upheaval in the Quiet Zone*, 7–8. On race, gender, paternalism, and labor, see also Glenn, "From Servitude to Service Work"; Cobble, "Spontaneous Loss of Enthusiasm"; and Nadasen, *Household Workers Unite*.

70. Quote from "Why We Strike!," folder 9-6, box 9, Sullivan Records. On public sector unionization and citizenship, see, for example, McCartin, "'Wagner Act for Public Employees'"; J. Hower, "Public Sector Unionism," *Oxford Research Encyclopedia of American History*, March 29, 2017, https://oxfordre.com/americanhistory/view/10.1093/acrefore/9780199329175.001.0001/acrefore-9780199329175-e-395/, accessed September 5, 2019.

71. Wimberli, "Workers Strike for Union Contract."

72. Quote from Letter, Bollard to Ames, October 21, 1969; Letter, Bob Bollard to Jerry Wurf, October 29, 1969, re: Cook County (Chicago) Hospital Strike, folder 15-21, box 15, AFSCME Central Files.

73. Ted Lacey, "End Seen in County Hospital Walkout: See End to Hospital Strike," *Chicago Defender*, November 5, 1969.

74. Ted Lacey, "Axe County Hospital Strikers," *Chicago Defender*, November 12, 1969; Letter, Robert J. Freeark to Lillie Buckles, November 7, 1969, folder 15-21, box 15, AFSCME Central Files; Letter, Robert J. Freeark to Willie D. Byrd, November 17, 1969, folder 15-21, box 15, AFSCME Central Files.

75. "Hospital Food Workers Ask for Union Pact," *Chicago Tribune*, November 7, 1969.

76. Nathaniel X, "Wages Still Inadequate: Black Woman Hospital Employees Fail to Get Support of 'Men,'" *Muhammad Speaks*, February 20, 1970, 10.

77. Interview with Jones, in Lewis, *Hospital*, 278.

78. Quotes from Wimberli, "Workers Strike for Union Contract"; interview with Jones, in Lewis, *Hospital*, 278.

79. A UAW representative wrote to George Dunne, "The obligation and responsibility [to bargain with striking workers] is yours, especially in this period when it is so important to rebuild the political coalition of labor, minorities and forward thinking people so that we can get the country moving again." Letter, Robert Johnston to George Dunne, November 6, 1969, folder 15-21, box 15, AFSCME Central Files. See also Everett Clark, President, Local 777, Seafarers International Union to Neal Bratcher, Cook County Council 19, November 20, 1969, folder 15-21, box 15, AFSCME Central Files; Memo, Bollard to Wurf, November 26, 1969.

80. Losier, "Rise and Fall of the 1969 Jobs Campaign," 118.

81. Memo, Bollard to Wurf, October 29, 1969.

82. Flyer, To ALL employees of Cook County Hospital, November 20, 1969, folder 15-21, box 15, AFSCME Central Files. Flyer attached to Letter from Hospital Director Robert J. Freeark to Mrs. Willie Byrd re: her dismissal from her position as food

service worker, November 17, 1969. On solidarity with Charleston hospital workers and the larger campaign for racial and economic justice, backed by the SCLC, see Mantler, *Power to the Poor*, 216–18.

83. Wimberli, "Workers Strike for Union Contract."

84. Nathaniel X, "Wages Still Inadequate."

85. The murders of Hampton and Mark Clark at the hands of state's attorney's officers prompted Jesse Jackson and Operation Breadbasket to pursue other campaigns and to register voters in order to defeat state's attorney Edward Hanrahan. Mantler, *Power to the Poor*, 235–38.

86. Flyer, To ALL employees of Cook County Hospital.

87. Quote from Letter, Eugene P. Moats to General President Sullivan, Subject: Local 46—Preliminary report, November 26, 1969, folder 9-5, Sullivan Records; Letter, David Sullivan to John Masse, December 2, 1969, folder 9-6, Sullivan Records.

88. John J. Masseto Member, December 1, 1969, folder 15-21, box 15, AFSCME Central Files.

89. "Hospital Union Row Breaks into Open," *Chicago Today*, December 3, 1969, folder 9–6, Sullivan Records; Thomas R. Donahue to James Gildea, December 11, 1969, folder 15-21, box 15, AFSCME Central Files.

90. Complaint, *Ida Mae Harris, et al., v. George W. Dunne, et al.*, no. 69 C 2547 (N. D. Ill, December 15, 1969), folder 9-6, box 9, Sullivan Records.

91. Transcript of Proceedings, *Ida Mae Harris, et al., v. George W. Dunne, et al.*, no. 69 C 2547 (N. D. Ill, December 15, 1969), folder 9-7, box 9, Sullivan Records. See also David Reed, "County Hospital Food Workers Sue, Charge Unfair Labor Practices," *Chicago Sun-Times*, December 11, 1969, folder 9-6, Sullivan Records; "Union Seeks Recognition," *Chicago Tribune*, December 11, 1969, folder 9-6, Sullivan Records. Attorney Gil Cornfield had represented tenants in the SCLC's organizing drive a few years earlier and continued to represent tenants in the years after. Gil Cornfield, Melody Heaps, and Norman Hill, "Labor and the Chicago Freedom Movement," in *Martin Luther King, Jr. and Civil Rights Activism in the North*, ed. Mary Lou Finley, Bernard LaFayette Jr., James R. Ralph Jr., and Pam Smith, 373–86 (Lexington: University of Kentucky Press, 2016).

92. Reporting on the number of striking workers varied. During the second week of November, WSO reporter Sig Wimberli reported 150 members on strike, of which 230 signed union cards. On November 26, an SEIU representative wrote that only 5 to 10 workers remained on the picket. *Chicago Today* reported 100 still on strike on December 3, and an AFSCME attorney said the same during court proceedings on December 15. The *Daily News* reported on December 18 that only 30 were on strike. On January 3, 1970, the *Defender* reported 100. Wimberli, "Workers Strike for Union Contract"; Moats to Sullivan, November 26, 1969; "Hospital Union Row Breaks into Open"; Transcript of Proceedings, *Harris v. Dunne*; "Strikers Lose Bid to Block Rival," *Chicago Daily News*, December 18, 1969, folder 9-6, box 8, Sullivan Records; "Striking Hospital Workers May Be Dismissed for Union Activities," *Chicago Daily Defender* (Big Weekend Edition), January 3, 1970.

93. Three who testified described being hired by precinct captains and then instructed by hospital management personnel to pay union dues. One was hired through civil service before being recruited as a Local 46 steward who herself collected Local 46 dues. Excerpt of Proceeding, *Ida Mae Harris, et al., v. George W. Dunne, et al.*, no. 69 C 2547 (N. D. Ill, December 15, 1969), folder 9-7, box 9, Sullivan Records. See also "Hospital Fights for Own Union, Court Is Told," *Chicago Sun-Times*, December 16, 1969, folder 9-6, box 9, Sullivan Records; "Forced into Union: Food Workers," *Chicago Sun-Times*, December 16, 1969, folder 9-6, box 9, Sullivan Records.

94. Letter, David Sullivan to George Meany, December 18, 1969, folder 9-6, box 9, Sullivan Records; Memorandum Opinion, *Ida Mae Harris, et al., v. George W. Dunne, et al.*, no. 69 C 2547 (N. D. Ill, December 15, 1969), folder 9-6, Sullivan Records; "County Hospital Strikers Lose Bid to Block Rival," *Chicago Daily News*, December 19, 1969, folder 9-6, Sullivan Records; "Refuse Injunction to Hospital Union," *Chicago Sun-Times*, December 19, 1969, folder 9-6, Sullivan Records.

95. "County Hospital Strike Over," *Chicago Sun Times*, March 26, 1970, folder 23, box 5, ILIR Clippings; "Striking Hospital Workers May Be Dismissed for Union Activities," *Chicago Daily Defender*, January 3, 1970.

96. Letter, David Sullivan to John J. Masse, March 23, 1970, folder 9-7, Sullivan Records. Sullivan had expressed similar concerns in the fall. Letter, David Sullivan to John J. Masse, October 10, 1969, folder 9-5, Sullivan Records.

97. Interview with Jones, in Lewis, *Hospital*, 278.

98. "Hospital Workers' Strike Right Upheld," *Chicago Sun Times*, November 26, 1969; Derber, "Hospital Employees Labor Program," 148. On RNs securing a contract, see "Cook County Hospital RNs in Job Accord," *Chicago Daily Defender*, January 6, 1970.

99. "'Sick' County X-Ray Aides Slow Transfers," *Chicago Sun Times*, April 14, 1970, folder 34, box 16, ILIR Clippings; Ronald Kotulak, "New County Crisis: X-Rays Help 'Sick,'" *Chicago Tribune*, April 14, 1970, folder 34, box 16, ILIR Clippings; "Offer X-Ray Technician Wage Hike," *Chicago Sun Times*, April 15, 1970, folder 34, box 16, ILIR Clippings; Bonne J. Nesbitt, "No End to X-Ray Protest," *Chicago Daily Defender*, April 21, 1970; Ronald Kotulak, "X-Ray Staff OK's Pay Hike, Ends Sick Out," *Chicago Tribune*, April 14, 1970, folder 34, box 16, ILIR Clippings.

100. On the "heal-in" as an activist tool in other locales, see "Interns and Residents . . . City Hospital Neglect Challenged," *Health PAC Bulletin* no. 3 (August 1968), http://www.healthpacbulletin.org/wp-content/uploads/2012/10/1968-Aug-32.pdf/.

101. The large number of "foreign medical graduates," as they were usually called, signified to some that the hospital's training program failed to attract American-trained students. The Hart-Celler Immigration and Nationality Act of 1965 made this possible. On this history and the precedent it set for decades following, see Eram Alam, "Cold War Crises: Foreign Medical Graduates Respond to US Doctor Shortages, 1965–1975," *Social History of Medicine* 33, no. 1 (2018): 132–51.

102. Betty Washington, "NMA Asks Hospital Probe," *Chicago Daily Defender*, November 1, 1967.

103. Barbara Bishop, "Health Movement: Storm in the Windy City," *Health PAC Bulletin* no. 30 (April 1971), 10.

104. Interview with Dr. Robert Freeark, in Lewis, *Hospital*, 113.

105. Quoted in Joseph Boyce, "Freeark Tells How Hospital Got in a Jam: Buildup of Crisis Detailed at Probe," *Chicago Tribune*, February 22, 1970. On bulging of wards in wintertime, see interview with Dr. Roger Benson, in Lewis, *Hospital*, 77; interview with Gertrude D'Anno, in Lewis, *Hospital*, 103.

106. Quote from hospital superintendent Freeark, in Ronald Kotulak, "Meeting Slated Today in County Hospital Crisis," *Chicago Tribune*, February 21, 1970.

107. Ronald Kotulak, "45 Hospitals Devise Plan to Ease Crisis in Emergency Rooms," *Chicago Tribune*, February 24, 1970. In a 1993 interview, Freeark described how the house staff had "already closed [the hospital] on a couple of nights when they thought they were overwhelmed, just to make a point, I suspect. And I had to defend them, because there was no question that they were overwhelmed." Dr. Robert Freeark interview, in Lewis, *Hospital*, 115.

108. Bonne J. Nesbitt, "McNeil: Reopen County Hospital," *Chicago Daily Defender*, February 25, 1970.

109. Faith C. Christmas, "Ask U.S. Aid in Hospital Crisis," *Chicago Daily Defender*, February 23, 1970.

110. Steven Pratt, "Staff Mourns as Hospital's 'Death' Nears," *Chicago Tribune*, May 20, 1970; Arthur Siddon, "Poor People Are Apprehensive about County Hospital Future," *Chicago Tribune*, May 21, 1970.

111. Sheryl Butler, "50 Picket County Hospital," *Chicago Daily Defender*, May 27, 1970; Ronald Kotulak, "Dunne Urges Bill to Turn Over Hospital," *Chicago Tribune*, May 28, 1970; Thomas Leroy, "Cook County Phase Out to Boost Care of Poor," *Chicago Daily Defender* (Big Weekend Edition), May 30, 1970; John Elmer, "Ogilvie Gets Bill to Keep County Hospital Running," *Chicago Tribune*, May 30, 1970; quote from Ronald Kotulak, "Ogilvie Gives Hospital Rein to Commission: Signs Two Bills Ending Board Domination," *Chicago Tribune*, June 18, 1970.

112. "Welcome Dr. Haughton," *Chicago Daily Defender*, October 6, 1970; Toni Anthony, "Challenges Turn Dr. Haughton On," *Chicago Daily Defender* (Big Weekend Edition), October 3, 1970.

113. "Inks Bills to Aid County Hospital," *Chicago Daily Defender*, June 24, 1970, 14.

114. Quote from Pat Girczyc, RN, and Lauren Crawford, Chicago Women's Liberation Union, untitled, n.d., Jenny Knauss Papers, folder 14, box 4, Northwestern Special Collections, Evanston, IL; "Nurses to Vote on County Strike," *Chicago Tribune*, October 22, 1972; Philip Wattley, "County Nurses OK Strike," *Chicago Tribune*, October 24, 1972.

115. "100 Protest Planned Firing of 1,000 at County Hospital," *Chicago Tribune*, December 5, 1972.

116. Quotes from Girczyc and Crawford, untitled.

117. Interview with Jones, in Lewis, *Hospital*, 278.

CHAPTER 9

The Meaning of Teachers' Labor in American Education

Change, Challenge, and Resistance

JON SHELTON

In the spring of 2018, teachers in West Virginia, Oklahoma, and Arizona staged massive statewide strikes. They were protesting their respective states' disinvestment from public education, and much of the public supported them. During the strike, Ashleigh Hardwick, a worker for a local florist and a parent of an elementary school student in Oklahoma, remarked, "[The strike] has been a hassle, that's for sure. But if it's going to better my child's future . . . I think I can handle missing a few days of work."[1] Hardwick's assumption about the strike—that improved education could enhance her daughter's economic future—provides us with an important window to understand how teachers' labor has changed throughout American history. It is clear that in the recent past, Americans have increasingly accepted the idea that economic opportunity is fundamentally linked to one's ability to acquire "human capital" in order to compete in a global labor marketplace. And because such human capital is supposedly enhanced by the work of teachers employed in the public sector, it is important to analyze how the labor of the teachers themselves has been perceived over time.

In his account of the early history of the public sector labor movement, Joseph Slater challenged scholars to consider that public employees, despite their obligation to serve the public, faced class dynamics just as any other worker does: "Certainly the goods and services government provides through its employees involve productive relations, and certainly these relations, which involve managers and subordinates at work, create class issues."[2] While Slater is undoubtedly correct, it is important to add that for teachers in particular among public employees, their supervisors (principals, superintendents, boards of education, etc.) do not manage their employees just as they please. Indeed, the assumptions of many different Americans about what the "product" of education should look like has undergirded the managerial decisions of employers in public education from the beginning of American history until the present. Teachers, therefore, have had to navigate a complex labor model in both their day-to-day work lives and whenever they sought to organize to affect their collective working conditions.

Of all the public services provided by the state, none has a longer history in the United States than education, and, arguably, none has been laden with such importance. Indeed, education is expected to instruct new generations of Americans in moral values and inculcate national identity, and, in modern America, education is viewed as integral in facilitating economic opportunity. Further, perhaps no American institution has been so directly connected to democratic governance as locally controlled schools.[3] In a very important sense, then, with regard to teachers, the "public" informs the employer's position in a more direct way than probably any other occupation in the United States.

This chapter considers a specific type of public employee—teachers—and explains how the expectations of their job duties have changed over time. I show how those expectations connect to broader social expectations related to class, race, gender, and economic opportunity, and I also examine how teachers have organized to shape both the conditions under which they work as well as some of the expectations undergirding those conditions.

Like all kinds of workers, American teachers have organized for better salaries, enhanced job security, and more control over their working conditions.[4] Perhaps more than any other workers, however, organizing by teachers has been structured by conflicts that transcend their own economic security. First, teachers have struggled for resources to do the work that they have signed up to do, which, beyond instruction, also includes emotional and social care for children. This struggle has been connected to salaries, health care, and pensions, but it has also included collective efforts for access to smaller classes, student supplies, and support services, all of which increase the cost to the state. Teachers have often negotiated this struggle within the broader context of race and class. After World War II, for instance, a largely white urban teaching force sought middle-class professional status by unionizing, but due process rights for teachers sometimes closed off opportunities to potential teachers of color, and both African American and Latino parents sometimes criticized white teachers for not responding to the needs of their children. Further, gender has played a large part in this conflict because

210   PUBLIC WORKERS IN THE NEOLIBERAL AGE

since the advent of universal public education, the teaching force has been overwhelmingly female.

Second, teachers have seen their labor enmeshed in social and political competition over what should be taught and who makes the decisions about what and how to teach. Indeed, since the beginning of the common schools movement in the nineteenth century, teachers have been enmeshed in public debates about the very purpose of education. Since they began organizing in unions in the late nineteenth century, teachers have sometimes done so in order to defend the democratic purpose of education in addition to seeking better material conditions. How Americans understand the purpose of education has shifted dramatically over the course of the past century, and this shift has had major implications for teachers and their unions in the recent past.

In the remainder of this chapter, then, I situate the efforts of teachers and their unions not only to improve their own working conditions but also to impact the broader terrain of public education. In the first section, I highlight the way Americans viewed the purpose of education in the nineteenth century, and then in the second section, I provide a very brief overview of the history of teachers' unions and the kinds of conflicts they faced from their inception in the 1890s through the fight for collective bargaining in the 1960s and '70s. Here I show how some of the earliest efforts to organize were undertaken to defend the democratic promise of education but that as unions sought institutional legitimacy, their concerns narrowed. In the third section, I examine the changing contours of public education and the labor of teaching since the 1970s, with a specific focus on antiunion conservatism, political economic neoliberalism, and the Democratic Party's shift toward a narrative around developing human capital as the primary means for economic opportunity in America. Examining the very recent past in the fourth section, I explain how teachers' unions responded to these developments. I argue that there has been a major shift in how many teachers' unions are organizing to defend and shape public education. As unions sought institutional legitimacy in the 1950s and '60s, they moved toward a much narrower form of "bread-and-butter" unionism. But in the past decade, the most successful teachers' unions returned to organizing for a broader vision of democracy. In the very recent past, many teachers are taking action to advance a more comprehensive social democratic vision for themselves and in the broader community. I show that the most successful teachers' unions now offer not just resistance to "neoliberalism" but also a vision of what an equitable education system in an equitable society should look like: connecting resources for public education and race and gender equity to the working conditions of teachers.

The Rise of Universal Public Education

Though the United States is often known for its spartan welfare state, the rapid and dramatic growth of public education across the nation in the nineteenth century represented a revolution in social welfare that would be emulated across the globe. Indeed, in just a few decades beginning in the 1830s, the expectation that primary education should be both fully publicly funded and universal spread across the country. Outside the South, the idea was virtually ubiquitous by the time of the Civil War.

Indeed, the advent of public education played a major role in the economic development of American citizens, as well as the nation writ large. According to historian Nancy Beadie, for instance, the social capital local communities invested in schools played an important role in the early nineteenth-century market revolution.[5] Economists Claudia Goldin and Lawrence Katz argue that the efforts of local constituencies in the nineteenth century to tax themselves were an instrumental "virtue" in the expansion of the education system that set the United States apart from other nations. This investment placed the nation on a trajectory to become a world leader in terms of both the skills of its citizens and economic development by the end of the nineteenth century.[6]

Despite the economic benefits, however, the primary purpose of common schools was to enhance individual moral and intellectual development and to inculcate a common understanding of American citizenship.[7] The advent of universal public education in the nineteenth century has not always been viewed as an unqualified good. Some Americans at the time argued about whether or not paying for public education was necessary. Further, there has been a robust debate among historians of education about whether common schools served primarily to discipline unruly (often Catholic immigrant) working families during a period of intense economic and social disruption.[8] It is clear, however, that the most important advocates of common schools, such as Horace Mann and William Ellery Channing, viewed their efforts as something more than enhancing the human capital of future generations. Channing, for instance, believed "a democratic education would open the riches of the natural and human worlds to all people—to allow each young person to gain insight into the nature of things. To offer some such a rich experience of the world and to leave others without it was an abrogation of the idea that all people in a democracy are equal."[9] Similarly, Mann specifically rejected arguments that common schools existed primarily to enhance the skills of future workers.[10] Indeed, accruing "human capital" was not a major concern of the most prominent advocates of common schools during the period of their expansion in the nineteenth century.

Most working people did not view the promise of public schools in this way either. Workingmen's parties in New York, Pennsylvania, and other states in the 1830s, '40s, and '50s advocated a universal school system that would train the next generation of workingmen to be citizens in a democratic society capable of organizing against the growing power of employers in a nation transitioning to a system of wage labor. As one workingmen's association put it in 1829, "Real liberty and equality have no foundation but in universal and equal instruction."[11]

By the end of the nineteenth century, the American education system continued to be a world leader. By that point, school districts across the country had begun to expand public access to high school.[12] Indeed, the average American young person likely received more education than students in any other nation.[13] Even African Americans in the South, who faced a separate and unequal system, valued education so much that Black communities often taxed themselves a second time (after paying taxes that mostly subsidized white schools) to ensure decent education for their children.[14] It may very well be the case that the expansion of public support for education in the nineteenth and twentieth centuries aided economic development by enhancing employees' skills, even among nonprofessional workers.[15]

Still, most working Americans did not view the purpose of education through the prism of skills development. Indeed, following the emergence of the "labor problem"—the dramatic conflict between working people and their employers in the late nineteenth century that suffused the American political economy—the key political questions around economic livelihood for most working people focused on jobs and workplace rights. By the end of the nineteenth century, however, a growing group of education reformers sought to centralize control over education and to shape it in ways that would subordinate it to business-style managerial techniques. This movement was rooted in efforts by reformer William Rainey Harper, president of the university created by John D. Rockefeller (the University of Chicago), to centralize education in Chicago in a way that took classroom autonomy away from a teaching force made up primarily of female teachers. This campaign, in part, impelled teachers in Chicago to organize the first teachers' union in the United States, the Chicago Teachers Federation (CTF).[16]

The Rise of Teachers' Unions

Organized in 1897, the CTF was initially formed by elementary school teachers, virtually all of whom were women, seeking better salaries and pensions. Indeed, the massive expansion of common schools in the nineteenth century had likely been possible only by feminizing the teaching profession. Though most teachers were men in the early nineteenth century, during the common school era, more women were hired as teachers. By 1850 a majority of American teachers were women, and by 1900 the teaching force was 70 percent female.[17] Though advocates praised female teachers' supposed natural abilities to guide children, there is a compelling argument that the gender shift mostly had to with finances: women could be paid less than men, allowing school districts to expand education with more limited resources.[18] Indeed, as late as 1906 the average female teacher made 38 percent less than a male teacher.[19]

Though teachers initially organized the union to push for economic security, the CTF was brought into the broader terrain of class politics in the city by sixth grade teacher Margaret Haley, who was elected vice president of the union in 1898. Haley connected teachers' working conditions to the growing inequality of the Gilded Age in order to mobilize the working-class community against Harper's education reforms. "By highlighting Harper's link to the millionaire Rockefeller and to moneyed interests," historian Kate Rousmaniere explains, "the debate over restructuring the city public school system was deflected to a debate about power and class interests in a democratic society."[20] The Harper plan was defeated, and Haley and the CTF would go on to engage in a years-long campaign, culminating in a court case, to force some of Chicago's wealthiest corporations to pay their fair share of taxes for public schools.[21] Haley and the CTF would also successfully organize against a business-derived plan to remake the public schools into a two-tiered system that would have narrowed the education of working-class children.[22]

It is worth spending a little space to fully appreciate how Haley thought about unions and public education. I am not making the case here that all Chicago teachers would have necessarily agreed with Haley, but it is instructive to firmly connect the roots of teacher unionism in the United States to a robust vision of public education and broader social democracy that transcended the notion that education merely enabled students to acquire "human capital."

Haley's most significant argument for the connection between the efforts of teachers' unions and the purpose of public education is her memorable speech, "Why Teachers Should Organize," at the annual meeting of the National Education Association (NEA) in 1904.[23] (The NEA, an organization that had been in existence since 1857, was not yet a union but a national organization led by school administrators that pushed for more funding for public education and shared best pedagogical practices. Haley was a member of both the CTF and the NEA.)

In the speech, Haley began by asserting that the American people were imperfectly prepared for democracy. Citing Mann, she argued that teachers' organizations must evidence the same democracy that public schools were meant to teach future American citizens. But the promise of public education was hamstrung, Haley argued, by the problems facing teachers, which included inadequate salaries, limited provisions for retirement, and overcrowded classrooms. As important as the diminished conditions under which teachers taught and students learned were, however, the teacher also faced the "increased tendency toward 'factoryizing education,' making the teacher an automaton, a mere factory hand, whose duty is to carry out mechanically and unquestioningly the ideas and orders of those clothed with the authority of position, and who may or may not know the needs of the children or how to minister to them." Connecting the struggles for teachers' autonomy to the efforts of industrial workers to organize, Haley argued teachers needed control over their workplace in order to best help students meet their needs.

Haley concluded that teachers must organize because of their special role in creating a more democratic society in the context of the inequalities of the industrial age. Indeed, she argued that teachers' "special contribution to society is their own power to think, the moral courage to follow their convictions, and the training of citizens to think and to express thought in free and intelligent action." Haley's articulation of why teachers should organize, then, showed that teachers were workers like any other, but they were also more than that: their work was also to teach other Americans to be citizens in a democracy.

Though the activism of Haley and the CTF helped prevent a dramatic transformation of the very premise of public education in Chicago, the effort to unionize met massive opposition from the teachers' employer. While the CTF was a charter member of the first national union, the American Federation of Teachers (AFT, formed in 1916), the Chicago Board of Education successfully attacked public school teachers' right to affiliate with other unions. Using a common tactic by private sector employers, school boards across the country sought to prevent teachers from unionizing by instituting yellow-dog contracts, or agreements in which workers agreed not to affiliate with a union as a condition of employment.[24] A yellow-dog policy passed by the school board in 1916 led the CTF to disaffiliate from the Chicago Federation of Labor and the AFT in 1917. Union membership fell by half.[25]

Teachers across the country continued to organize in the 1920s and '30s but without statutory rights to bargain (and in some cases with complete prohibitions on joining unions); they had to use various forms of less formal collective pressure to improve salaries and working conditions. After World War II, some teachers—the first were in Norwalk, Connecticut, in 1946, and teachers went on strike in Buffalo, St. Paul, and Minneapolis, too—withheld their labor in order to get higher salaries and better conditions for their students. In St. Paul, for example, teachers' demands included lowering enormous class sizes and ensuring all students had textbooks. But teacher strikes right after the war were dealt with harshly, as states passed a series of punitive laws to prevent public employees from exercising collective leverage by striking. These laws assumed that strikes violated government sovereignty since they were tantamount to disobeying the orders of the state.[26]

In the 1960s and 1970s, teachers across the country gained institutional collective bargaining relationships with their school boards. The struggle to grasp and hold on to institutional legitimacy during this era, however, limited the demands of teachers' unions and sometimes set them in opposition to the communities in which they taught. It is difficult to summarize the trajectory of bargaining rights in this era, as there was a great deal of state and local idiosyncrasy. But there was clearly a dialectical relationship at play. With stronger labor unions in the United States and the growth of government efforts to solve social problems (I employ the term "labor-liberalism" for this combination in my book *Teacher Strike!*), public employee unions faced a less hostile legislative terrain and worked within a political economic structure in which labor unions had dramatically improved the wages and working conditions of millions of industrial workers. Public employee unions lobbied for laws that allowed them to collectively bargain, and Wisconsin was the first state to pass such a law in 1959. The Wisconsin Council of County and Municipal Employees (WCCME) was integral in pushing for a collective bargaining law.[27] Still, even with more liberal labor laws, teachers often had to strike to get school boards to agree to meaningful bargaining relationships in the 1960s and '70s. There were a lot of teacher strikes in the 1960s, largely confined to industrial states on the East Coast and Midwest with strong private sector labor movements, but most were short, rarely lasting more than a week.[28]

The length of strikes grew in the late 1960s and '70s, as teachers' unions were embroiled in two interrelated conflicts: first, urban school systems' abject failures to provide equal education to African American and Puerto Rican students, and, second, fiscal crises caused by long-term suburbanization and capital flight, and, in the 1970s, the energy crisis and economic downturn. In 1968 a series of strikes by New York City's United Federation of Teachers (UFT) to defend teachers' due process rights from the legitimate

216   PUBLIC WORKERS IN THE NEOLIBERAL AGE

demand of Black parents to end racial inequality in the school system shut down schools and brought simmering racial tensions into the streets.[29]

In a similar conflict, teachers were on strike in Newark for about four weeks in 1970 and eleven weeks in 1971. In 1973, teachers in Chicago, St. Louis, and Philadelphia were on strike at the same time. In 1974, the entire membership of the rural Hortonville Education Association in Wisconsin was fired and replaced by the school board. In the 1975–1976 school year, there were over two hundred teacher strikes in the United States, including an illegal, weeklong strike by teachers in New York City protesting education cuts during the city's fiscal crisis. In 1979, St. Louis teachers were on strike for fifty-six days. In Cleveland teachers were on strike from mid-October 1979 until January 1980. And in 1981, right after Reagan had summarily fired and replaced striking air traffic controllers, educators in Philadelphia undertook the last lengthy teacher strike in American history, a seven-week walkout, in which teachers mostly held the line against concessions demanded by Democratic mayor William Green III.[30]

After the smoke had cleared, teachers' unions had successfully defended their right to collectively bargain and for the most part had been accepted, often grudgingly, as legitimate actors in both the labor movement and in American public education. Still, the public reputation of teachers' unions had been battered. The massive problems that existed in many metropolitan school systems (on which contentious teacher strikes had powerfully shone a light in the 1960s and '70s) had not improved. Urban school systems were still beset by racial segregation, capital flight, the shift of property taxes to the suburbs, and student populations facing all of the problems that come with a systemic lack of economic opportunity. In some cities, particularly where contentious strikes pitted communities of color against largely white teaching forces, unions continued to absorb a good deal of blame for persistent institutional racism. Further, a growing conservative explanation for the political economic crisis of the 1970s blamed both political liberalism and teachers' unions for high taxes and a supposedly unproductive public sector.

Teaching in a Neoliberal World

Over the past fifty years, two interrelated developments have dramatically altered the structure of the American education system. In the 1970s, as teachers' unions battled school district administrations, American industry faced increasing competition from abroad, and corporations began a decades-long war to diminish unions, shift production elsewhere, and increase profits by reducing labor costs.[31] From this era came two different visions for facilitating economic opportunity in the United States. Conservatives, such as economist Milton Friedman and President Ronald Reagan, pushed to reduce taxes and government regulations and to weaken unions. Republicans trained their sights on weakening the power of public employee unions, especially those of teachers, as part of this effort. Neoliberal Democrats, their base shifting away from blue-collar workers and toward suburban, college-educated liberals, began to make a different argument: a meritocratic system that enhanced access to education would allow working people hard hit by economic crisis, deindustrialization, and capital flight in the 1970s and '80s to gain the "human capital" necessary to compete in a global labor marketplace.[32]

These "new" Democrats' growing emphasis on education built on existing assumptions regarding the notion of "human capital," which had been woven into earlier iterations of liberalism and grew alongside the battles for teachers' collective bargaining rights. Lyndon Johnson's Great Society program, through the Elementary and Secondary Education Act (1965), included explicit federal calls to reduce social and economic inequalities through compensatory education as well as the dramatic expansion of federal support for higher education funding through the Higher Education Act. During this era, in fact, the American economics field, led by the University of Chicago's Gary Becker, even began employing the term "human capital" to refer to the higher wages Americans workers would earn from investing in education. This terminology represented a significant shift in how Americans viewed economic production.[33]

There was certainly no shortage of Republicans in the 1980s and '90s arguing that education was significant in facilitating American economic growth and opportunity. This argument, for instance, was one of the premises of the landmark report *A Nation at Risk* in 1983, an effort led by Reagan's secretary of education Terrel Bell.[34] And in fact, as Becker noted in the third edition of his economics text *Human Capital: A Theoretical and Empirical Analysis with Special Reference to Education*, in the 1992 U.S. presidential campaign both George H. W. Bush and Bill Clinton employed the term "investing in human capital," terminology, he pointed out, that "would have been inconceivable in a Presidential campaign" just twelve years before.[35]

But Democrats—particularly Clinton, who became chair of the five-year-old Democratic Leadership Council (DLC) in 1990 before resigning to run for president, and economist Robert Reich, secretary of labor during Clinton's first term—would push most forcefully in the 1990s the notion that American workers must accommodate to the new reality of a "knowledge economy." Reich argued that as the American economy became more global, American workers could guarantee themselves a livelihood only if they were able to become "symbolic analysts," whose primary tasks were to "solve, identify, and broker problems by manipulating symbols." These workers included engineers, financial and management consultants, research scientists, public relations executives, journalists, and others. Most symbolic analysts, according to Reich, were college graduates, and he supposed that from the 1950s to the 1990s, the percentage of such workers had more than doubled. He believed the key in getting all Americans to succeed in the growing knowledge economy was simply to bring more of them into it. Doing so necessitated major public investment in education—at the primary, secondary, and tertiary levels. Clinton, a longtime friend, made Reich's argument a centerpiece of his campaign in 1992.[36]

The ascendance of Clinton and the DLC in the 1990s put this vision of economic opportunity at the center of the Democratic Party. The growing importance of education in narratives around facilitating economic opportunity, in turn, abetted market-based reforms aimed at the public school system, and Democrats have since been some of the most important proponents of disciplining teachers to ensure they are supposedly better able to meet the needs of the nation's employers. It makes intuitive sense for Democrats to push for such changes given the shifting premises for economic opportunity in the United States: if the global economy is a meritocracy, and education is the means by which to get the skills to make it, then those schools that do not graduate students with such skills—no matter the structural impediments their students face—are, by definition, failing. Further, Democrats have operated under growing pressure from a far-right chorus blaming teachers' unions for stifling education reform and protecting incompetent teachers. This argument's roots can be traced back to the late 1960s, particularly with the work of the National Right to Work Committee (NRTWC), which focused both legal challenges and public relations on public employees, especially teachers.[37]

Since the early 1990s, most states have experimented with different forms of education based on the principle that "competition"—typically from non-union schools—will improve traditional public schools and enhance educational outcomes for everyone without significant increases in state investment. A surprising coalition in Wisconsin, for example, included African American civil rights activists in the legislature and conservative Republican governor Tommy Thompson, who brokered a deal in 1989 to become the first state to provide public dollars for private school vouchers. The voucher program has since been expanded several times, siphoning tax dollars from public schools. Ohio has also instituted a voucher program, and a handful of other states have experimented with it, but vouchers have not yet broadly undermined public education.[38]

The Meaning of Teachers' Labor in American Education   219

Charter schools, however, which are vouchers' more palatable cousin, have exploded since the Clinton years. Initially envisioned as a way for teachers to experiment with different pedagogical techniques, charters allow various community groups to run schools with public dollars, but they are less accountable to the governance of school boards. The first such school, created in Minnesota, was chartered in 1991; as of 2012–2013, there were almost six thousand charter schools responsible for instructing about 5 percent of the total number of students in the country.[39] Though many charters, like many public schools, are excellent, there is little evidence that charters have, on the whole, significantly improved educational outcomes for students, and in some places, private corporations have managed them with the idea of extracting a profit. Almost all charters, whether for-profit or nonprofit, however, employ teachers who are not in unions and can be disciplined or fired much more easily than those in public schools represented by strong unions.

In traditional public schools and charters alike, the accountability movement, fortified by the bipartisan No Child Left Behind Act (a reauthorization of the Elementary and Secondary Education Act in 2001) and "Race to the Top" (part of the Barack Obama administration's implementation of the American Recovery and Reinvestment Act in 2009), have sought to tie teachers' livelihoods to their students' performance on standardized tests. There is little evidence that this emphasis on testing is even doing what it is intended to do: improving Americans kids' aggregate performance on test scores. There is evidence, however, that these efforts have placed the public school system under serious threat from market-based reforms and the efforts of private capital, which manages charter schools for profit in many states and now makes lucrative profits in the testing and test preparation industries.

In contrast to the rhetoric of corporate reformers, traditional public schools actually provide high-quality education to the majority of students, as Diane Ravitch notes, and the real impediments to better educational outcomes are structural poverty and racial segregation. Liberals, she argues, "have lent their support to a project that is antithetical to liberalism and progressivism. By supporting market-based 'reforms,' they have allied themselves with those who seek to destroy public education. They are being used by those who have an implacable hostility toward the public sector." Indeed, perhaps no better example of this shift in thinking about public education can be found in the 2010 film *Waiting for "Superman."* Directed by liberal Davis Guggenheim (lauded for his documentary chronicling Al Gore's attempts to fight climate change) and funded and promoted by the Gates Foundation, the film furthered the narrative that teachers' unions represent the most significant impediment to poor children's ability to access economic opportunity through education, and that more choice for parents—specifically in the form of charters—represents the panacea that will help alleviate inequality in the United States.[40]

At the same time, the massive investments in public education Reich called for in *The Work of Nations* never materialized. Indeed, in many cities, neoliberal Democrats have since undermined public school systems by closing neighborhood schools, opening charters, and funneling money meant for public education to corporate development. Chicago has represented the tip of this spear. Mayors Richard Daley and Rahm Emanuel, the latter of whom had been Obama's chief of staff, moved to shift the trajectory of the school district away from the needs of the city's poorest students and to discipline unionized teachers. Other cities, such as Newark, whose mayor Cory Booker was deeply connected to Democrats for Education Reform, effectively turned the school district over to corporate consultants in one of the greatest boondoggles in the history of American cities, and federal policymakers such as Obama's education secretary Arne Duncan, the "CEO" of Chicago's schools before becoming the architect of "Race to the Top," followed suit.[41]

Since 2010, in the purple states of Wisconsin, Ohio, Michigan, and Iowa, extreme right-wing conservatives have built on years of efforts to blame public employees for deindustrialization and capital flight, connecting private sector workers' livelihoods to higher taxes by passing laws to diminish public sector unions.[42] Wisconsin's Act 10, the signal accomplishment of Republican governor Scott Walker, represented the most prominent effort in this battle. Teachers, of course, represented the largest group of public employees impacted by the law. Since Act 10, teacher turnover and the state's educational outcomes have been demonstrably hampered.[43]

In many red states, as the teacher strikes of the "education spring" in 2018 revealed to the entire country, Republican lawmakers had simply starved the schools of funds to pay for tax cuts for extractive industries, particularly in the years after the economic crisis of 2008. In Oklahoma, for instance, where the GOP had cut taxes and the legislature could not increase taxes without a 75 percent supermajority, 20 percent of the state's school districts moved to four-day weeks to accommodate chronic budget shortfalls.[44]

* * *

There has thus been a great irony within the trajectory of public education over the course of the past four decades. Education has been laden with ever greater significance as Americans' acquisition of "human capital" represents a major part of the explanation for how to access economic opportunity. At the same time, disinvestment in public education and increased accountability measures have put extreme pressure on teachers and their unions. In fact, from the 1990s to the present, teacher salaries, in aggregate, have actually declined, and fewer than half of Americans now want to see their children to go into the teaching force.[45] Teachers have voted with their feet by opting for other occupations, and many states now face chronic teacher shortages.

Further, since the early 1970s, the teaching force has been increasingly comprised of women (and now about 76 percent of teachers are women, compared to about 65 percent in 1971). It is an open question whether the profession has become more gendered as a consequence of the downward pressure on teacher salaries and diminished autonomy in the classroom or if gendering has played a constitutive role in those developments.[46] More than likely, the answer is dialectical: the greater percentage of the teaching force that is female, the easier it is for policymakers to employ sexist notions of care work to keep budgets tighter and salaries lower and to surveil and discipline teachers, and the more diminished the profession gets, the more likely it is that men seek work elsewhere.

Another open question is the extent to which teachers' unions bear responsibility for accommodating neoliberal developments. For years, representatives of the AFT and the NEA, for strategic reasons, endorsed neoliberal Democratic politicians and at least tacitly accepted neoliberal discourses about economic opportunity. For instance, in a speech at an Education International meeting in 1996, NEA president Bob Chase attempted to defend public education from Republicans' voucher schemes and to advocate for greater racial equity in America's schools. In the speech Chase conceded that public education needed to be reformed in order to accommodate its important function of facilitating human capital acquisition in a global economy.

Indeed, we should note how closely Chase's account of the changing landscape in the United States resembles Reich's: "The constant realignment going on in the world—and the nation—demands a labor force that is well educated, increasingly versatile and continually learning to reshape itself to the needs of the economy. And that brings added urgency to the need for all schools to do a better job. But transformation within the public school system has been less rapid, less encompassing, and less understood." Chase would even go on to assert that educators should "view their students as clients and partners—capable of performing to higher standards, given enough time and adequate resources." The speech invoked management techniques like Total Quality Management and asked if schools could be modeled along business practices, but there was no mention of the structural barriers an increasingly diverse student population faced in American cities. Nor did Chase assert

222   PUBLIC WORKERS IN THE NEOLIBERAL AGE

that teachers bore much responsibility in the classroom beyond building the capacities of students to "possess higher-level thinking skills and to utilize the tools of the Information Era."[47] More research must be done to answer the question, but it seems obvious that some teachers' union leaders were complicit in furthering a narrative around economic opportunity that has been partially responsible for diminishing teachers' working conditions.

Social Democratic Teachers' Unionism

In the last decade, some teachers' unions have organized a systematic response to neoliberalism, and, notably, it has come from below. Just as Margaret Haley argued was necessary a century ago, these teachers have increasingly advanced an organizing vision that places the needs of the community in which they teach alongside their working conditions. For the growing number of social democratic teachers' unions in the past decade, calls for a more robust public sector and a more equitable society rightly include better salaries and working conditions for teachers. But these calls also include an attack on a narrow curriculum centered on standardized testing and social support services for students and their families.

In Chicago in 2010, a dissident caucus of activist teachers (the Congress of Rank and File Educators—CORE), tired of union leadership in the Chicago Teacher Union (CTU), which had done very little to contest the designs of Daley and Emanuel, won a competitive election to take over the leadership of the union. CORE then spent two years building connections with the communities most impacted by racism and neoliberalism in the city and in 2012 won an overwhelming victory in a strike that centered on the needs of students in contract negotiations.[48] In Seattle, St. Paul, and elsewhere, teachers' unions, embracing the notion of "bargaining for the common good," have used either a strike or the threat of a strike to prevent budget cuts, gain teachers' voices in programs to fight racism, and reduce onerous standardized tests.[49] In 2018 the grassroots-driven red-state teacher strikes, which began in West Virginia's coal country and then led to statewide walkouts in Oklahoma and Arizona (in addition to protests in Kentucky, Colorado, and North Carolina), galvanized a national conversation about the connection between teachers' working conditions and students' learning conditions. Teachers in all of those states powerfully argued that they had to go on strike not only for livable salaries and health care but also to ensure that their students had the necessary facilities and materials to succeed in school.[50]

In January 2019, teachers in Los Angeles won a major strike. In one of the nation's wealthiest cities, teachers struggled to pay their bills, and years

Figure 9.1. Arizona teachers on strike, April 26, 2018. Invoking the slogan #RedforEd, teachers successfully organized a statewide walkout, galvanizing public support to dramatically increase education funding from a Republican-dominated state government. (Photo by Gage Skidmore for Arizona Education Association. Courtesy of Wikimedia.)

of sparse state aid forced the city's students into classrooms with unconscionable numbers of students. Further, the city's schools had been significantly undermined by corporate education reform. At the time of the strike, the LA Unified School District city had two hundred charter schools. A $12 million school board election in 2017 brought a charter-friendly majority to the board and elevated corporate Democrat Austin Beutner to the superintendent position.[51] Led by Alex Caputo-Pearl, Union Power, an insurgent caucus that won leadership in the United Teachers of Los Angeles (UTLA), spent the better part of a year organizing for a potential strike. With a 98 percent strike vote and clear public support for the walkout, UTLA was able to negotiate smaller class sizes, a major reduction of standardized testing in LA schools, a commitment from the school district to protect immigrant rights, the guarantee of a full-time nurse in every school, and a moratorium on district-authorized charter schools. The latter showed that the union would prioritize the fight to limit the takeover of public schools in the city by the charter industry.[52]

224   PUBLIC WORKERS IN THE NEOLIBERAL AGE

Clearly, the last decade has brought a significant shift in the direction of teacher unionism in the United States. Indeed, as their employers—backed by corporate money and ideology—have shifted American public education to meet the needs of employers and, to use the words of Haley back in 1904, to "factoryize" it by deprofessionalizing teachers, teachers, as workers often do, have begun fighting back. Indeed, unions like the CTU and UTLA, in addition to the grassroots efforts in red states in 2018, are once again consciously embracing the kind of social movement unionism that Haley so powerfully articulated in 1904. These teachers are building a critique of neoliberal logic, but most importantly, in fighting for more stable funding for education, health care for students, diminishing the number of standardized tests students must take, and racial equity, they have been articulating a different vision of what our world might look like: one in which people represent more than human capital and everyone is entitled to the social goods they need to live safe and secure lives.

Further Reading

Blanc, Eric. *Red State Revolt: The Teachers' Strike Wave and Working-Class Politics*. London: Verso, 2019.

Clifford, Geraldine. *Those Good Gertrudes: A Social History of Women Teachers in America*. Baltimore: Johns Hopkins University Press, 2014.

Murphy, Marjorie. *Blackboard Unions: The AFT and the NEA, 1900–1980*. Ithaca, NY: Cornell University Press, 1989.

Perrillo, Jonna. *Uncivil Rights: Teachers, Unions, and Race in the Battle for School Equity*. Chicago: University of Chicago Press, 2012.

Podair, Jerald. *The Strike That Changed New York: Blacks, Whites, and the Ocean Hill–Brownsville Crisis*. New Haven, CT: Yale University Press, 2004.

Rousmaniere, Kate. *Citizen Teacher: The Life and Leadership of Margaret Haley*. Albany: SUNY Press, 2005.

Shelton, Jon. *Teacher Strike! Public Education and the Making of a New American Political Order*. Urbana: University of Illinois Press, 2017.

Weiner, Lois. *The Future of Our Schools: Teacher Unions and Social Justice*. Chicago: Haymarket Books, 2012.

Notes

1. "Oklahoma Teachers Risk Losing Support as Walkout Continues, Some Say," *CBS News*, April 5, 2018, https://www.cbsnews.com/news/oklahoma-teachers-risk-losing-support-as-walkout-continues-some-say/.

2. Joseph Slater, *Public Workers: Government Employee Unions, the Law, and the State, 1900–1962* (Ithaca, NY: ILR Press, 2004), 4.

3. Campbell Scribner, *The Fight for Local Control: Schools, Suburbs, and American Democracy* (Ithaca, NY: Cornell University Press, 2016).

4. Though there is a long history of private schools in the United States, for the purposes of "teachers" in this chapter, I mean to refer only to public school teachers.

5. Nancy Beadie, *Education and the Creation of Capital in the Early Republic* (Cambridge: Cambridge University Press, 2010), 17.

6. Claudia Goldin and Lawrence Katz, *The Race between Technology and Education* (Cambridge, MA: Harvard University Press, 2008), 1–8, 139–49.

7. Johann Neem, *Democracy's Schools: The Rise of Public Education in America* (Baltimore: Johns Hopkins University Press, 2017).

8. See, for example, Michael Katz, *The Irony of Early School Reform* (Cambridge, MA: Harvard University Press, 1968).

9. Neem, *Democracy's Schools*, 15.

10. Ibid., 21–22.

11. Wayne Urban and Jennings Wagoner, *American Education: A History*, 5th ed. (New York: Routledge, 2014), 100–101. See also Ira Katznelson and Margaret Weir, *Schooling for All: Class, Race, and the Decline of the Democratic Ideal* (New York: Basic Books, 1985), ch. 2 (28–57). Quotation from Helen Sumner, "Rise and Growth in Philadelphia," in John Commons and Associates, *History of Labour in the United States*, vol. 1 (New York: MacMillan, 1926), 224.

12. See, for example, William Reese, *America's Public Schools: From the Common School to "No Child Left Behind"* (Baltimore: Johns Hopkins University Press, 2011), 180–83.

13. Goldin and Katz, *Race between Technology and Education*, 12.

14. James Anderson, *The Education of Blacks in the South, 1860–1935* (Chapel Hill: University of North Carolina Press, 1988), 148–85.

15. Goldin and Katz, *Race between Technology and Education*, 63–67.

16. Marjorie Murphy, *Blackboard Unions: The AFT and the NEA, 1900–1980* (Ithaca, NY: Cornell University Press, 1989), 23–34. See also Kate Rousmaniere, *Citizen Teacher: The Life and Leadership of Margaret Haley* (Albany: SUNY Press, 2005), 49–58.

17. Neem, *Democracy's Schools*, 118; Geraldine Clifford, *Those Good Gertrudes: A Social History of Women Teachers in America* (Baltimore: Johns Hopkins University Press, 2014), 35.

18. Neem, *Democracy's Schools*, 118. Marjorie Murphy frames the explanation even more explicitly: "The major reason for the feminization of teaching was purely economic." Murphy, *Blackboard Unions*, 14.

19. Clifford, *Those Good Gertrudes*, 49.

20. Rousmaniere, *Citizen Teacher*, 52.

21. Ibid., 59–91.

22. Ibid., 158.

23. Margaret Haley, "Why Teachers Should Organize," National Education Association, *Journal of Proceedings and Addresses of the Forty-Third Annual Meeting,*

St. Louis, MO, June 27–July 1, 1904. For more analysis of this speech, see Shelton, "Teaching Guide for 'Why Teachers Should Organize,'" for Labor and Working-Class History Association's Teaching Labor's Story Project, http://www.lawcha.org/wp-content/uploads/7-2-Why-Teachers-Should-Organize-FINAL.pdf/.

24. Slater, *Public Workers*, 40, 69–70.

25. Rousmaniere, *Citizen Teacher*, 159–64.

26. Murphy, *Blackboard Unions*, 182–84.

27. Slater, *Public Workers*, 158–92.

28. Jon Shelton, *Teacher Strike! Public Education and the Making of a New American Political Order* (Urbana: University of Illinois Press, 2017).

29. Jerald E. Podair, *The Strike That Changed New York: Blacks, Whites, and the Ocean Hill–Brownsville Crisis* (New Haven, CT: Yale University Press, 2004).

30. Shelton, *Teacher Strike!* On the air traffic controllers' strike, see Joseph McCartin, *Collision Course: Ronald Reagan, the Air Traffic Controllers, and the Strike That Changed America* (New York: Oxford University Press, 2011).

31. Lane Windham, *Knocking on Labor's Door: Union Organizing in the 1970s and the Roots of a New Economic Divide* (Chapel Hill: University of North Carolina Press, 2017).

32. On the shifting base of the Democratic Party, see Lily Geismer, *Don't Blame Us: Suburban Liberals and the Transformation of the Democratic Party* (Princeton, NJ: Princeton University Press, 2017).

33. See Gary Becker, *Human Capital: A Theoretical and Empirical Analysis with Special Reference to Education*, 3rd ed. (Chicago: University of Chicago Press, 1993).

34. United States Department of Education, *A Nation at Risk: The Imperative for Educational Reform* (Washington, DC: National Commission on Excellence in Education, 1983).

35. Becker, *Human Capital*, xix.

36. Robert Reich, *The Work of Nations: Preparing Ourselves for Twenty-First Century Capitalism* (New York: Vintage, 1992); Bill Clinton and Al Gore, *Putting People First: How We Can All Change America* (New York: Times Books, 1992). For instance, "Putting people first demands a revolution in lifetime learning, a concerted effort to invest in the collective talents of our people. Education today is more than the key to climbing the ladder of opportunity. In today's global economy, it is an imperative for our nation. Our economic life is on the line" (16).

37. Jon Shelton, "'Compulsory Unionism' and Its Critics: The National Right to Work Committee, Teacher Unions, and the Defeat of Labor Law Reform in 1978," *Journal of Policy History* 29, no. 3 (2017): 378–402.

38. See Jim Carl, *Freedom of Choice: Vouchers in American Education* (Santa Barbara, CA: Praeger, 2011), chs. 4–5, for the best accounts of the voucher programs set up in Milwaukee and Cleveland.

39. National Conference of State Legislatures, "Charter Schools," http://www.ncsl.org/research/education/charter-schools-overview.aspx/.

40. Diane Ravitch, *Reign of Error: The Hoax of the Privatization Movement and*

the Danger to America's Public Schools (New York: Alfred A. Knopf, 2013), quotation on p. 4. Discussion of *Waiting for "Superman,"* pp. 40–41. For further discussion of the film, see Shelton, *Teacher Strike!*, 194.

41. Pauline Lipman, *The New Political Economy of Urban Education: Neoliberalism, Race, and the Right to the City* (New York: Routledge, 2011); Dale Russakoff, *The Prize: Who's in Charge of America's Schools?* (Boston: Houghton Mifflin Harcourt), 2015.

42. Jon Shelton, "Walker's Wisconsin and the Future of the United States," in *Labor in the Time of Trump*, ed. Jasmine Kerissey, Eve Weinbaum, Clare Hammonds, Tom Juravich, and Dan Clawson, 69–86 (Ithaca, NY: Cornell University Press, 2019).

43. David Madland and Alex Rowell, "Attacks on Public-Sector Unions Harm States: How Act 10 Has Affected Education in Wisconsin." *Center for American Progress*, November 15, 2017, https://www.americanprogressaction.org/issues/economy/reports/2017/11/15/169146/attacks-public-sector-unions-harm-states-act-10-affected-education-wisconsin/.

44. Pat Donachie, "Oklahoma School Districts Enact Four-Day School Week," *Education Dive*, May 31, 2017, https://www.educationdive.com/news/oklahoma-school-districts-enact-four-day-school-week/443871/.

45. Sylvia Allegretto and Lawrence Michel, "The Teacher Pay Penalty Has Hit a New High," *Economic Policy Institute*, September 5, 2018, https://www.epi.org/publication/teacher-pay-gap-2018/.

46. I have explored these ideas in more depth elsewhere. See Shelton, "Women's Work, Women's Walkouts," *Gender Policy Report*, October 16, 2018, https://genderpolicyreport.umn.edu/womens-work-womens-walkouts/.

47. Bob Chase, "Education Reform: Into the New Millennium," Education International Roundtable of Teacher Organizations, December 1996, National Education Association Collection, series 7, box 2443, George Washington University Archives, Washington, DC.

48. Jane McAlevey, *No Shortcuts: Organizing for Power in the New Gilded Age* (New York: Oxford University Press, 2016); and Micah Uetricht, *Strike for America: Chicago Teachers against Austerity* (London: Verso, 2014). See also Dylan Scott, "The Strike That Brought Teachers Unions Back from the Dead," *Vox*, July 5, 2019, https://www.vox.com/the-highlight/2019/6/28/18662706/chicago-teachers-unions-strike-labor-movement/.

49. See Joseph McCartin, "Bargaining for the Common Good, *Dissent*, Spring 2016, https://www.dissentmagazine.org/article/bargaining-common-good-community-union-alignment/; Gillian Russum and Samantha Winslow, "Teachers Union Caucuses Gather to Swap Strategy," *Labor Notes*, August 17, 2017, https://www.labornotes.org/2017/08/teachers-caucus-together/; and Solvejg Wastvedt, "Strike Averted after St. Paul School District, Teachers Reach Tentative Agreement," *MPR News*, February 12, 2018, https://www.mprnews.org/story/2018/02/12/st-paul-teachers-district-avert-strike/.

50. The best single account of the red state teacher strikes so far is Eric Blanc's *Red State Revolt: The Teachers' Strike Wave and Working-Class Politics* (London: Verso, 2019).

51. Nelson Lichtenstein, "L.A. Teachers Prepare to Strike," *Dissent*, January 7, 2019, https://www.dissentmagazine.org/blog/l-a-teachers-prepare-to-strike/.

52. Sarah Jaffe and Michelle Chen, "Belabored Podcast #167: L.A. Teachers Shut It Down, with Alex Caputo-Pearl," January 14, 2019, *Dissent*, https://www.dissent magazine.org/blog/belabored-podcast-167-l-a-teachers-shut-it-down-with-alex -caputo-pearl/; "Summary of Tentative Agreement/UTLA and LAUSD," *UTLA*, January 22, 2019, https://www.utla.net/sites/default/files/V3%20Summary%20of%20 Tentative%20Agreement%20012219_1.pdf/; "School Board Approves Moratorium on Charters," *UTLA*, January 29, 2019, https://www.utla.net/news/school-board -approves-moratorium-charters/.

Afterword

EILEEN BORIS

In an era of privatization and contracting out, in which the responsible employer disappears into a maze of arrangements, the line between private employment and the public sector has increasingly blurred.[1] The U.S. Supreme Court exacerbated such ambiguity. Writing for the majority in 2014, Associate Justice Samuel A. Alito argued that personal attendants under the Illinois Department of Rehabilitation "are quite different from full-fledged public employees." In *Harris v. Quinn* (573 U.S. 616 [2014]), the Court designated care workers for the welfare state as "partial public employees" or "quasi-public employees," a newly made-up term, because their unions neither bargained for pay nor handled grievances against their "customers"—that is, the needy elders and people with disabilities who qualified for such services. Despite the State of Illinois claiming to be a joint employer with receivers of home care, Alito and the antiunion majority on the Court determined that free-speech rights trumped long-accepted fair share and agency fees.[2] Consequently, workers who refused to join the union turned into free riders, paying nothing even though the union remained responsible for representing them before management. The question than became: Why should anyone pay union dues under such circumstances? But perhaps that was the point, to cripple public employee locals from serving government workers by cutting off resources.

For home care, the Court rejected the precedent set by *Abood vs. Detroit Board of Education* (432 U.S. 209 [1977]), a case involving another group of public employees—teachers. *Abood* held that the union shop was necessary for "industrial peace" and that public sector unions could draw a line between expenditures for collective bargaining and membership services and monies for "political or ideological purposes." In contrast, *Harris* contended that even issues of wages and benefits in the public sector were "political." However, the very classification of home attendants as not real public employees made it impossible for Alito to use *Harris* to overturn *Abood*. That he soon would accomplish in *Janus v. AFSCME* (585 U.S. ___ [2018]).

To cement his opinion in *Harris*, Alito noted the place of the household in industrial relations, one that kept the boundaries of the private cordoned off from the public. "Federal labor law reflects the fact that the organization of household workers like the personal assistants does not further the interest of labor peace," he insisted. "'[A]ny individual employed . . . in the domestic service of any family or person at his home' is excluded from coverage under the National Labor Relations Act."[3] With the same women combining jobs in domestic work with home care, with a shared location and overlapping tasks, no wonder that personal assistants became conflated with domestic service and thus outside of the labor law. The characteristics of the worker—disproportionately "female," Black, and increasingly women of color, often older (defined as midlife)—justified the devaluing of the work, which involved intimate labor—that is, aid with the quotidian and personal activities of daily life. In short, such workers were unworthy to be considered public employees.[4]

The fate of home care workers underscores enduring themes in the history of public employment that these deeply researched histories illuminate. Though coeditors Frederick W. Gooding Jr. and Eric S. Yellin have collected essays on workers "whose labor was directly managed by public servants inside public institutions," these legible public employees share much with less visible ones, like Illinois's personal attendants. First, the law has hardly been a stalwart friend of public workers. As a number of chapters reveal, it took protests and strikes for governments at state, local, and federal levels to recognize teacher, sanitation, hospital, and federal agency unions and then to agree that they had the legal authority to bargain over conditions. The American Federation of State, County, and Municipal Employees (AFSCME), for one, ultimately found the courts inhospitable when it came to gaining comparable worth in the 1980s. However, Katherine Turk shows that they sometimes transformed defeat at the bar into victories in the state legislature. As Joseph Slater chronicles, police unions long set the legal landscape for other public employees, even when then they gained greater rights, as with Wisconsin's Act 10 in 2011.

After all, there are no public workers without the political, a second similarity crossing types and statuses. Whether as products of patronage or political appointees outside of civil service regulations, whether seen as corruption or compatible staffing, state, county, municipal, and federal workforces exist to carry out the program of elected officials—that is, to make government

232   Afterword

work. Yellin especially traces these connections for the federal government. Taxation and spending, as well as "home rule" and the sovereign powers of government, have framed the hiring of labor, manufacturing of goods, and provision of services. The politics of public employment shaped police unions, as Slater reveals, no less than municipal garbage collection, presented by both William P. Jones and Francis Ryan; county hospital staffing, highlighted by Amy Zanoni; and elementary and secondary education, discussed by Jon Shelton. Third, according to chapters by Cathleen D. Cahill, Gooding, and Turk, Black men, Indigenous peoples, and women from various racial and ethnic backgrounds have found greater security through jobs in the public sector even if the rationale for hiring was their status as cheap labor. The work was steadier and compensation better as a charwoman for the government than as a domestic servant in the residences of those whose offices such public employees cleaned. Fourth, fiscal crisis can undermine social needs so that the power of police can disrupt the workings of the police power when it comes to providing for the common good.

Even before the rise of schools and hospitals as engines of economic growth during the last decades of the twentieth century, before the care work, service, and knowledge economies displaced manufacturing as the locus of employment, public employees served as agents of social reproduction.[5] That is, they engaged in the maintenance and perpetuation of the society by sustaining people as well as the institutions and infrastructure surrounding them. Schools, clinics, water and sanitation systems, welfare offices, agricultural bureaus, and labor inspectors all stand as public forms of social reproduction.[6] Municipal sanitation workers sought to turn their leverage over public health to win concessions from politicians in the South, as Jones demonstrates in providing a longer context for the famous "I Am a Man" Memphis walkout, as well as in the North, as Ryan uncovers through the fracturing of Philadelphia's Democratic Party coalition.

The white women sent to reservations, Cahill emphasizes, were agents of assimilation, who generated new avenues of professionalization for themselves in the process of reforming their charges. We might reframe their mission as a double reproduction of labor power—their own and those of Indigenous peoples, each placed within an occupational hierarchy by race, gender, and citizenship. Shelton's public school teachers perhaps stand as the emblematic reproductive laborers for educating the next generation in the conduct of life along with lessons in academic subjects. So too nurses and other health professionals, such as those at the underfunded Cook County Hospital, whose plight in the late 1960s and 1970s Zanoni dramatizes. They engaged in actual reproductive labor, birthing babies and trying to sustain

Afterword   233

the lives of the uninsured. Even police, whose special treatment Slater analyzes, appear as reproducers—of order. Public servants engaged in service: necessary, often affective labor, expected to be freely given.

Public sector jobs allowed for reproducing individuals, households, and communities daily and generationally. Thus, Yellin highlights the difference that access to federal employment made for the emergence of a Black middle class, especially in Washington, DC—though Woodrow Wilson segregated the agencies and reinforced racial discrimination. In an original and important argument, Gooding casts African American federal employees as builders of American democracy itself. They become, we might say, reproducers of the mythical American Dream, even as limited opportunities cast the laborers among them into the abyss of "zombie capitalism." Defined as essential workers, African Americans were overrepresented among government employees who had to labor without pay during recent shutdowns. The employment security of the federal step system rarely brought the same compensation offered others in the private sector.

Public employees not only have undertaken reproductive labor but have produced goods, services, and other intangibles. During the Civil War, women clerks made money when they cut sheets of paper currency into distinct, individual bills. Other federal workers produced knowledge. Expanding the rich literature on the U.S. Women's Bureau, Bureau of Labor Statistics, and New Deal planners, now we have Cahill's Office of Indian Affairs and women like Flora Warren Seymour, a white graduate of the Washington College of Law who penned popular books on various Native American tribes, and Gertrude Bonnin, who under her Dakota name, Zitkala-Ša, countered misapprehensions of Indigenous cultures. Government-employed technical writers and researchers investigated social conditions, generating reports that offered an evidentiary basis for policy. A wide range of knowledge workers were government employees, but race and gender shaped where they landed within federal agencies or state systems.[7]

The very organization of the collection highlights how politics and identity intersect in public employment. Race and gender, what I have named "racialized gender," informs class experiences.[8] In contrasting the activism and allegiances of Indigenous and white employees of the Indian Service, Cahill lays out the benefits of intersectional analysis. In searching for equal rights, Indigenous women engaged in intertribal activism more than women's suffrage, while white women led suffrage groups and became key members of the National Federation of Federal Employees. White women benefited from the civilizing mission directed to Native peoples, who had to fight their own forms of exclusion and discrimination. Likewise, Turk considers a

234   Afterword

century-long struggle for pay equity against gender norms that set boundaries to proper work for women and pervaded even some public sector unions. AFSCME, however, sought to meet the demands of its large membership of women, as it tried to do so when it came to Black men as well as women, seen in the pieces by Jones, Ryan, and Zanoni. These community studies probe sometimes flat-footed, other times opportunistic alliances between civil rights and Black empowerment organizations and unions. When local people in both arenas joined to fight political bosses as well as their hand-picked directors, African Americans had a fighting chance for better jobs and better services.

In ending with pillars of the care-work economy, *Public Workers in Service of America* recognizes the ways we take for granted the sacrifices of essential workers. We depend on them. In bargaining for the common good, teachers and others who maintain human as well as physical infrastructure—including home health care attendants, nurses and sanitation workers—carry forward a vision of social interdependence countering those would starve government under an ideology of personal responsibility.

Notes

1. David Weil, *The Fissured Workplace: Why Work Became So Bad for So Many and What Can Be Done to Improve It* (Cambridge, MA: Harvard University Press, 2014).

2. Opinion, *Harris v. Quinn*, 573 U.S. 616 (2014), at 16–17, 27, and its Syllabus, 3.

3. Ibid., at 32.

4. Eileen Boris and Jennifer Klein, *Caring for America: Home Health Workers in the Shadow of the Welfare State* (New York: Oxford University Press, 2012). The 2015 paperback edition discusses *Harris v. Quinn*.

5. Gabriel Winant, *The Next Shift: The Fall of Industry and the Rise of Health Care in Rust Belt America* (Cambridge, MA: Harvard University Press, 2021).

6. Eileen Boris, "Reproduction as Production: Thinking with the ILO to Move beyond Dichotomy," *Labor and Society* 22, no. 2 (2019): 283–98.

7. For example, Judith Sealander, *As Minority Becomes Majority: Federal Reaction to the Phenomenon of Women in the Workforce, 1920–1963* (New York: Praeger, 1983); Mark Hendrickson, "Gender Research as Labor Activism: The Women's Bureau in the New Era," *Journal of Policy History* 20, no. 4 (2008): 482–515; Alice O'Connor, *Poverty Knowledge: Social Science, Social Policy, and the Poor in Twentieth-Century America* (Princeton, NJ: Princeton University Press, 2001); Patrick D. Reagan, *Designing a New America: The Origins of New Deal Planning* (Amherst: University of Massachusetts Press, 2000).

8. Eileen Boris, "The Racialized Gendered State: Constructions of Citizenship in the United States," *Social Politics: International Studies in Gender, State, & Society* 2, no. 2 (1995): 160–80.

Contributors

EILEEN BORIS is Hull Professor of Feminist Studies at the University of California, Santa Barbara.

CATHLEEN D. CAHILL is Professor of History at Penn State University.

FREDERICK W. GOODING JR. is Associate Professor of African American History and Dr. Ronald E. Moore Professor of Humanities at Texas Christian University.

WILLIAM P. JONES is Professor of History at the University of Minnesota.

JOSEPH A. McCARTIN is Professor of History and Executive Director of the Kalmanovitz Initiative for Labor and the Working Poor at Georgetown University.

FRANCIS RYAN is Director of the Master of Labor and Employment Relations Program and Assistant Teaching Professor at Rutgers University.

JON SHELTON is Associate Professor of Democracy and Justice Studies at the University of Wisconsin, Green Bay.

JOSEPH E. SLATER is Distinguished University Professor and Eugene N. Balk Professor of Law and Values at the University of Toledo College of Law.

KATHERINE TURK is Associate Professor of History at the University of North Carolina, Chapel Hill.

ERIC S. YELLIN is Associate Professor of History at the University of Richmond.

AMY ZANONI is a historian of social welfare and movements in the twentieth-century United States.

Index

Abood vs. Detroit Board of Education, 231
Adams, Stuart W., 159
Addonizio, Hugh J., 156
AFSCME Local 201 v. City of Muskegon, 118
AFSCME v. State of Washington, 96
Agricultural Adjustment Agency, 89–90
air traffic controllers, 6, 115
Alito, Samuel A., Jr., 6–7, 231–32
American Arbitration Association, 125
American Civil Liberties Union, 63, 155
American Federationist, 111
American Federation of Labor (AFL)/ AFL-CIO, 25, 110–11, 132; organizations affiliated with, 111; sanitation workers and, 131–34, 139–40; support for police unions, 111–14, 122
American Federation of State, County, and Municipal Employees (AFSCME), 8, 89, 92, 232; cases involving public employer bans on unionizing and, 115–16; Cook County Hospital (CCH) workers and, 185–92; expansion into the South, 132–34, 138–44; food service workers and, 185–92; gender equality and, 92–97; in Philadelphia, 163–64; police unions and, 114; prominence of, 107–8; sanitation workers and, 138–44; wildcat strike and, 185
American Federation of Teachers (AFT), 89, 111, 114, 115
American Indian Stories, 29
American politics: black-and-tan organizations of, 40; bureaucracy and, 39; corruption in, 48–49, 50–51, 164–65; fights over public sector unions in, 119–22; patronage politics and, 37, 38–43, 45, 47, 49; political parties and, 38–42, 45–46; scandals in, 39; tokenism in, 41
Americans for Democratic Action, 155
Appropriations Act of 1932, 89
Aron, Cindy, 18
Atkins v. City of Charlotte, 118
Atlanta Constitution, 134–35
Atlantic, 28

Baker, Frazier, 42
Baldwin, Marie Bottineau, 21–23, 24, 26, 27
Baptist, Edward, 78
Barry, Marion, 48, 59n80
Beaumont, Gustave de, 3
Becker, Gary, 218
Bell, John, *142*
Bell, Terrel, 218
Bennett, Wallace Foster, 95
Benson, Renita, 99
Berson, Lenora, 166
Beutner, Austin, 224
Biden, Joseph R., 2
Birmingham News, 144
Birmingham sanitation workers strike, 1960, 130–32, 134–35. *See also* sanitation workers
Birmingham World, 131
Black, Bob, 180–81

black-and-tan organizations, 40
Black bourgeoisie, 85
Black-collar workers, 68; appeal of "good government jobs" for, 76–77; in dead-end jobs, 78–80; John Henryism and, 74–75; restricted from the free market, 75–76
Black Lives Matter movement, 110
Black Panther Party, 191
Black Political Forum, 157–58, 165, 166
Black politicians, 37–38, 42; aftermath of Reconstruction and, 47–50; corrupt, 48–49, 59n80
Black Power movement, 50, 161, 179
Black public workers, 15–16, 36–38; in dead-end jobs, 78–80; difficulties in obtaining promotions, 63–64; discrimination against, 61–62, 69–71, 234; early appointments of, 40–43, 44; Fair Employment Practices Committee (FEPC) and, 46–47; federal recruitment of, 71–73; female, 43–45, 71–73; Great Migration of, 37, 46, 67; growth in numbers of, 66; in the Jim Crow era, 46, 49, 50, 68; John Henryism and, 74–75; patronage politics and, 37, 38–43, 45; restricted from the capitalist experience and free market, 75–76; statistics on, 51n3; unique conditions for, 66–69; violence against, 42; wage disparities for, 49, 61, 69, 74, 75
Blackwell, Lucian, 167
Blackwell, Lucy Stone, 19
Board of Indian Commissioners (BIC), 25
Bonnin, Gertrude Simmons, 27–30, 234
Bonnin, Raymond, 28
Booker, Cory, 221
Borland, William P., 25
Boston police strike of 1919, 110–15
Bottineau, Jean B., 21
Bowser, Charles, 166
Brooks, Thomas R., 160–61
Brosius, Marriott, 42
Brotherhood of Sleeping Car Porters, 90
Brown, Elsa Barkley, 45
Brown, Harold, 155
Brown, Jerry, 93
Bruce, Blanche K., 40, 45, 48
Building Service Employees International Union (BSEIU), 89
Burleson, Albert, 66, 111
Bush, George H. W., 218

Bush, George W., 119
Business Week, 137

Cahill, Cathleen, 7, 15, 233
Cainon, Ray, *142*
Caldwell, John, 140
Campbell, Edgar C. Sr., 158
Capers, Florence, *142*
capitalist system, American, 75–76, 79
Carroll, Vincent A., 154
Cates, H. J., 134–35, 136
Channing, William Ellery, 212
charter schools, 220
Chase, Bob, 222–23
Cheatham, Henry, 45
Chicago Daily Defender, 178, 180–82, 189
Chicago Teachers Federation (CTF), 213–15
Chicago Tribune, 183
City of Jackson v. McLeod, 115–16
Civil Rights Act of 1964, 69–70, 77, 91, 93, 95
civil rights movement, 49; sanitation workers and, 143–44
Clark, Joseph S., 152
Clark, Kathleen, 45
Clinton, Bill, 218–19
Coalition for United Community Action (CUCA), 187
Coalition of Black Trade Unionists (CBTU), 161
Cohen, David, 158
Cold War era, 90–91, 138, 140
Coleman, Joseph, 167
Collette, Cathy, 97
Communism, 90, 138
comparable worth, 86, 92, 96–97
Connolly, N. D. B., 49
Connor, "Bull," 139, 143
Constitution of the United States of America, 1
Cook County Hospital (CCH), 177–80, 233–34; democratic organizing tradition in the 1970s and, 194–95; employees building an organizing momentum at, 182–85; exposing labor and patient conditions at, 180–82; "heal-in" at, 192–94; strike by, 186–92
Coolidge, Calvin, 6, 110, 137
Corleto, Fred T., 150–51, 159
corruption, 48–49, 50–51, 59n80, 164–65
County of Washington v. Gunther, 95

COVID-19 pandemic, 1–2, 10, 10n1
Curtis, Edwin, 112–13

Dade, Charles, 163, 165
Dailey, Jane, 40
Daley, Richard, 221, 223
dead-end jobs, 78–80
Democratic Party, 39, 40, 46; emphasis
  on education, 218–21; Philadelphia, 151,
  153–54, 156–58, *159*, 163, 167–68
Department of Homeland Security (DHS),
  119
Derber, Milton, 182
Detroit Labor News, 114
Devlin, William J., 156
Dilworth, Richardson, 152
Dissent, 160
Dorchester, Merial, 18, 19
D'Ortona, Paul, 154
Dothard v. Rawlinson, 97
Douglass, Frederick, 45
Doyle, Robert, 153
Du Bois, W. E. B., *44*
Duncan, Arne, 221
Dunne, George, 186, 188, 191
Dunston, Merle Stokes, 90
Durand, E. Dana, 38–39

Eastern Band of Cherokee Indians, 21
Edwards, Don, 63
Elementary and Secondary Education Act
  of 1965, 218
Emanuel, Rahm, 221, 223
Equal Employment Opportunity Act of
  1972, 69, 71, 91
Equal Employment Opportunity Commis-
  sion (EEOC), 77, 79, 92, 96
Equal Pay Act of 1963, 92, 95–96
Era of Enslavement, 78
Etheridge, Florence, 17, 23–26
Evans, Daniel, 93
Evening Star, 42

Fader, Jamie J., 132
Fair Employment Practices Committee
  (FEPC), 46–47, 90
Fair Labor Standards Act, 96
Farris, William, 144
Fauntroy, Walter E., 63
Federal Employee, The, 25
Federal Housing Administration (FHA),
  70, 71

Feldman, Joseph G., 162
feminism, 24–25, 86, 92–93
feminization of public work, 15, 17, 23–26,
  92, 213–14, 222
Five Civilized American Indian Tribes, 26
Fletcher, Alice, 18, 19
Fletcher, James C., 72, 73
Florence, W. A., 134–35, 141
Foglietta, Thomas, 166
food service workers, 185–92
Fraternal Order of Police, 115, 155
free market, 75–76
free speech rights, 6–7, 13n22
Fulwiley, Lena, 180–82

Garrity v. New Jersey, 118
Gates Foundation, 220
gay men and lesbians in the public sector,
  90–91
Gillett, Emma, 20–21
Gilmore, Glenda, 43
Godkin, E. L., 39
Goldin, Claudia, 212
Goldstein, Leo, 159
Goluboff, Risa, 49
Gompers, Samuel, 112
Goode, W. Wilson, 166–67
Gooding, Frederick W., Jr., 8, 47, 61, 232,
  234
Gore, Al, 220
Great Depression, 3, 89, 133
Great Migration, 37, 46, 67
Great Society, 4, 46, 47, 91, 161, 180, 218
Green, Cooper, 139
Green, William J., III, 163, 166, 217
Grootemaat, Oliver, 117
Guggenheim, Davis, 220

Haas, Al, 160
Haigler, Carey, 139
Haley, Margaret, 214–15
Halferty, Joseph F., 150–54, 158–59
Hall, Charles E., 43
Halttunen, Karen, 43
Hampton, Fred, 191
Hanrahan, Edward, 188, 190
Harding, Warren, 25
Hardwick, Ashleigh, 209
Hare, B. B., 47
Harlem Renaissance, 49
Harper, William Rainey, 213
Harper's Monthly, 28

Index   241

Harris, Ida, 188
Harris, John, *142*
Harris, Ruth Bates, 71–73
Harrison, Benjamin, 40, 43
Harris v. Quinn, 231–32
Hartsfield, William B., 136–38
Hatch Act of 1939, 5
Haudenosaunee Confederacy, 27
Haughton, James G., 194
Hay, Leon G., *142*
Hayes, Luther, *142*
Hayter, Julian, 48
Hazell, Jon, 99
Henry, John, 74
Higginbothan, Evelyn Brooks, 43
Higher Education Act, 218
History of the New York Indians, 26
History of Woman Suffrage, The, 17, 19
Honeggar, Frances, 85
Honey, Michael, 7
Hood, Henry, 88
Hopkins, Albert J., 43
hospital staff, Chicago. *See* Cook County Hospital (CCH)
Housing and Urban Development (HUD), Department of, 70–71
Human Capital: A Theoretical and Empirical Analysis with Special Reference to Education, 218

Ikenberry, John, 40
Illinois Nurses Association (INA), 183
Indian Agents of the Old Frontier, 26
Indian School Service, 18
Indians of the Pueblos, 26
Indians Today, The, 26
Indigenous feminism, 17, 19
Institute for Government Research, 42

Jackson, Emory O., 131
Jackson, Helen Hunt, 18
Jackson, Jesse, 185
Jackson, Maynard, 167
Jackson, Willa Mae, 191
Janus v. AFSCME, 6–7, 13n22, 98, 120
Jim Crow era, 46, 49–50, 68, 80
John Henryism, 74–75
Johnson, Lyndon B., 4, 46, 70, 91, 218
Joint Commission on the Accreditation of Hospitals (JCAH), 180
Jones, James, 162

Jones, Lillie, 177, 181–82, 184–85, 189–90, 192, 195
Jones, William P., 8, 107, 233

Kagan, Elena, 7, 13n22
Kasich, John, 121
Katz, Lawrence, 212
Katz, Michael B., 132
Kellogg, Laura Cornelius, 27–30, 35n45
Kennedy, Edward, 63
Kennedy, John F., 91, 118
Kilson, Martin, 49
King, Martin Luther, Jr., 50, 91, 130–31, 150, 161
King v. Priest, 116
Kohler, Walter Jr., 117
Krislov, Samuel, 46
Ku Klux Klan, 143

labor protections, 6
Labor World, 113
Lathrop, Julia, 30n1
Law Enforcement Officer Bill of Rights Laws (LEOBORs), 122, 124
law schools, 20–21
League for Revolutionary Black Workers, 161
Leeds, Alton, *142*
Levi, Ruby, 191–92
Lewis, Michael, 1, 10n2
Lim, Daniel, 1
Lincoln, Abraham, 40, 42, 49
Lockwood, Belva, 21
Longstreth, W. Thacher, 163
Lucy, William, 161
Lynch, John Roy, 40
lynchings, 42

Madison nurses, 85–86
Mancuso, Nicholas, 98
Mann, Horace, 212
March on Washington for Jobs and Freedom, 90, 144
Massachusetts Officer Standards and Training Commission, 125–26
Masse, John, 185
Mattachine Society of Washington, 91
Mayers, Lewis, 42
Mazique, Jewal, *67*
McCall, Howard, 157, 162–63
McCarthyism, 90

242   Index

McCartin, Joseph, 7
McCoy, Ernest, 141
McEntee, Bill, 152–53
McEntee, Gerald, 95
McGhee, Hazel, 91–92
McIntosh, Thomas, 158
McKinley, William, 41, 42, 43
McMahon, Ed, 154
McNorriell, Mozell, 92–93
Meany, George, 140
Medicaid, 180
Medicare, 180
Mendoza, Carmen, 186, 188
Mitchell, Michele, 43
Montague, W. H., *142*
Montezuma, Carlos, 27
Morgan, James, 143
Morgan, J. W., 138–39
Muhammad Speaks, 189
Murphy, Marjorie, 7
Musgrove, Derek, 39
Mussey, Ellen Spencer, 20

Napier, James, 45
National Aeronautics and Space Administration (NASA), 71–73
National American Woman Suffrage Association (NAWSA), 19
National Association for the Advancement of Colored People (NAACP), 73, 155, 157
National Association of Letter Carriers, 111
National Civil Service Reform League, 41
National Education Association (NEA), 115, 214
National Federation of Federal Employees (NFFE), 18, 25, 111
National Independent Political League, 45
National Institutes of Health (NIH), 63–64
National Labor Relations Act of 1935, 8, 109, 115, 138, 182
National Right to Work Committee (NRTWC), 219
Nation at Risk, A, 218
Nation of Islam, 189
Native Americans, 7–8; female public workers, 17–18, 26–30, 234; Indigenous feminism and, 17, 19; Office of Indian Affairs (OIA) and, 17–20; U.S. citizenship and, 29; white feminists and, 24–26
Native nationalism movement, 20
Nelson, Gaylord, 117

neoliberalism, 217–21
New Deal, 4, 37, 46, 90, 151
new federalism, 4
Newman, Winn, 92, 95
New Republic, 122
New York Call, 112, 113
New York Times, 137, 143
Nicholas, Henry, 166
Nixon, Richard, 4
Norton, Clifford, 91
Norton, Eleanor Holmes, 92, 95–96
Norton v. Macy, 91
nurses, Chicago. *See* Cook County Hospital (CCH)

Obama, Barack, 36, 219, 221
Obama, Michelle, 49
Office of Indian Affairs (OIA), 17–20, 27
Ogilvie, Richard, 186
O'Meara, Steven, 112
O'Neill, June, 95
Osborne, David, 39
Our Democracy and the American Indian, 29

patronage politics, 37, 38–43, 45, 47, 49; Jim Crow era and, 46, 49, 50
Pearlman, Nancy, 92
Pendleton, Clarence, 96
Pendleton Civil Service Reform Act, 1883, 15, 87
Perez v. Board of Police Commissioners, 116
Perkins, Frances, 88
Philadelphia: Black Political Forum of, 157–58, 165, 166; Black politicians of, 167–69; community alliances in, 155–60; Joseph F. Halferty and, 150–54, 158–59; limits of social justice unionism in, 164–68; sanitation workers strike in, 1970, 149–50, 160–61; support for public sector workers in, 160–64
Philadelphia Evening Bulletin, 151–52
Philadelphia Inquirer, 160, 166
Philadelphia Tribune, 155, 158
police unions, 107, 109–10; Boston police strike of 1919 and, 110–15; debate over, as obstacle to reform, 122–26; first state public sector collective bargaining law in Wisconsin and, 116–18; and law in the mid-twentieth century, 115–16; political fights over public sector unions and,

police unions (*continued*)
119–22; rise of public sector labor laws and, 118–19

political activism and female federal employees, 23–30

political significance, 40

private sector, 4, 64–65, 79–80; boundary between public sector and, during World War II, 90; dismal jobs available to Black workers in, 76–77

private sector unions, 6

Professional Air Traffic Controllers Union (PATCO), 6, 115

Progressive Era, 86, 133

Prophet-Riley, Ida, 23

Protecting Soldiers and Mothers, 39

public education: disinvestment in, 222; neoliberal, 217–21; rise of universal, 212–13

Public Employees Organized for Political Empowerment (PEOPLE), 161

Public Safety, 89

public sector unions, 6, 64–65; comparable worth theory and, 96–97; Cook County Hospital and, 182–85; first state public sector collective bargaining law in Wisconsin and, 116–18; gender norms and, 88–89, 98–99; political fights over, 119–22; rise of public sector labor laws and, 118–19. *See also* police unions

public work and workers: 1960s and 1970s militance in, 119; boundary between private and, during World War II, 90; bureaucracy of, 39, 232–33; continuing gendered boundaries in, 97–98; critical role of government and, 2–3; defining, 4–7; diversity of, 3, 71–73; feminization of, 15, 17, 23–26, 92, 213–14, 222; gay men and lesbians in, 90–91; gender and race defining, 86–91; and handling of COVID-19, 1–2; historical perspective on, 3–4, 9–10; in hospitals (*see* Cook County Hospital); labor protections for, 6; as largest group of employees globally, 64, 81n9; legislation affecting, 69–70; partial or quasi, 231; police (*see* police unions); postwar growth in numbers of, 91; and private *versus* public sector competition model, 4; racial and gender discrimination in, 61–62, 69–71; rule of three in, 56n40; strikes by, 6; teachers (*see* teachers); visibility and political

accountability of, 5–6; wage system in, 64–65, 68, 74. *See also* Black public workers; women public workers

Railway Mail Carriers, 111

Randolph, A. Philip, 90

Randolph, Oliver M., 38–39

Raspberry, William, 63

Ravitch, Diane, 220

Reagan, Ronald, 4, 6, 115, 218

Reconstruction, 36–37, 39, 45, 55n35, 80; aftermath of, 47–50

red power movement, 20

Reed, Adolph, 47–48, 59n77

Reel, Estelle, 18, 19

Reich, Robert, 218–19, 221, 222

Republican Party: Black voters taken for granted by, 45–46; involvement of Black politicians and delegates in, 38–42; Philadelphia, 156, 158, 166

Rizzo, Frank L., 151–52, 163, 164–65

Rockefeller, John D., 213

Roosevelt, Franklin D., 46, 88, 90, 137

Roosevelt, Theodore, 41, 42

Rowe, W. A. "Shorty," 141–42, *142*

Rowel, Hoover, 63–64, 68, 73

rule of three, 56n40

Rung, Margaret, 9

Ryan, Francis, 8, 107–8, 233

Ryan, Paul, 39

Sacagawea: Bird Girl, 26

sanitation workers: AFSCME and, 131–32, 134–35; Birmingham strike by, 1960, 130–32, 134–35; civil rights leaders and, 143–44; collective bargaining by, 139–40; community support for, 160; organizations affiliated with, 135–36; Philadelphia strike by, 1970, 149–50, 160–61; Southern cities fighting back against strikes and, 136–38

Sealander, Judith, 88

Service Employees International Union (SEIU), 184–85, 191–92

Seymour, Flora Warren, 23, 25–26, 35n45, 234

Seymour, John, 23

Shaw, Anna Howard, 19

Shelton, Jon, 9, 175, 176, 233

Sherrod, Shirley, 48

Simmons, Samuel J., 70

Skocpol, Theda, 39, 40

244   Index

Slater, Joseph, 8, 107, 138, 209, 233, 234
Smalls, Robert, 48
Smallwood, David, 150
Smith, Adam, 92
Smith, Robert C., 47
Socialism, 90
Society of American Indians (SAI), 18, 24, 27–30
Somersett, W. A., 141
Southern Christian Leadership Conference (SCLC), 131, 144
Spero, Sterling, 7
Spinner, Francis, 87
Stanek, Ann, 191
State, County, and Municipal Workers of America (SCMWA), 133–34
Stein, Eileen, 96
Stern, Mark J., 132
Stewart, E. H., *142*
Story of the Red Man, 26
Story of the Sioux Indians, 26
Stout, Earl: Philadelphia sanitation workers and, 149, 152–53, 156, 159–60; political influence of, 162–63, 165–67
Strickland, Ruth, 90
suffrage movement, 17, 18, 20, 23, 28–29, 30n1
Sullivan, David, 185

Taft, William Howard, 41
Tanner, Jack, 95
Tate, James H. J., 151–54, 156–58, *159,* 164
Taylor, Jim, 21
Taylor, Ocea, 38–39
Taylor, Robert R., 151
teachers, 231–32; American Federation of Teachers (AFT) and, 89, 111, 114, 115; changing landscape for, 222–23; disinvestment in education and, 222; long history as public employees, 210–11; multistate strikes by, 2018, 209–10; rise of teachers' unions and, 213–17; rise of universal public education and, 212–13; social democratic teachers' unionism and, 223–25; strikes by, 216–17; teaching in neoliberal world, 217–21
Teamsters, 134, 144
Terrell, Robert, 45
Thomas, Clarence, 96
Thomas, Edna, 158
Thomas, Hortense, 181
Thompson, J. Philip, III, 47

Thompson, Tommy, 219
Tocqueville, Alexis de, 2–3, 61
tokenism, 41
Trotter, William Monroe, 45
Trump, Donald, 1, 10nn1–2, 36
Turchi, Ray, 163
Turk, Katherine, 8, 61
Turtle Mountain Chippewa Nation, 21

United Black Labor Political Committee (UBLPC), 162
United Public Workers of America (UPWA), 137–38
United Southern Employees Association (USEA), 141
United States v. Cherokee Nation, 21
U.S. Census Bureau, 43
U.S. Commission on Civil Rights, 96

Van Riper, Paul, 7
Voting Rights Act, 47–48
vouchers, school, 219

Waggoner, J. T., 130, 131, 143–44
Waiting for "Superman," 220
Walker, Scott, 99, 120
Wall Street Journal, 115
Washington, Betty, 180–81
Washington American, 38
Washington Bee, 41
Washington College of Law (WCL), 20–23
Washington Post, 40, 63
We Called Them Indians, 26
West Side Torch, 189
Whaley, Lenta, 191
What Do We Mean by Indian?, 35n45
White, Jan, 93
White, John F., Sr., 157–58
White, John S., Sr., 165, 166
white feminism, 24–26
Williams, Hardy, 163
Wilson, Woodrow, 39, 45–46, 66–67, 234
Wimberli, Sig, 189
Wisconsin Educ. Ass'n Council v. Walker, 120
Wisconsin Oneida Nation, 27
Womack, John E., 70–71, 73
Woman's Journal, The, 23–24
Women of Trail and Wigwam, 26
women public workers, 15, 17, 86–91; as attorneys, 20–26; Black, 43–45, 71–73; comparable worth theory and, 86, 92,

Index   245

women public workers (*continued*) 96–97; continuing gendered boundaries for, 97–98; feminism and, 24–25, 92–93; in food service, 185–92; Native American, 17–18, 26–30, 234; as nurses (*see* Cook County Hospital); in the Office of Indian Affairs (OIA), 17–20; political activism and, 23–30; suffrage movement and, 17, 18, 20, 23, 28–29, 30n1; as teachers (*see* teachers); wage disparities for, 92–95

Women's Bureau, 88

Women's Journal and Suffrage News, The, 19

Woods, Georgie, 156

Workingmen's parties, 213

Work of Nations, The, 221

World War II, 90

Wurf, Jerry, 161–62, 166, 189

Yellin, Eric S., 8, 15–16, 88, 232, 233, 234

Young, Coleman, 48

Young, Wendell W., III, 165

Youngman, Emma, 89–90

Zander, Arnold, 133–35, 140, 141

Zanoni, Amy, 8–9, 175, 176, 233

Zeiger, Robert, 167

Zitkala-Ša, 27, 28, 234

The Working Class in American History

Worker City, Company Town: Iron and Cotton-Worker Protest in Troy and
Cohoes, New York, 1855–84   *Daniel J. Walkowitz*

Life, Work, and Rebellion in the Coal Fields: The Southern West Virginia Miners,
1880–1922   *David Alan Corbin*

Women and American Socialism, 1870–1920   *Mari Jo Buhle*

Lives of Their Own: Blacks, Italians, and Poles in Pittsburgh, 1900–1960
John Bodnar, Roger Simon, and Michael P. Weber

Working-Class America: Essays on Labor, Community, and American Society
Edited by Michael H. Frisch and Daniel J. Walkowitz

Eugene V. Debs: Citizen and Socialist   *Nick Salvatore*

American Labor and Immigration History, 1877–1920s: Recent European Research
Edited by Dirk Hoerder

Workingmen's Democracy: The Knights of Labor and American Politics
Leon Fink

The Electrical Workers: A History of Labor at General Electric and Westinghouse,
1923–60   *Ronald W. Schatz*

The Mechanics of Baltimore: Workers and Politics in the Age of Revolution,
1763–1812   *Charles G. Steffen*

The Practice of Solidarity: American Hat Finishers in the Nineteenth Century
David Bensman

The Labor History Reader   *Edited by Daniel J. Leab*

Solidarity and Fragmentation: Working People and Class Consciousness in
Detroit, 1875–1900   *Richard Oestreicher*

Counter Cultures: Saleswomen, Managers, and Customers in American
Department Stores, 1890–1940   *Susan Porter Benson*

The New England Working Class and the New Labor History
Edited by Herbert G. Gutman and Donald H. Bell

Labor Leaders in America   *Edited by Melvyn Dubofsky and Warren Van Tine*

Barons of Labor: The San Francisco Building Trades and Union Power in the
Progressive Era   *Michael Kazin*

Gender at Work: The Dynamics of Job Segregation by Sex during World War II
Ruth Milkman

Once a Cigar Maker: Men, Women, and Work Culture in American Cigar
Factories, 1900–1919   *Patricia A. Cooper*

A Generation of Boomers: The Pattern of Railroad Labor Conflict in Nineteenth-
Century America   *Shelton Stromquist*

Work and Community in the Jungle: Chicago's Packinghouse Workers, 1894–1922
James R. Barrett

Workers, Managers, and Welfare Capitalism: The Shoeworkers and Tanners of
Endicott Johnson, 1890–1950   *Gerald Zahavi*

Men, Women, and Work: Class, Gender, and Protest in the New England Shoe Industry, 1780–1910 *Mary Blewett*

Workers on the Waterfront: Seamen, Longshoremen, and Unionism in the 1930s *Bruce Nelson*

German Workers in Chicago: A Documentary History of Working-Class Culture from 1850 to World War I *Edited by Hartmut Keil and John B. Jentz*

On the Line: Essays in the History of Auto Work *Edited by Nelson Lichtenstein and Stephen Meyer III*

Labor's Flaming Youth: Telephone Operators and Worker Militancy, 1878–1923 *Stephen H. Norwood*

Another Civil War: Labor, Capital, and the State in the Anthracite Regions of Pennsylvania, 1840–68 *Grace Palladino*

Coal, Class, and Color: Blacks in Southern West Virginia, 1915–32 *Joe William Trotter Jr.*

For Democracy, Workers, and God: Labor Song-Poems and Labor Protest, 1865–95 *Clark D. Halker*

Dishing It Out: Waitresses and Their Unions in the Twentieth Century *Dorothy Sue Cobble*

The Spirit of 1848: German Immigrants, Labor Conflict, and the Coming of the Civil War *Bruce Levine*

Working Women of Collar City: Gender, Class, and Community in Troy, New York, 1864–86 *Carole Turbin*

Southern Labor and Black Civil Rights: Organizing Memphis Workers *Michael K. Honey*

Radicals of the Worst Sort: Laboring Women in Lawrence, Massachusetts, 1860–1912 *Ardis Cameron*

Producers, Proletarians, and Politicians: Workers and Party Politics in Evansville and New Albany, Indiana, 1850–87 *Lawrence M. Lipin*

The New Left and Labor in the 1960s *Peter B. Levy*

The Making of Western Labor Radicalism: Denver's Organized Workers, 1878–1905 *David Brundage*

In Search of the Working Class: Essays in American Labor History and Political Culture *Leon Fink*

Lawyers against Labor: From Individual Rights to Corporate Liberalism *Daniel R. Ernst*

"We Are All Leaders": The Alternative Unionism of the Early 1930s *Edited by Staughton Lynd*

The Female Economy: The Millinery and Dressmaking Trades, 1860–1930 *Wendy Gamber*

"Negro and White, Unite and Fight!": A Social History of Industrial Unionism in Meatpacking, 1930–90 *Roger Horowitz*

Power at Odds: The 1922 National Railroad Shopmen's Strike *Colin J. Davis*

The Common Ground of Womanhood: Class, Gender, and Working Girls' Clubs, 1884–1928   *Priscilla Murolo*

Marching Together: Women of the Brotherhood of Sleeping Car Porters   *Melinda Chateauvert*

Down on the Killing Floor: Black and White Workers in Chicago's Packinghouses, 1904–54   *Rick Halpern*

Labor and Urban Politics: Class Conflict and the Origins of Modern Liberalism in Chicago, 1864–97   *Richard Schneirov*

All That Glitters: Class, Conflict, and Community in Cripple Creek   *Elizabeth Jameson*

Waterfront Workers: New Perspectives on Race and Class   *Edited by Calvin Winslow*

Labor Histories: Class, Politics, and the Working-Class Experience   *Edited by Eric Arnesen, Julie Greene, and Bruce Laurie*

The Pullman Strike and the Crisis of the 1890s: Essays on Labor and Politics   *Edited by Richard Schneirov, Shelton Stromquist, and Nick Salvatore*

AlabamaNorth: African-American Migrants, Community, and Working-Class Activism in Cleveland, 1914–45   *Kimberley L. Phillips*

Imagining Internationalism in American and British Labor, 1939–49   *Victor Silverman*

William Z. Foster and the Tragedy of American Radicalism   *James R. Barrett*

Colliers across the Sea: A Comparative Study of Class Formation in Scotland and the American Midwest, 1830–1924   *John H. M. Laslett*

"Rights, Not Roses": Unions and the Rise of Working-Class Feminism, 1945–80   *Dennis A. Deslippe*

Testing the New Deal: The General Textile Strike of 1934 in the American South   *Janet Irons*

Hard Work: The Making of Labor History   *Melvyn Dubofsky*

Southern Workers and the Search for Community: Spartanburg County, South Carolina   *G. C. Waldrep III*

We Shall Be All: A History of the Industrial Workers of the World (abridged edition)   *Melvyn Dubofsky, ed. Joseph A. McCartin*

Race, Class, and Power in the Alabama Coalfields, 1908–21   *Brian Kelly*

Duquesne and the Rise of Steel Unionism   *James D. Rose*

Anaconda: Labor, Community, and Culture in Montana's Smelter City   *Laurie Mercier*

Bridgeport's Socialist New Deal, 1915–36   *Cecelia Bucki*

Indispensable Outcasts: Hobo Workers and Community in the American Midwest, 1880–1930   *Frank Tobias Higbie*

After the Strike: A Century of Labor Struggle at Pullman   *Susan Eleanor Hirsch*

Corruption and Reform in the Teamsters Union   *David Witwer*

Waterfront Revolts: New York and London Dockworkers, 1946–61   *Colin J. Davis*

Black Workers' Struggle for Equality in Birmingham   *Horace Huntley and David Montgomery*

The Tribe of Black Ulysses: African American Men in the Industrial South   *William P. Jones*

City of Clerks: Office and Sales Workers in Philadelphia, 1870–1920   *Jerome P. Bjelopera*

Reinventing "The People": The Progressive Movement, the Class Problem, and the Origins of Modern Liberalism   *Shelton Stromquist*

Radical Unionism in the Midwest, 1900–1950   *Rosemary Feurer*

Gendering Labor History   *Alice Kessler-Harris*

James P. Cannon and the Origins of the American Revolutionary Left, 1890–1928   *Bryan D. Palmer*

Glass Towns: Industry, Labor, and Political Economy in Appalachia, 1890–1930s   *Ken Fones-Wolf*

Workers and the Wild: Conservation, Consumerism, and Labor in Oregon, 1910–30   *Lawrence M. Lipin*

Wobblies on the Waterfront: Interracial Unionism in Progressive-Era Philadelphia   *Peter Cole*

Red Chicago: American Communism at Its Grassroots, 1928–35   *Randi Storch*

Labor's Cold War: Local Politics in a Global Context   *Edited by Shelton Stromquist*

Bessie Abramowitz Hillman and the Making of the Amalgamated Clothing Workers of America   *Karen Pastorello*

The Great Strikes of 1877   *Edited by David O. Stowell*

Union-Free America: Workers and Antiunion Culture   *Lawrence Richards*

Race against Liberalism: Black Workers and the UAW in Detroit   *David M. Lewis-Colman*

Teachers and Reform: Chicago Public Education, 1929–70   *John F. Lyons*

Upheaval in the Quiet Zone: 1199/SEIU and the Politics of Healthcare Unionism   *Leon Fink and Brian Greenberg*

Shadow of the Racketeer: Scandal in Organized Labor   *David Witwer*

Sweet Tyranny: Migrant Labor, Industrial Agriculture, and Imperial Politics   *Kathleen Mapes*

Staley: The Fight for a New American Labor Movement   *Steven K. Ashby and C. J. Hawking*

On the Ground: Labor Struggles in the American Airline Industry   *Liesl Miller Orenic*

NAFTA and Labor in North America   *Norman Caulfield*

Making Capitalism Safe: Work Safety and Health Regulation in America, 1880–1940   *Donald W. Rogers*

Good, Reliable, White Men: Railroad Brotherhoods, 1877–1917   *Paul Michel Taillon*

Spirit of Rebellion: Labor and Religion in the New Cotton South   *Jarod Roll*

The Labor Question in America: Economic Democracy in the Gilded Age
Rosanne Currarino

Banded Together: Economic Democratization in the Brass Valley   *Jeremy Brecher*

The Gospel of the Working Class: Labor's Southern Prophets in New
Deal America   *Erik Gellman and Jarod Roll*

Guest Workers and Resistance to U.S. Corporate Despotism   *Immanuel Ness*

Gleanings of Freedom: Free and Slave Labor along the Mason-Dixon Line,
1790–1860   *Max Grivno*

Chicago in the Age of Capital: Class, Politics, and Democracy during the Civil
War and Reconstruction   *John B. Jentz and Richard Schneirov*

Child Care in Black and White: Working Parents and the History of Orphanages
Jessie B. Ramey

The Haymarket Conspiracy: Transatlantic Anarchist Networks
Timothy Messer-Kruse

Detroit's Cold War: The Origins of Postwar Conservatism   *Colleen Doody*

A Renegade Union: Interracial Organizing and Labor Radicalism   *Lisa Phillips*

Palomino: Clinton Jencks and Mexican-American Unionism in the
American Southwest   *James J. Lorence*

Latin American Migrations to the U.S. Heartland: Changing Cultural Landscapes
in Middle America   *Edited by Linda Allegro and Andrew Grant Wood*

Man of Fire: Selected Writings   *Ernesto Galarza, ed. Armando Ibarra and
Rodolfo D. Torres*

A Contest of Ideas: Capital, Politics, and Labor   *Nelson Lichtenstein*

Making the World Safe for Workers: Labor, the Left, and Wilsonian
Internationalism   *Elizabeth McKillen*

The Rise of the Chicago Police Department: Class and Conflict, 1850–1894
Sam Mitrani

Workers in Hard Times: A Long View of Economic Crises   *Edited by Leon Fink,
Joseph A. McCartin, and Joan Sangster*

Redeeming Time: Protestantism and Chicago's Eight-Hour Movement, 1866–1912
William A. Mirola

Struggle for the Soul of the Postwar South: White Evangelical Protestants and
Operation Dixie   *Elizabeth Fones-Wolf and Ken Fones-Wolf*

Free Labor: The Civil War and the Making of an American Working Class
Mark A. Lause

Death and Dying in the Working Class, 1865–1920   *Michael K. Rosenow*

Immigrants against the State: Yiddish and Italian Anarchism in America
Kenyon Zimmer

Fighting for Total Person Unionism: Harold Gibbons, Ernest Calloway,
and Working-Class Citizenship   *Robert Bussel*

Smokestacks in the Hills: Rural-Industrial Workers in West Virginia
Louis Martin

Disaster Citizenship: Survivors, Solidarity, and Power in the Progressive Era
Jacob A. C. Remes

The Pew and the Picket Line: Christianity and the American Working Class
Edited by Christopher D. Cantwell, Heath W. Carter, and Janine Giordano Drake

Conservative Counterrevolution: Challenging Liberalism in 1950s Milwaukee
Tula A. Connell

Manhood on the Line: Working-Class Masculinities in the American Heartland
Steve Meyer

On Gender, Labor, and Inequality   *Ruth Milkman*

The Making of Working-Class Religion   *Matthew Pehl*

Civic Labors: Scholar Activism and Working-Class Studies
Edited by Dennis Deslippe, Eric Fure-Slocum, and John W. McKerley

Victor Arnautoff and the Politics of Art   *Robert W. Cherny*

Against Labor: How U.S. Employers Organized to Defeat Union Activism
Edited by Rosemary Feurer and Chad Pearson

Teacher Strike! Public Education and the Making of a New American
Political Order   *Jon Shelton*

Hillbilly Hellraisers: Federal Power and Populist Defiance in the Ozarks
J. Blake Perkins

Sewing the Fabric of Statehood: Garment Unions, American Labor, and the
Establishment of the State of Israel   *Adam Howard*

Labor Justice across the America   *Edited by Leon Fink and Juan Manuel Palacio*

Frontiers of Labor: Comparative Histories of the United States and Australia
Edited by Greg Patmore and Shelton Stromquist

Women Have Always Worked: A Concise History, Second Edition
Alice Kessler-Harris

Remembering Lattimer: Labor, Migration, and Race in Pennsylvania
Anthracite Country   *Paul A. Shackel*

Disruption in Detroit: Autoworkers and the Elusive Postwar Boom
Daniel J. Clark

To Live Here, You Have to Fight: How Women Led Appalachian Movements for
Social Justice   *Jessica Wilkerson*

Dockworker Power: Race and Activism in Durban and the San Francisco
Bay Area   *Peter Cole*

Labor's Mind: A History of Working-Class Intellectual Life   *Tobias Higbie*

The World in a City: Multiethnic Radicalism in Early Twentieth-Century
Los Angeles   *David M. Struthers*

Death to Fascism: Louis Adamic's Fight for Democracy   *John P. Enyeart*

Upon the Altar of Work: Child Labor and the Rise of a New American
Sectionalism   *Betsy Wood*

Workers against the City: The Fight for Free Speech in *Hague v. CIO*
Donald W. Rogers

Union Renegades: Miners, Capitalism, and Organizing in the Gilded Age
  Dana M. Caldemeyer

The Labor Board Crew: Remaking Worker-Employer Relations from Pearl Harbor
  to the Reagan Era   *Ronald W. Schatz*

Grand Army of Labor: Workers, Veterans, and the Meaning of the Civil War
  Matthew E. Stanley

A Matter of Moral Justice: Black Women Laundry Workers and the Fight f
  or Justice   *Jenny Carson*

Labor's End: How the Promise of Automation Degraded Work   *Jason Resnikoff*

Toward a Cooperative Commonwealth: The Transplanted Roots of Farmer-Labor
  Radicalism in Texas   *Thomas Alter II*

Working in the Magic City: Moral Economy in Early Twentieth-Century Miami
  Thomas A. Castillo

Where Are the Workers? Labor's Stories at Museums and Historic Sites
  Edited by Robert Forrant and Mary Anne Trasciatti

Labor's Outcasts: Migrant Farmworkers and Unions in North America, 1934–1966
  Andrew J. Hazelton

Fraying Fabric: How Trade Policy and Industrial Decline Transformed America
  James C. Benton

Harry Bridges: Labor Radical, Labor Legend   *Robert W. Cherny*

Strong Winds and Widow Makers: Workers, Nature, and Environmental Conflict
  in Pacific Northwest Timber Country   *Steven C. Beda*

Purple Power: The History and Global Impact of SEIU   *Edited by Luís LM Aguiar
  and Joseph A. McCartin*

The Bosses' Union: How Employers Organized to Fight Labor before the
  New Deal   *Vilja Hulden*

Workers of All Colors Unite: Race and the Origins of American Socialism
  Lorenzo Costaguta

The Ruined Anthracite: Historical Trauma in Coal-Mining Communities
  Paul A. Shackel

On the Waves of Empire: U.S. Imperialism and Merchant Sailors, 1872–1924
  William D. Riddell

The Way We Build: Restoring Dignity to Construction Work   *Mark Erlich*

Public Workers in Service of America: A Reader   *Edited by Frederick W. Gooding
  Jr. and Eric S. Yellin*

The University of Illinois Press
is a founding member of the
Association of University Presses.

University of Illinois Press
1325 South Oak Street
Champaign, IL 61820-6903
www.press.uillinois.edu